...ning

The East Germ...

CITY AND ISLINGTON
COLLEGE

MANCHESTER
1824
Manchester University Press

The East German revolution of 1989

GARETH DALE

Manchester University Press
Manchester and New York

distributed exclusively in the USA by Palgrave

Published by Manchester University Press
Oxford Road, Manchester M13 9NR, UK
and Room 400, 175 Fifth Avenue, New York, NY 10010, USA
www.manchesteruniversitypress.co.uk

Distributed in the United States exclusively by
Palgrave Macmillan, 175 Fifth Avenue,
New York, NY 10010, USA

Distributed in Canada exclusively by
UBC Press, University of British Columbia, 2029 West Mall,
Vancouver, BC, Canada V6T 1Z2

British Library Cataloguing-in-Publication Data is available

Library of Congress Cataloging-in-Publication Data is available

ISBN 978 0 7190 7478 3 paperback

First published by Manchester University Press 2006

First reprinted 2013

The publisher has no responsibility for the persistence or accuracy of URLs for any external or
third-party internet websites referred to in this book, and does not guarantee that any content
on such websites is, or will remain, accurate or appropriate.

Printed by Lightning Source

For Yola and Zora

Contents

Preface and acknowledgements

The fall of the Berlin Wall was a landmark historical event. It has come to symbolise the end of the Cold War, the ensuing rearrangement of geopolitical furniture and the incursion of market capitalism into Eastern Europe. Not quite so well known is the history of the uprising of which it was but one event. In the face of a gargantuan security apparatus, protests were organised in the streets, squares, schools and workplaces of East Germany, which forced open democratic space, overthrew Erich Honecker's regime and propelled his successors to introduce a slew of reforms – including the liberalisation of the border regime – that culminated in the transition to parliamentary democracy in March 1990. That rising is the subject of this book.

There already exists, it is true, a prodigious literature on this period of East German history. There are diplomatic histories and economic histories, as well as numerous descriptive accounts of the events through the lens of particular social groups and institutions. There are volumes that explore aspects of the 1989 uprising, such as the behaviour of the state and SED apparatuses, the role of the Churches, or the influence of State Security (Stasi) informants within the 'civic groups,' as well as numerous studies of localities (notably Leipzig) and of specific sections of the movement. Yet only a handful of these deal analytically with the movement as a whole, and still fewer thematise the relationship between street protests and the civic groups. The monograph that fits these descriptions most closely is available only in German.[1]

This lacuna in contemporary research on East Germany is a manifestation of a wider problem, one which Jürgen Kocka has drawn attention

---

1 Timmer, *Aufbruch*. Of monographs in English, the best known are either conceived on a very broad historical canvas and devote little space to the uprising itself (e.g. Maier's *Dissolution*), or focus upon the unification process to the neglect of the autumn democracy movement (e.g. Jarausch's *Rush*).

to in a recent survey. There is, he observes, a wealth of detailed empirical studies of the revolution, unification and so on, but the field, considered as a whole, evinces 'a high degree of self-referentiality and self-isolation'. The literature has become 'terribly fragmented', and this may reflect the fact that the bulk of research has been conducted by 'individuals who research exclusively on the GDR'. It is time for scholars working in this area to engage more intensively with research in related fields (such as German, European and world history), to pursue different questions, to reconsider old ones and to develop novel approaches.[2]

In a sense, this book may be regarded as an attempt to meet Kocka's challenge. Its author's background is in sociology, political science and German literature. The approach is informed by social movement theory, a body of work that draws upon the study of collective action globally, thus facilitating analysis of the dynamics characteristic of the wider collective action repertoire, in addition to historical contingencies. In the text, social-movement theoretical concepts are not discussed separately but are worked in at relevant points.

The historiography of the GDR was, inevitably, powerfully affected by the Cold War, and this remains the case today. Even some of the better studies characterise the differences between the two Germanies in black-and-white terms. One, for example, describes 'tyranny' in the East and 'freedom' in the West; an 'indoctrination apparatus' is contrasted with 'a free education system' and a 'servile judiciary' with a system geared to the defence of civil rights. The same scholar suffers from an ailment that may be described as 'Cold Warrior's nose': he opposes 'the unmistakable Eastern smell ... of body odor' to 'the soaped and perfumed aroma of the West.'[3] This work, by contrast, finds the differences to be more accurately portrayed in shades of grey. It is not a continuation of the Cold War by other means.

The questions that form the backbone of this study can be grouped into three clusters. The first concerns the protest movement in general. Given the lack of traditions of public protest and the regime's determination to crush resistance, what explains its emergence in September 1989? What was the scale of the movement; did it, as Mancur Olson contends, last but a few days and involve 'a tiny percentage' of the population? And was that minority faced by an 'apathetic' majority, as Klaus von Beyme has argued? How did the movement evolve, in terms of its social composition and political complexion? Why did the demand for German unification become so popular? And why did collective action

2 Kocka, *Bilanz*, p. 768.
3 Jarausch, *Rush*, pp. 162, 194.

ebb away in spring 1990? Was it because by then, as Roland Bleiker avers, 'every single demand that the people had taken to the streets in the fall' had been met (as 'utopia turned into reality')?[4]

The second cluster concerns the strategy of the regime – in particular, its response to the movement. Why did it not unleash armed force, as it had done in 1953? What explains its abandonment of an intransigent stance in favour of 'dialogue'? Why did it open the Berlin Wall? And what motivated its desire to cooperate with the civic groups at 'round-table' negotiations?

The third set of issues concerns the civic groups. What were their ideological commitments? How did they relate to the mass movement – were they of it, or a separate force? Why did they seek rapprochement with the regime, and how did this relationship evolve? What were their attitudes towards unification, and why did they fare so poorly in the elections of March 1990?

I have touched upon some of these issues in previous publications and, although the present work is a stand-alone monograph, some readers may find a brief précis of three earlier works helpful.[5] The first, *Between State Capitalism and Globalisation*, is an economic history of East Germany, one that pays particular attention to the international context. It analyses the GDR as a state-capitalist formation: although its businesses were not geared to making profits for private owners their behaviour was dictated by the exigencies of capital accumulation – not unlike nationalised industries in market economies, or not-for-profit firms, such as Mozilla or Manchester University Press (if my publisher will forgive the comparison with the GDR). The book explores the forces that pulled GDR policymakers between centrally planned autarky and greater engagement with West Germany and the global economy. The first option spelled stagnation; the second steered towards indebtedness and dependence upon Cold War enemies. Its diminishing room for manoeuvre in economic policy contributed to the SED leadership's paralysis when confronted, in rapid succession, by Moscow's 'new thinking', the crumbling of Comecon and the mass emigration and protests of GDR citizens. These momentous events resolved the economic dilemma, and newly promoted SED leaders set course towards market capitalism and German unification, attempting all the while to contain the protest

4 Olson, 'Logic', p. 18; von Beyme, *Transition*, p. 41; Bleiker, *Nonviolent*, p. 9.
5 In addition to the three mentioned below, these include articles in the journals *Historical Materialism*, *Debatte* and *Socialism and Democracy* and a chapter in *To Make Another World* (edited by Colin Barker and Paul Kennedy).

movement and to maximise the transmutation of bureaucratic power into property and position in the new Germany. Although this strategy appeared at first to succeed, only a relatively thin layer of East Germany's ruling class was able to survive, as the country's industry collapsed in the catastrophic recession of the early 1990s.

As to how the transition process is best characterised, I suggest in a recent article (' "A very orderly retreat" ') that the East German case was one of transition 'by extrication'.[6] As with cases of 'regime collapse', this entailed a sharp departure from the formal rules of the old order, yet, as with 'negotiated transitions', the old regime retained sufficient strength to dictate important terms of the transition, and entered a pactmaking process with opposition forces. The pillars of the old regime suffered from demoralisation and indiscipline but the outgoing rulers managed to hold on until spring 1990 and, even after free elections, political office passed to the SED's former allies in the Christian Democratic Union (CDU). In the process, East German elites, like their counterparts elsewhere in Eastern Europe, adapted to parliamentary democracy and the market. The surprisingly easy abandonment of previous beliefs, the article concludes, suggests that Communism was adhered to for pragmatic purposes: it symbolised the SED's alliance with Moscow, a relatively autarkic economy, and one-party rule, but these commitments could be – and were – abandoned without undue fuss.

Moving from a focus on elites to the masses, a second monograph, *Popular Protest in East Germany, 1945–1989*, examines, among other things, two major sets of actors in the 1989 uprising – the 'civic groups' and the workers and technicians in factories and other workplaces. For both groups, the situation in East Germany had become intolerable and both participated in the street demonstrations, but before long they went their separate ways: the former into coalition government under the leadership of reformist Communists, the latter towards the Deutschmark. In addition to a brief narrative of the events of the summer and autumn of 1989, the book analyses the relationship between these two sections of the movement, and assesses the claim that 1989 was a 'revolution of the intellectuals'.

While preparing this book, I have incurred many debts. Research has been assisted by overseas fieldwork awards from the Economic and Social Research Council and the Deutsche Akademische Austauschdienst. Chapter 3 was completed while a research fellow at the London School of Economics. I am grateful to these three bodies for the time and resources that contributed to the completion of this study.

6　Dale, ' "Retreat" '.

For encouragement and constructive criticism in its initial stages, I owe more than can be gracefully expressed to Colin Barker. Carsten Johnson and Karl-Dieter Opp generously donated copies of their survey data. My thanks are also due Hans-Jochen Vogel, for supplying copies of files from the Leipzig and Dresden Stasi and police archives, and Gideon Saunders, for the transcript of his interview with Pastor Christian Führer. Meredith Dale translated some quotations, although I am responsible for the majority. East Germany's streets in 1989 witnessed a renaissance of the rhyming couplet not seen since W. S. Gilbert was at his prime; in translating them, poetic licence has been freely taken.

Timeline, 1989–90

1989

5 Jun.	Slaughter at Tiananmen Square, Beijing
4 Sept.	Resumption of Leipzig 'Peace Prayer' after the summer recess
10 Sept.	New Forum publishes 'Awakening '89'
11 Sept.	Hungary opens its western border for East Germans
30 Sept.	Thousands of East Germans who had sought refuge in West German embassies in Czechoslovakia and Poland permitted to exit to West Germany
2 Oct.	15,000–25,000 march through Leipzig, demanding legalisation of opposition groups and democratic reform
3 Oct.	In a move to stem the exodus, East Germany suspends unrestricted travel to Czechoslovakia; would-be emigrants gather at Dresden's Central Station; bloody repression by security forces
7 Oct.	Mikhail Gorbachev joins in festivities in Berlin marking fortieth anniversary of the German Democratic Republic (GDR); demonstrations in East Berlin and elsewhere brutally suppressed
9 Oct.	80,000 or more demonstrate in Leipzig
14 Oct.	New Forum announces membership figure of 25,000
16 Oct.	150,000+ demonstrate in Leipzig
18 Oct.	After eighteen years in power, Erich Honecker resigns as head of state and as leader of Socialist Unity Party (SED); succeeded as SED leader by Egon Krenz
23 Oct.	250,000+ demonstrate in Leipzig
24 Oct.	Krenz assumes post of chair of Council of State
1 Nov.	East Germany reopens its border with Czechoslovakia; tens of thousands flee to the West
4 Nov.	Up to a million East Germans fill the streets of East Berlin for pro-democracy rally

7 Nov.	GDR government resigns
8 Nov.	In attempt to strengthen his leadership, Krenz ousts much of ruling Politburo and brings in reformers
9 Nov.	Berlin Wall is stormed
24 Nov.	Czechoslovakia's hard-line Party leadership resigns following mass protests
27 Nov.	General strike in Prague
1 Dec.	GDR Parliament abolishes SED's constitutional guarantee of supremacy; Karl-Marx-Stadt New Forum proposes political general strike
3 Dec.	SED Politburo resigns
4 Dec.	Occupations of Stasi headquarters in several towns
5 Dec.	Former SED leaders, including Honecker, placed under house arrest
6 Dec.	Krenz resigns as Chair of Council of State; political strikes in South
7 Dec.	Central Round Table holds its first meeting

1990

11–12 Jan.	Strikes and demonstrations against reconstitution of the Stasi
15 Jan.	Storming of Stasi headquarters, Berlin
Late Jan.	Strike wave; prime minister Modrow declares for German unification
18 March	General elections held
1 Jul.	Treaty of Currency/Economic/Social Union with Federal Republic (FRG)
Aug.	Unification Treaty signed
3 Oct.	Formal German Unification

Map of the German Democratic Republic

1

Prelude: sensing opportunities

In early 1989, SED leader Erich Honecker famously promised that the Berlin Wall would still be standing a century later. In retrospect, this may seem risible. Possibly, the regime's confidence resulted from media censorship; like its Prussian predecessors, it 'heard only its own voice, which it mistakes for that of the people, whose actual voice is suppressed'.[1] Yet the state's omnipotent image also rested upon brute facts. It had always been able to crush public protest, and from June 1953 the GDR experienced a dearth of collective action.

The SED leadership was not alone in assuming the permanence of its rule. Even in the summer of 1989 few inhabitants of Soviet Eastern Europe believed that major political and geopolitical transformation was imminent, and still fewer that uprisings were about to begin. Among Western social scientists, the dominant emphasis was upon the innate stability of Soviet-type societies. Sociologists described Communism 'as a machine for the generation of political stability', and few Soviet-type societies appeared to be more stable than East Germany. Its citizens, argued Oxford scholar Timothy Garton Ash, would remain quiescent so long as a minimum of material security was guaranteed. Barely a year before its collapse, Zbigniew Brzezinski concluded that the GDR was one of the least crisis-prone of fifteen communist states he surveyed.[2]

There were, however, other, less sanguine voices. In the mid-1980s, *The Economist* magazine noted that the economic crisis afflicting the Soviet bloc was catalysing political strains and dissent throughout the region. A British Quaker reporting on a visit to East Germany, to give a second example, observed that although many social institutions compared favourably with the West,

1 Marx, in Fine, *Democracy*, p. 67.
2 David Lane, in Denitch, *End*, p. 193; Ash, *Bruder*, p. 82; Brzezinski, *Failure*, p. 234.

most of the problems of a system which is still tightly controlled do remain. Freedom of movement, opinion, publication and assembly are all very restricted, which necessarily creates frustration and the potential, therefore, for fundamental and unpredictable change.

Others drew upon recent East European history to predict economic crisis and revolutionary change. The historian Günter Minnerup prophesied that against a background of 'deep economic crisis, social and political polarisation, and political and military destabilisation' worldwide, the 1980s would 'submit the GDR to the sternest test of its ability to survive since its foundation'.[3] Chris Harman anticipated that if reforms were not carried through, economic crisis would worsen, and if they were, 'a split of the proportions that characterized Hungary in 1956 and Czechoslovakia in early 1968' was likely, and this would be the prelude to a general crisis 'in which the extra-bureaucratic classes would mobilize behind their own demands'.[4]

In the late 1980s something resembling this scenario did occur, as tensions over Mikhail Gorbachev's reform programme emerged within and between the countries of the Soviet bloc. Already in 1986 East Berlin signalled that it would not follow Gorbachev's lead, and relations with Moscow deteriorated. The GDR owed its existence to the Soviet Union, and the Kremlin's 'new thinking' raised fears that it could be cut adrift from its parent and guardian. Such fears were stoked when senior Soviet officials hinted that the modalities of German division might be opened up for renegotiation within a prospective 'common European home'. If these early portents of geopolitical change were verbal, practical steps soon followed – notably, in December 1988, the announcement of a major unilateral reduction in Soviet forces in Eastern Europe. Given that Soviet forces had long served to police Eastern Europe, the announcement was a powerful symbol of change, as was the new electoral law adopted in the Soviet Union that introduced multi-candidate elections at all levels of the polity.[5]

The crisis of the Soviet system, culminating in Gorbachev's reforms, gave rise to what Ruud Koopmans calls an 'opportunity cascade',

---

3 However, he also insisted, 'spontaneous mass movements "from below" are unlikely, unless economic conditions take a catastrophic turn for the worse . . . The decisive stress point in the coming years', he wrongly predicted, 'will therefore be the Party itself'. Minnerup, 'GDR', pp. 3, 13; Minnerup, 'Politische', p. 74; *The Economist*, 2 April 1988.

4 Jonathan Dale, 'Report to Quaker Yearly Meeting on Visit to the GDR 4–14 April 1981', in possession of the author; Callinicos, *Revenge*, p. 19. For further examples of analyses that predicted crisis and revolt, see Pryce-Jones, *War*, p. 21.

5 Light, 'USSR/CIS', p. 139.

whereby Moscow's unwillingness to intervene against reformist governments in Eastern Europe made the position of remaining hardliners more precarious, heightening the problems they faced in containing opposition.[6] In East Germany, the political opportunity structure was transformed.[7] Within the SED, Moscow's 'new thinking' catalysed a differentiation process, and criticisms of the leadership were widely felt if rarely articulated. Among the public at large much evidence points to a 'silent breaking' with the regime. By the spring of 1988, Jürgen Kuczynski, the 'Nestor of GDR social science', was worrying that 'a chasm between leadership and masses is opening up absolutely everywhere – in both civilian and military populations. If the leadership does not change course soon a serious situation could arise'. Yet, equally, a change of course could well require a change of leadership, and that itself would spell trouble. As one SED leader put it: 'Over decades, unfortunately, real life has proved this axiom correct: The replacement of the leader of a socialist state has always led to social upheaval.'[8]

Although the crisis of the Soviet bloc was there for all to see, not least when Hungary began dismantling the Iron Curtain in May 1989, such developments were neither automatically nor inevitably perceived as a 'signal'. The newly available political opportunities did not translate directly into collective action. Latent conflicts within political elites, and other regime weaknesses, have first to be made manifest and perceived before they affect contention. Expanding opportunities must be scented, interpreted and tested; actors must believe that possibilities exist, and that they have the capacity to effect change. In the East German case, the road to public protest began at Hungary's western border where GDR holidaymakers, hearing of the dismantling of fortifications, attempted to exit to Austria. In fact the changes to the border regime were cosmetic. Fences and other defences remained in place, as the would-be emigrants discovered upon arrival. A quarter of them managed to battle their way

6 Koopmans, 'Protest', p. 26.
7 The political opportunity structure refers to 'consistent dimensions of the political environment which either encourage or discourage people' from engaging in collective action (Tarrow, *Power*, p. 18). Changes to the political opportunity structure result from, for example, shifts in regime strategy, leadership change or divisions within elites. It is not the most parsimonious of concepts, but is a category that can be helpful in identifying short- and medium-range variables that mediate between 'big structures' and social movements.
8 Interviews with Michael Brie, Helmut Meier and Rolf Richter. See also Dale, *Between*, chs. 7, 8; Schlegelmilch, 'Politische', p. 136; Flam, *Mosaic*, p. 93; Pfaff, 'Collective', p. 102; Kuczynski, *Probleme*, p. 189; Krenz, *Herbst*, p. 67.

through but it was no easy trip; thousands were apprehended by border guards and there was even one fatality.[9]

If those who fought through did much to expose the Soviet bloc's brittle architecture, those that were returned were the innovators in collective action. Instructed by the Hungarian authorities to leave the country within twenty-four hours, many opted instead to occupy the West German (FRG) embassy in Budapest. This heightened the visibility of the crisis, accelerating the flow of would-be emigrants to Hungary and exacerbating tensions between Budapest and East Berlin. It also provided an opportunity for Bonn to involve itself in the affair: although FRG diplomats sought to avoid actions that would directly destabilise East Germany, by providing Budapest with a DM500 million loan they deepened the rift between Hungary and East Berlin.[10] In August, embassy occupants were permitted to exit to the West, and the mass emigration could no longer be stemmed.

The summer 1989 exodus was a historical singularity. One scholar portrays it as 'a curious blend between domestic labor movement and international search for political asylum' – but seldom do asylum-seekers find such a welcoming host state and rarely are labour movements manifested through such 'serial' behaviour.[11] By contrast, in a reprise of patrician dismissals of the irrational and gullible mob, Fritz Haug describes it as a mixture 'of psychosis and plebiscite' – but in fact emigrants were quite sane. They were motivated, in the analysis of one GDR oppositionist, by a desire for improved living conditions, including 'freedom to travel, luxury goods and better cars' but also basic necessities ('a telephone line, floorboards, drainpipes, roof tiles and tools for D.I.Y'). For some, an appetite for more creative work also played a part ('to work with the most modern machines and computers, or to research at the cutting edge of science.') The Stasi's interviews with would-be emigrants suggested that pull factors included western living standards and career prospects, freedom of travel and the quality and variety of educational opportunities, while push factors included media censorship as well as resentments at bullying by managers and state officials. In addition, growing numbers were impelled by fears of approaching repression.[12]

9 Koopmans, 'Protest', p. 24; Timmer, *Aufbruch*, pp. 98–9.
10 Adomeit, *Imperial*, p. 390.
11 Jarausch, *Rush*, p. 25. 'Serial' refers, following Sartre (*Critique*, p. 829), to 'an ensemble each of whose members is determined in alterity by the others (in contrast to a group)'.
12 Haug, *Perestrojka-Journal*, p. 31; Reich, 'Freiheit', p. 199; Mitter and Wolle, 'Ich liebe', pp. 144–6.

Many East Germans shared these dreams and dreads, and it is this that explains the voice-promoting consequences of the exodus. Although 'exit' can undermine 'voice', by removing potential dissenters, in East Germany the dominant effect was the opposite. It was a repressive society in which extra-local communication was difficult and the degree to which grievances were shared was poorly known. The exodus turned up the volume, as it were, rendering the 'silent breaking' with the regime suddenly audible. Exiters exposed regime vulnerability and also signalled to others that they were not alone in their discontent and opposition. This new-found realisation of shared grievances, Steven Pfaff and Hyojoung Kim suggest, may motivate voice. 'A commonly understood signal of the magnitude of public grievances will likely raise the expectation that others will speak out.'[13]

And others did speak out. Political debate erupted – within families, on public transport, in workplaces. Courageous individuals began to test the limits of public expression and organisation. One wrote to New Forum to report that 'on October 3 at around 17.15 I came out of the delicatessen and onto Pirna's market square where, out of frustration and pent-up anger, I shouted: "Down with Honecker," "Honecker, you rascal, give the little children bananas" and "We want free elections."' Naturally, Stasi officers arrived swiftly but what was remarkable, he continues, was 'that so many onlookers shouted: "leave the man be, he's speaking the truth."'[14]

Sensing the new opportunities, church-based oppositionists began to organise. Already in early 1989 several people had proposed that independent political platforms be established on the national stage and in May oppositionists supervising local elections had been pleasantly surprised to see that their activities were finding a significant echo among the public.[15] With the arrival of a signal political crisis in the summer, activists decided the hour to establish political platforms had arrived. 'It was clear to us', Katrin Eigenfeld recalls, 'that we had to bring the opposition onto the streets and into the public realm. The time was ripe to leave the shelter of the Church in order to gain influence in society at large.'[16] Albeit unintentionally, the emigrants, oppositionists and sundry discontents were paving the way towards mass uprising.

13 Pfaff and Kim, 'Exit-Voice'.
14 Klenke, *Rationalisierung*; Krone, *Briefe*, p. 116.
15 Including Hans-Jochen Tschiche, Martin Gutzeit and Markus Meckel; see also Mühlen, *Aufbruch*, p. 243.
16 Eigenfeld, 'Neues', p. 80.

2

A movement arises

It was in Leipzig, where space for collective action was prised open by the emigration movement, that the uprising began. With little to lose in terms of career prospects, and hopeful that participation in protest might speed their exit, the 'protest threshold' of would-be emigrants was comparatively low. From early 1989 they gathered on Mondays at the Nikolai Church before marching out, to chants of 'We want out!' Although small, these events were highly charged; the simple act of demonstrating in public undermined the state's aura of omnipotence. They inspired and provoked a response from others who retained hopes of domestic political change and who now began to join the demonstrations, raising slogans critical of both the regime and, implicitly, the emigrants. Already on 4 September the usual strains of 'We want out!' were accompanied by the counter-slogan 'We're staying here!'

Dynamics and tactics: numbers, vigils, milling

These first demonstrations were tentative affairs, attesting to a movement that was only beginning to experience its existence. Numbers were small; participants were unsure of themselves. Support from the Church was lacking – as late as 18 September even the radical Pastor Christian Führer enjoined the congregation at peace prayers to return home quickly and quietly. Attesting to East Germany's lack of recent protest traditions and the high level of arrests, potential participants would mill around in the Nikolai churchyard, refraining from indicating whether they were participants, onlookers or passers-by. This behaviour was presumably deliberate, and certainly made it harder for the security forces to intervene. But the threat from the police was also confronted directly. On Monday 11 September, for example, security forces attacked the demonstration, made almost one hundred arrests and imposed several fines. In response, activists organised daily

'solidarity worships' to 'pray-demand' the release of protestors who
remained in custody.[1]

Despite police intimidation, morale grew as September wore on. The
regime's impotence in the face of Budapest's decision to allow unhindered
emigration of GDR citizens helped, as did the launch of the opposition
platform New Forum. Crucial, too, was the 'logic of numbers': larger
demonstrations are more visible, make a greater impact and impair a
regime's ability to police the crowds.[2] By their size, demonstrations also
signal the level of support enjoyed by protest movements. As growing
numbers of Leipzigers scented expanding political opportunities and witnessed the increasing size of demonstrations, greater numbers chose to
look on, and onlookers became participants. As Table 1 indicates, attendance curved upwards while the likelihood of being arrested declined. A
turning point was reached on 18 September when the 1,800 inside the
Nikolai Church emerged to witness over 1,000 onlookers milling
around. For the first time, large numbers of 'millers' joined the protest.

The next Monday saw the movement take a further step forward.
Following peace prayers – during which the question of police brutality
was broached, in an atmosphere described by the Stasi as 'inflamed
and aggressive' – churchgoers and 'millers' did not remain, as usual,
in the vicinity of the church but marched through the town, singing
the *Internationale* and 'We Shall Overcome', chanting 'Freedom' and
'Legalise New Forum!' and encouraging onlookers to join in. Significantly,
given recent orders from Berlin to 'nip enemy activity in the bud', the
police did not intervene to prevent the march forming. Later, they did
make every effort to disperse it, including driving vans into the crowd, but
determined resistance was displayed and at least one van was forced to
retreat. Although dozens of protestors nursed injuries victory was theirs:
the march had gone ahead despite the concerted efforts of the security
forces. Police assessments of the day's events noted with concern that 'a
qualitatively new situation has been reached' in terms of the protestors'
ability to gain public attention.[3]

In mid-September the Leipzig model began to catch on elsewhere.
Typically, would-be emigrants would engage in protests, encouraging
'here-stayers' to follow suit – although the line between the two
constituencies was seldom hard and fast. In Weißenfels, for example,

1 Bartee, *Time*, p. 70; On 'milling', see Timmer, *Aufbruch*; For reports on the
  11 September demonstration, see Wagner, *Freunde*, pp. 386–91.
2 Della Porta and Diani, *Movements*, p. 174.
3 Report from BDVP Leipzig, 12 October 1989; Mitter and Wolle, *Befehle*,
  p. 175; Sievers, *Revolution*, p. 38.

Table 1 Leipzig demonstrations, 1989

	Jan.–Jul.[a]	Sept. 4/11	Sept. 18	Sept. 25	Oct. 2	Oct. 7[b]	Oct. 9
Estimates of attendance	80–300	1,000–1,300	2,300	4–6,000	10–25,000	4–10,000	70–95,000
Arrests, percent of protestors	10–40	8–11	2–8	0.1	0.1	2–5	0

Notes:

[a] According to Leipzig district police force records, at least seventeen demonstrations took place in this period.
[b] This was the first demonstration to take place without 'peace prayers' beforehand.

emigration applicants led a protest (that developed in the aftermath of what the Stasi termed a 'disco gathering'), in which around twenty young people occupied a street, chanting slogans such as 'Stasi out!' and 'We want New Forum!' In other towns the initiative was taken by 'here-stayers'. In Arnstadt, a policeman's son typed dozens of flyers advertising a demonstration, which he then pinned around the town. Some 200 attended, and an improvised rally ensued: 'One woman summons up courage and begins to speak, on the subject of low pensions. Others follow her example.'[4]

Firm orders, infirm structures

As protests mushroomed the regime ratcheted up its response, notch by notch. It signalled unmistakably that democratisation was not on its agenda. Senior cadre from the Party and security forces were brought together in regional 'crisis cabinets' to ensure the rigorous and unified implementation of repressive measures. The security forces were put on alert. Weapons were issued. Before deployment, soldiers received extra rations. Officers were apprised of the seriousness of the situation and informed that the opposition must at all costs be prevented from becoming a mass force. On 22 September Honecker ordered regional SED chiefs to 'isolate the organisers of counter-revolutionary activity' in order to prevent them from gaining a 'mass following'. Three days later New Forum was ordered to cease all activity with immediate effect. Stasi officers were instructed to arrest anyone distributing oppositional literature and to take 'offensive measures to block and disrupt conspiratorial assembly'. Lists, drawn up in the previous year, of thousands of oppositionists to be 'isolated' in internment camps in the event of a crackdown were brought out ready for use.[5] Then, on 5 October, Stasi chief Erich Mielke issued the infamous order: 'enemy-negative activities to be decisively prevented *by any means* . . . Allow no surprises! Allow the opponent no opportunity to undertake activities on the assumption that we are not present!'[6]

During this period oppositionists were aware that the regime was taking a repressive tack, but not of the more extreme plans such as mass internment. Neither did we know that some sections of the state were signalling a slightly less severe approach. In late September, for instance, the Stasi issued the draconian instruction to arrest anyone copying and

4 Editors of *Das Andere Blatt, Überraschung*, p. 62; Lindner, *Revolution*, p. 70.
5 Fortunately, the order to action the internment programme never came.
6 Bahr, *Sieben*, p. 57; Lasky, *Wortmeldung*, p. 33.

distributing leaflets, but added that the only sanction should be a warning, except in cases of repeat offence. Some senior functionaries, meanwhile, were urging a differentiated response to the movement. Stasi Colonel-General Mittig, for example, proposed that more attention be paid to understanding the causes of discontent and listening to citizens, and suggested that branding all emigrants and opposition supporters as enemies was counterproductive.[7]

Such deviations from the prevailing hard line attested to a lack of confidence in the prospects of all-out repression and this, I would hazard, reflected a recognition of the dire internal state of the SED and security forces. Already in July an internal SED report had revealed considerable discontent among Party members (as well as a widespread reluctance to perceive the West as the 'class enemy'). 'The Party is not behaving as we imagine it should – it's not going on the offensive', a Stasi general complained. His organisation's reports in September depicted a catastrophic situation in the SED and warned that 'the people's trust in the Party is in continuous decline', while in early October they recorded a 'sharp rise in signs of uncertainty, confusion and resignation among Party members and employees of the state apparatus' and Party members' concern that the country was 'already in a situation resembling the one immediately before the counter-revolutionary events of 17.6.1953'. SED members were overwhelmed by the wrath directed at their Party. Many felt unable or even unwilling to defend the 'line' and would concur with the sharp, even aggressive, criticisms of their non-Party fellows. At SED meetings even 'full-time Party functionaries seem "helpless" in their arguments', the Stasi's informants reported. SED members in higher education

> are going into lectures and seminars with growing unease because students are addressing politically sensitive topics ever more frequently and are asking questions to which they cannot give adequate answers without calling the fundamental positions of the Party into question.

Faith in the leadership was rapidly disappearing, with many members feeling torn between support for the system and condemnation of its leaders. The most common grievances concerned the regime's inability to organise the provision of a decent quality of life for citizens and its failure to take problems seriously – in particular, to allow proper discussion in the media. Many at the grassroots shared the popular revulsion at the SED leadership's attitude of 'good-riddance' to emigrants, and some even emigrated themselves. But a more common form of exit was from the Party: resignations rose rapidly, reaching 100,000 by early October. Even

---

7 Krone, *Briefe*, p. 25.

the Central Committee was not exempt from this surge of discontent, with some of its members feeling 'left in the lurch' by the top leadership.[8]

The 'bloc parties'[9] were likewise affected by dissent and demoralisation. One witness describes 'an avalanche of resentment' among ordinary CDU members against their leadership's unceasing support for hard-line policies; others reported that party meetings had had to be halted due to 'chaos'. Gradually, the party leaderships began to reflect some of the criticism bubbling within the ranks. The Liberal Democrat Party (LDPD) in particular, but also the CDU, began to make 'off-message' statements. 'We must not prevent change, but foster and channel it', one declared. 'The GDR needs questioning, impatient, curious people', said another; 'it needs those awkward types, people who cut against the grain of "normality"'. In early October LDPD functionaries even offered meeting rooms to the (still outlawed) civic groups. For such heretical thoughts and deeds they were roundly condemned by SED hardliners, and accused of 'fomenting counter-revolution'.[10]

Nor were the security forces exempt from the general disquiet. Dissent flourished among conscript soldiers, particularly regarding the prospect of domestic deployment of the army. From August, the number of soldiers deserting either army or country increased dramatically and several dozen officers, including a colonel, joined the exodus. Many reservists refused to sign up for baton training, and the prospect of intervention against unarmed civilians brought some army units to the threshold of mutiny. In one, when officers requested volunteers for deployment at demonstrations not a single soldier stepped foward, and there was at least one case of an army officer being arrested for joining a demonstration.[11]

Even the Stasi was affected. Its employees were more aware than most of the depth of the crisis. In the late 1980s some officers had expressed irritation at the SED leadership's tendency to request that

8 Pfaff, 'Revolution', p. 323; Mitter and Wolle, *Befehle*, pp. 204, 149, 127; Mitter and Wolle, *Untergang*, p. 510; Wolle, *Diktatur*, p. 317; Krenz, *Wenn*, p. 13.
9 The bloc parties were SED allies that had been created 'to intercept the political energy of non-Communists and to divert it from a possible opposition and channel it to the support of the Communist establishment'. Krejci, *Social*, p. 138.
10 Opie, 'Views', p. 33; Keithly, *Collapse*, p. 148; Knabe, *Aufbruch*, p. 303; Neubert, *Opposition*, p. 847; Gerlach, *Mitverantwortlich*, p. 7.
11 Hertle, *Chronik*, pp. 121, 195; *Friedrichsfelder Feuermelder*, December 1989; Opp *et al.*, *Volkseigene*, p. 290; Liebsch, *Dresdner*, p. 95; Mitter and Wolle, *Untergang*, p. 537.

what were in reality long-term political problems be addressed by the Stasi with its short-term 'administrative, repressive' techniques. In 1988 a group of senior officers had met conspiratorially to discuss prospects of reforming and slimming their organisation. By 1989 many were exasperated that their forecasts of impending trouble had been ignored. Throughout the summer and autumn a stark contrast existed between the Stasi's near-omniscient cognisance of social problems and its lack of ability to master them. It may be, one West German intelligence source speculated, that 'the Stasi had so much information coming in to its headquarters that it was immobilised in trying to digest it'. More to the point, I suspect, was that the lack of political direction from SED leaders generated paralysis in their 'sword and shield'. As Elizabeth Pond contends, it was 'the failure of the top leadership to act in response to the exodus of mid-1989' that demoralised Stasi officers. 'We didn't know what we should do', one confessed. 'No signals came from above.'[12]

The battle of Dresden Station

Thus far, we have charted the diminishing room for manoeuvre available to the regime, and the manner by which citizens 'scented' and acted upon opportunities to emigrate and to engage in public protest, and we have portrayed the emergence of a consciousness of political crisis among the population at large. During the first week of October this sense of crisis sharpened greatly, due to the inter-section between a succession of ham-fisted policy decisions, repressive police tactics and sustained pressure from would-be emigrants and the nascent democracy movement. The site of the lengthiest – and bloodiest – confrontation was Dresden. In the country's far south east, Saxony's second city was a natural embarkation point for travel to nearby Czechoslovakia. As such, its railway station was to provide the arena for a major contest, provoked by the regime's attempts to solve its emigration problem.

Two related decisions led to a convergence of would-be emigrants upon Dresden. The first was a concession to the occupants of the FRG embassy in Prague. Under pressure from Czechoslovakia's Communist leaders it was announced on 30 September that East Germans in Prague

---

12 Wilkening, *Staat*, p. 56; Knauer, 'Opposition', p. 726; *Der Spiegel*, 23 April, 1990; Rüddenklau, *Störenfried*, p. 360; Allen, *Germany*, p. 198; Pond, *Beyond*, p. 125; Riecker, *Stasi*, p. 238. See also Peterson, *Secret*, Hartung, *Neunzehnhundertneunundachtzig*, p. 49.

would be permitted to emigrate to West Germany.[13] The decision, however, carried a crucial rider: that they exit not by the shortest route – across the Czech–FRG border – but via a detour through the GDR. This condition was widely interpreted as an undignified attempt to mask a defeat with a display of hubris, an impression that can only have been confirmed by the scenes that greeted the trains as they passed through Saxony. Handkerchiefs were waved from the balconies of housing estates as the emigrants sped by. Workers absented themselves from work in order to wish them well. 'They've made it!', was the phrase on many lips, expressing acclaim as well as surprise.[14]

Having decanted their troublesome citizens from the embassy in Prague the East German authorities were not so naïve as to assume that the crisis had blown over. For the termination of the occupation raised the thornier question of how to prevent the embassy from filling up again. In preceding weeks functionaries had been detailed to consider a range of options for ameliorating the border regime problem. One, backed by the security chief Wolfgang Herger, was to extend the right of citizens to receive visas for travel to the West. Even this comparatively liberal option, Herger fretted, risked provoking a 'social conflagration' yet his superordinate, Egon Krenz, favoured a more hazardous course of action: the immediate closure of the border to Czechoslovakia to visa-free travel, combined with a pledge that some sort of border regime relaxation would ensue in the not-too-distant future. In the event the policy adopted was yet more draconian than this, and by some way: on 3 October the border was closed, without even the palliative of a promised future liberalisation.

More than any other policy decision, the border closure escalated the sense of crisis. Far from solving problems of travel and emigration, it exacerbated them. Passport offices filled with desperate, often enraged, citizens demanding visas. Applications for emigration soared – by around a thousand a day – throughout October.[15] And among the 'staying put' majority hostility to the policy was widespread. Strikes broke out in several towns, partly in reaction to the border closure, and hundreds of miners in Altenberg began a go-slow, demanding the reopening of the border and wider freedoms of movement.

13 The Czechoslovaks did not mince their words in their appeals to Berlin to remove protesting East Germans and reported with alarm that 'opposition groups in the CSSR are linking up with GDR citizens'. Przybylski, *Tatort 2*, p. 336.
14 Küttler and Röder, *Volk*, p. 118.
15 Hertle, *Chronik*, p. 89.

Objections to the border closure, according to one Stasi report, could be heard from 'countless sources, who represent the most diverse groups of the population'. In the factories of Saxony, it continues, non-party members greeted the move with derision but numerous branches of the 'bloc parties', notably the LDPD, expressed vehement opposition, too. The sample of opinions listed therein attest to the passions involved: it is 'the government's declaration of bankruptcy'; 'we are now imprisoned'; 'there's nothing for it but to emigrate'.[16] These stark statements tally with the recollections of my interviewees. For them, the first week of October stands out as the darkest of the autumn. Ollie, from Dresden, after describing the summer months as a period which for the most part had been experienced under the sign of hope, added that 'when they closed the Czech border, then we did feel imprisoned – which, despite the Wall, we never really had before'. Antje, the most relaxed and optimistic of interviewees, singled out the border closure as *the* moment of genuine anxiety:

> Most of us [in my milieu] were fairly relaxed about the prospects of a crack-down. We were pretty confident, because the state was up against such constraints, and because of the Russian politics of the time. But that changed when the border to Czechoslovakia was closed. Things did then get a bit scary.

Those who felt the force of the border closure most keenly were the emigrants themselves, particularly those who had already packed their suitcases, kissed their friends and relatives goodbye, bought their tickets, or even already begun their journey to Prague. It is not difficult to imagine their emotions upon hearing that the border gates were closing, particularly given that trainloads of fellow emigrants were about to leave Prague, bound for West Germany. To some, the opportunity of boarding these trains represented a final hope. In their thousands they began to flock towards the stations, notably Dresden, through which the emigration trains were due to pass.

First to arrive in Dresden, on 3 October, were several hundred visa-less occupants of successive trains that had been halted at the border crossing point of Bad Schandau. Fearful of being refused exit from East Germany, they had barricaded their compartments to prevent customs officials from entering. In a fateful decision some of these carriages were now towed back to Dresden Central Station. In the heat of the moment, little thought had been given to the potential consequences. Upon arrival some 800 of the emigrant hopefuls occupied an empty train on a Prague-facing platform. Ejected from the carriages by police, around half of them either sat down on or walked along the tracks, forcing an inter-

---

16 Mitter and Wolle, *Befehle*, p. 192.

ruption of train services in the area. Others gathered in the forecourt. According to police reports some 1,600 were present, along with several hundred onlookers. The station rang to chants of 'We want out!' and strains of the *Internationale*.

On its own, this gathering could quite conceivably have been contained. However, as noted earlier, the stations through which the Westbound trains were due to pass had become magnets for would-be emigrants. Thousands converged on Dresden station and set about blocking the tracks in the hope of forcibly boarding the trains. By the evening of 4 October, the crowd in and around the station was swelling towards 15,000.[17] 'There was a real danger', in the judgement of Stasi officers, 'that the entire station area would come under complete occupation'.[18] One eyewitness, an engineer from a local factory, has described the scenes that followed:

> It was ordered that the station be cleared. A chain of uniformed officers pressed forward, pushing people back and toward the exits. Those who resisted were beaten, pulled off the ground by their hair and arrested. Eventually the station was cleared, but then it filled up again. Another attempt was made to clear it. This time the police beat their clubs against their shields, making a deafening noise that frightened and intimidated the crowd.[19]

At this point the region's SED chief, Hans Modrow, ordered that batons and water cannon be deployed, and even called in the army.[20] The security forces ran riot, making literally thousands of arrests and treating demonstrators with no mercy. Dozens were injured. As the full force of the state was unleashed, protestors responded in kind. Missiles were hurled and a police vehicle torched.

His reformist image notwithstanding, Modrow's record in dealing with resistance was the match of any of his peers. Ulrich Albrecht's contention that he was 'extremely hesitant to unleash the use of force' is difficult to reconcile with his words and deeds. In previous years he had been responsible for a succession of police assaults against environmental campaigners.[21] In the autumn of 1989 his stance, initially at least,

17 Some Stasi reports put the figure at 20,000.
18 Hertle, *Chronik*, p. 79.
19 Paraphrased by Dyke, *Dresden*, p. 213. See also Bahr, *Sieben*.
20 Although 'when no water sprayed from the first one, laughter burst out amongst the crowd – they were accustomed to technical failures of this sort'. Zwahr, 'Umbruch', p. 429.
21 Albrecht, 'Movements', p. 154; Richter and Sobeslavsky, *Gruppe*; Süß, 'Bilanz', p. 598. For Modrow's spin on events, including an explanation of his later amnesia before the courts, see Modrow, *Deutschland*, pp. 264–72.

remained hawkish and his speeches at rallies were greeted by boos and jeers.[22] In his autobiography he describes himself as formed by 'the old framework of order and security'. As regards the battle itself, there is some dispute as to whether Modrow personally encouraged police and army brutality or whether greater culpability attaches to Mielke, Defence Minister Heinz Kessler or to commanders on the ground. But there is no doubt that Modrow was as determined as his colleagues in Berlin to disperse the protests, and that the army was deployed on his authority. In telegrams to Honecker he praised the 'courage' of the security forces and justified their uglier deeds by labelling the demonstrators 'terrorists'.[23]

Following the riots, protestors regrouped and formed what became in effect a semi-permanent demonstration that fluctuated in size from several thousand to 30,000. Emigrants occupied three churches in an attempt to press the authorities to meet their demands. Others continued on their feet. For over three days, crowds milled around the station and peregrinated through the city to chants of 'We want out!' and 'New Forum'. With each passing day the proportion of emigrants to locals shifted in favour of the latter.[24]

The battle at Dresden Station remains an under-illuminated moment of East Germany's revolutionary autumn. Even some of the most comprehensive and accomplished histories of the period relegate it to a single sentence or footnote. As to why there is this neglect, a variety of factors suggest themselves. One involves a relative scarcity of data: in contrast to Leipzig, in Dresden there were few connections to western journalists, and these were noticeable by their absence. Others stem from the interpretive schemas employed by historians. To those for whom 1989 was a 'velvet revolution', the army's bloody intervention, the thrown stones and broken bones, appear anomalous. And for historians whose accounts treat the exodus and democracy movement as separate threads the Dresden events – involving a combination of emigrants and 'here-stayers' – fit awkwardly.[25]

Whether or not these explanations are convincing the fact remains that the battle was a key event, and for a number of reasons. First, Dresden witnessed a major street battle, and this was not lost on the population.

22 On 22 September, for example, when Honecker called simply for the organisers of protests to be 'isolated', Modrow insisted upon the *systematic* isolation of *all* counter-revolutionary forces'. Hertle, *Fall*, p. 110, emphasis added. See also Greenwald, *Berlin*, p. 256.
23 Telegram dated 4 October 1989, GVS E1 602339; GVS 05–6/89; in BDVP Abt. Information; Modrow, *Aufbruch*, p. 23
24 Police and Stasi reports both note this development. BDVP, Abt. Information.
25 E.g. Maier, *Dissolution*, pp. 120–46, esp. p. 131.

News spread throughout the land that people had begun to respond to state force with counterforce. Despite the use of clubs, water cannon and the deployment of the army, protestors had held their ground. In testing the security forces and finding them wanting, they contributed to the public *perception* that the regime was vincible, and thus to its *actual* weakness. The Dresden events produced a demonstration effect. Reports, broadcast in the western media and – albeit negatively – in the domestic media, encouraged what the Stasi termed 'unlawful gatherings of predominantly young people' in cities and towns throughout Saxony and Saxony-Anhaltine.[26]

Second, the events issued the regime with a stark reminder of the potential of repressive policies to backfire. As Krenz described in his diary, they 'exposed the contradictions of our society' – these included the rise of the emigration and democracy movements. In closing the border the regime had unwittingly provoked a potent alliance between these two movements, as Dresden revealed.[27] Third, for a hardline course to succeed the security forces would have to be steeled, and in this regard, too, the evidence from Dresden was not encouraging. At least sixteen soldiers mutinied on 3–4 October. Although not an especially high figure, if one sets it against the risk of court martial that mutiny incurs it is significant. Those sixteen, moreover, represented the tip of an iceberg – many other police officers and soldiers sought to evade duty while not actually disobeying orders. Dresden district police files contain numerous reports of serious discontent among soldiers and reservists, and reveal that senior police officers felt uncertain, exasperated and at times quite unable to cope with the crisis. 'What mistakes have we made in the education of the younger generation?', one of them asked. 'I am sick of this; these people are peaceful', a police officer yelled when he witnessed troops attacking demonstrators, 'now our image is completely ruined'. And he was right, for – and fourthly – the Dresden events further vitiated the SED's self-representation as a 'Party of peace'.[28]

Turning points in Saxony

In the second week of October, the SED leaders still hoped to succeed in suppressing protest without recourse to arms. As this tactic began to run

26 Timmer, *Aufbruch*, p. 75; Editors of *Das Andere Blatt*, 'Überraschung', p. 14.
27 Krenz, *Herbst*, p. 75. Krenz took rough notes at the time and wrote them up later as memoirs.
28 BDVP Abt. Information, Drs. 1/4773. See also Richter and Sobeslavsky, *Gruppe;* Pfaff, 'Revolution', p. 332.

aground, however, differences appeared over whether or not to escalate repression. None, according to Günther Schabowski, were prepared for an open outbreak of conflict and still less for the development of a reform programme. Some were disinclined to risk civil war, a group that seems to have included Siegfried Lorenz and Schabowski, and also a number of SED leaders in command of the police and army (Krenz, Herger and Rudi Mittig). Others, notably Honecker and perhaps Mielke, were quite prepared to unleash armed force. They perceived the situation to be akin to the eve of the 1953 uprising and were determined to avoid a reprise.[29] Senior functionaries who shared this position included Politburo member Werner Krolikowski as well as Gera's Party boss, who announced that: 'We shall deal with these agitators and counter-revolutionaries after the fortieth anniversary [of the GDR's foundation], just as it was done in China.'[30] Interior Minister Friedrich Dickel may have belonged to this group, too. On 8 October he ordered the police to crush resistance using 'any means necessary', and he certainly had few qualms about resorting to violence. 'I would prefer', he bragged to colleagues,

> to go in there and beat up these scoundrels so their own mother's wouldn't recognise them. I was in charge here in Berlin in 1953. Nobody needs to tell me what those counterrevolutionary scum get up to. I went to Spain as a Young Communist and fought against the scoundrels, the fascist trash.[31]

In early October hard-liners appeared to have the upper hand. Indeed, the similarities between, and the violence of, police assaults on demonstrators and onlookers in Dresden, Magdeburg, Leipzig, Karl-Marx-Stadt, Halle and Potsdam suggest that senior officers and functionaries deliberately aimed to provoke a civil war atmosphere in order to furnish a pretext for military crackdown.[32]

Perhaps the cruellest policing occurred in Berlin, during the GDR's fortieth anniversary celebrations, but this event is best known for the startling behaviour of Free German Youth (FDJ) members. They had been assembled in the usual manner, to create a spectacle and the pretence of acclaim for Honecker and his guests (including Gorbachev); yet by this stage in the deterioration of East German society FDJ members could no longer be counted on to act as drones. Consider the recollection of one

---

29 Schabowski, *Politbüro*, p. 189; Hertle, *Fall*, pp. 121, 422.
30 On October 3. *Der Spiegel*, 48, 1989, p. 28.
31 At a meeting on 21 October. Even if only bravado on Dickel's part, the tone implies the prevalence of a civil war mentality. Hollitzer, 'Verlauf', p. 286.
32 Wolle, *Diktatur*, p. 323. On police brutality on 7 October in Dresden see Bahr, *Sieben*, p. 89.

young Dresdner, who took the opportunity to travel to the event as a legitimate way of missing school for the day. It was a cold wet day in Berlin but he and the other Free German Youth were obliged to have their blue shirts showing:

> There we were, standing at Friedrichstrasse, right next to an expensive hotel that only westerners could afford. We were not even allowed in, and we couldn't even think of staying overnight there. We stood there in the cold drizzle with our torches and we were supposed to celebrate the 40th birthday of the GDR. And here these rich West Germans and other westerners looked down on us from windows in a hotel where we could never go. We felt like fools.

When the parade started he and his friends shouted not 'The Party, the Party is always right' but 'Down with the Prussians' and 'Saxony Number One!' Others intoned a German–Russian song of friendship, or chanted 'Gorby', as legitimate yet unmistakable signals of their support for reform.

In addition to the Gorby-chanting blue-shirts, opposition activists gathered to disrupt the official anniversary celebration. 'None of the eager plainclothes Stasi officials', according to one report, 'knew whether the chants of "Gorby, Gorby" hailed from loyal FDJ members or from "disgusting" oppositionists'.[33] From within the Palace of the Republic where Honecker's guests were assembled, one official described the scene:

> On all floors there was top-class entertainment with famous artists and comedians, refreshments, and delicacies – and through it all, unmistakably audible from outside, on the bank of the Spree, came the chants of the demonstrators: 'Freedom, Freedom!' It was eerie. An oppressive mood pervaded the event . . . It was just like on the Titanic.[34]

When the protestors moved away from the Palace, police and Stasi officers attacked. Over a thousand demonstrators were arrested and many were subjected to physical and verbal abuse. Undaunted, they stood their ground. One of those present recalls her three abiding memories: 'The

33 Dyke, *Dresden*, p. 226; *Der Spiegel*, 23 April 1990; Schabowski, *Absturz*, p. 180; Hall, *Fernseh-Kritik*, p. 106.
34 Reuth and Bönte, *Komplott*, p. 109. Of the jokes that reportedly circulated at the gathering, one concerned the activities of three countries, the USA, USSR and GDR, at work on the salvage of the Titanic. Each was driven by a pressing motive. The USA was after the gold in the safes. The USSR wished to study the technology of the engines. And the GDR? Its leaders were desperate to discover which pieces had been played by the ship's courageous orchestra as it went down.

cops were vicious. We were scared, of course. And the whole thing felt unreal, like in a movie.'[35] Another eyewitness remembers the presence of locals: 'Normal people, some of them still in their slippers, came downstairs and joined in.' A third describes

> how uneasy the [police] making the cordon looked when verbally attacked by women. The women reproached them, 'Aren't you feeling ashamed of yourself, standing against your own population? I could be your mother, yet you stand here with your truncheon. Put it away!'

Here, as in Dresden a few days earlier, the forces of order failed to triumph despite outnumbering the 'counterrevolutionaries' by a wide margin. In a series of letters to Honecker, Berlin's SED secretary Schabowski concluded that the security forces had not intervened swiftly enough and 'were not sufficiently prepared for such massive resistance'.[36] Stubborn resistance was forcing the SED leadership to reassess its assumption that the movement could be crushed by police methods alone.

On the same day as the Berlin clashes the first signs of an alternative trajectory appeared, in Plauen. This Saxon town had already been brushed by collective action at the start of October when crowds had arrived at the station to hail the trainloads of emigrants heading West. (Although the sealed trains had passed through at speed, a scheduled train from Berlin was stormed.)[37] As elsewhere, the protest agenda passed swiftly from emigration to domestic reform. On 7 October a demonstration took place, attended by 10,000–20,000. Although commonly described as 'spontaneous' it was triggered by somebody (or - bodies) who typed a flyer that announced the event, including time and venue. The flyer also presented demands: civil liberties and free elections, the legalisation of opposition groups and the right to strike. It was disseminated by bikers who criss-crossed the town at night stuffing them into letterboxes, and thence by that word-of-mouth grapevine known as 'whisper propaganda'.[38]

35 Behrend and Prenzel, *Republikaner*, p. 111; Hilke, interview. The scene has been memorialised in film, as the opening sequence of Wolfgang Becker's magnificent *Goodbye Lenin*.
36 Marcus Bahr, interview; Reich, 'Reflections', p. 87; Letters dated 7, 8 and 9 October, published in *Die Andere*, 10, 1991. In his memoirs, Schabowski adopts an 'I knew nothing' stance towards the police violence of these days (*Politbüro*, p. 79).
37 This and the next paragraph rely upon the accounts compiled by Thomas Küttler and Jean Röder, *Volk*, and John Connelly, 'Moment'.
38 As one journalist described it: 'Doctors called mechanics. Mechanics called construction workers. Construction workers called nurses. Nurses called

In line with prevailing policy the security forces were bent upon physically preventing the demonstration. In one sense, there was nothing exceptional about the event. Protests of similar size had occurred in Leipzig and Dresden. Yet, relative to its population (74,000) and its comparatively small police force, this was an enormous gathering. The police, though heavily armed, were surrounded, while the mayor found himself barricaded in the town hall. Police attempted to disperse the crowd with water cannon but this backfired. Compounded by their irritation at the menacing circling of a police helicopter, the water cannonade only antagonised protestors, who responded with a hail of bottles and stones, forcing the police to retreat (and badly damaging the water cannon).

At this juncture, events took an unexpected turn. A first small chink in the regime's armour was observed. On the basis of a rapport achieved between a local pastor and a police commander an arrangement was concluded in which the former urged the crowd to go home, promising that the mayor had agreed to hold discussions on reform, while the latter ordered his forces to retreat and sent the helicopter away. Although several thousand demonstrators remained and, together with passers-by, endured repeated attacks by police and army, the facts remained that a police commander, faced with a much greater crowd than expected, had pulled his forces back before demonstrators dispersed and that the informal deal bore the prospect of negotiations between the authorities and movement representatives.

On the next day Dresden witnessed a similar break in the established pattern of confrontation, albeit on a larger scale and without the police's relapse into violence that had marred the close of play in Plauen.[39] Here, too, demonstrators faced a heavily armed opponent. In addition to police and factory militias Hans Modrow again deployed the army. Initially, and in line with Politburo policy, the security forces assaulted protestors with little mercy and made mass arrests. However, as in Plauen, the size of the demonstration took the authorities by surprise and exposed a lack of resolve among police and army units. Dresden district police documents reveal that senior army and police officers were acutely aware of growing doubts and indiscipline in the ranks. Some expressed sympathy with the

doctors. Neighbors called neighbors. This is how the demonstrations came to life.' (Rosenau, 'Relocation', p. 268.) This was, incidentally, how most of my acquaintances in Potsdam and Berlin learned of demonstrations – at least if 'called' is understood loosely, for few East Germans possessed a telephone connection.

39 Many historians (e.g. Jarausch, *Rush*, p. 45), identify this event as the first break in the pattern of confrontation. In fact, the accolade belongs to Plauen.

demonstrators; a few were especially troubled when they spotted their own fathers in the crowds. In the police force similar doubts could be observed as the demonstration proceeded, and a growing number of officers disobeyed orders to attack.[40] In implicit acknowledgement of these facts a senior police officer broke with established tactics and, after consultation with a curate, issued an unauthorised order for truncheons to be sheathed in order that negotiations could take place. Demonstrators voted twenty of their number, soon to be known as the 'Group of Twenty' (G20), as their representatives and Dresden's mayor, Wolfgang Berghofer, agreed to meet them on the following morning.

This was a momentous event. For protestors, relishing their accepted presence on the streets, a signal victory had been won. It was the first major example of a regional leadership abandoning offensive tactics and agreeing to 'dialogue'. Although in the negotiations that followed Berghofer opposed the legalisation of New Forum and refused to recognise the G20 as a legitimate negotiating partner, he did nonetheless make significant concessions – notably an amnesty for 'non-violent' political prisoners – and even hinted that he sympathised with the demand for free elections. The fact that negotiations had gone ahead at all attested to divisions and uncertainties among SED leaders. Faint fissures were appearing in the regime.

On 9 October a demonstration in Leipzig widened those fissures into cracks. The previous Monday had seen an impressive gathering, of some 20,000, that held firm against the security forces. Demonstrators had suffered heavy beatings, serious injuries and arrests but were not cowed. Some had counter-attacked, drumming on police cars (with the occupants inside) and confiscating eight or more police hats. On 9 October Leipzigers expected a ruthless crackdown. When Marianne Pienitz, a hospital psychotherapist, and her colleagues wrote a letter to Mielke to plead that the security forces practise restraint 'we said "farewell" to one another when we sent it off, fearing that our next meeting would be in prison'. Fears of a bloodbath were assiduously stoked by the authorities. On the preceding Friday the local paper published a letter from a factory militia commander that made the state's position ominously clear. It warned that the security forces were determined to 'finally and decisively thwart [the protests]; if necessary, with arms at the ready!' Pastor Führer received anonymous threatening phone calls; to give one example: 'If you hold another Peace Prayer in this church, it will go up in flames.'[41]

40 *Der Spiegel*, 23 April 1990.
41 Zwahr, *Selbstzerstörung*, p. 48; Neues Forum Leipzig, *Jetzt*; Bartee, *Time*, p. 167.

The threats of violence were not idle. At least some SED leaders wished to quell the rising with armed might. The security forces were mobilised, and ordered to contain or crush the protest. Helmut Hackenberg, the acting Leipzig SED chief, informed Krenz that all necessary measures had been taken to nip any 'provocation' in the bud. The army was put on alert and extra troops from outside Leipzig were brought in to replace a local unit that had mutinied the previous Monday. In all, tens of thousands of security force members, including mobile police (a conscript force), army, factory militias and Stasi, were deployed – very visibly – around the city centre. Many were issued with live ammunition. Officers impressed the urgency of the task upon their troops. One battalion of mobile police was told: 'Comrades, today the class war begins. Today is the day – it's them or us. If truncheons prove inadequate, arms are to be used.'[42]

If the authorities' 'Plan A' centred on the prospect of bloodshed deterring demonstrators from reaching the centre, when this looked hopeless the emphasis switched to 'Plan B' – to prevent a march from forming following the peace prayers. Hundreds of SED members were sent to occupy the Nikolai Church in order to disrupt the protest-worship and to demoralise the congregation. Yet this plan, too, was unsuccessful. Not only were churchgoers undeterred but Leipzig clergy had ensured that the Nikolai Church would not be the only consecrated source of the march. Local clergy were not a particularly subversive group – at the time only a third of pastors believed that the Church should support the protest movement, and a decision whether to allow New Forum even to meet in churches was postponed. But when, on the Wednesday before 9 October, the city's 300 pastors were summoned to a meeting at which the Bishop of Leipzig urged them to cancel all further peace prayers, they not only rejected the proposal but voted in a clear majority that they be spread to all the city's churches.[43]

As evening approached, Leipzig's four central churches filled to overflowing. Despite calls by Rainer Eppelmann and several Church worthies – including Bishop Forck and Manfred Stolpe, a Church leader and Stasi collaborator – for citizens to refrain from demonstrating, tens of thousands remained in, or made their way to, the town centre.[44] People

---

42 See, e.g., Rudi Mittig, interviewed in Riecker, *Stasi*, p. 171; Hollitzer, 'Verlauf', p. 272; Neues Forum Leipzig, *Jetzt*, p. 92
43 Bartee, *Time*, p. 72; Schlegelmilch, 'Politische', p. 132.
44 It is one-sided at best to claim, with Edward Tiryakian ('Effervescence', p. 278), that the demonstrations received 'the *active* support of the church'. See also *die tageszeitung*, 1990, Nr. 1, p. 43; Reuth and Bönte, *Komplott*, p. 110; Kuhn, *Entscheidung*, p. 125. On Stolpe's collaboration with the Stasi, see Miller, *Narratives*.

lined the streets – 'hesitant sympathisers pretended to be onlookers', one demonstrator recalls.[45] As in Plauen and Dresden, young people predominated, but all generations were present. The authorities had failed to deter protestors from gathering. They had failed to disrupt the peace prayers. This left only 'Plan C': to disperse the demonstration by force.

A peaceful victory

The atmosphere in the centre of Leipzig was exceptionally tense. Police were present in huge numbers and indicated their intentions by drumming truncheons on shields. Yet, in a dramatic moment that came to be seen as the fatal blow to Honecker's regime, the security forces were pulled back.

Some debate, and still a little mystery, surrounds the questions of why the regime lost this signal battle in its 'class war' against protestors and why the event was non-violent. That it proceeded without bloodshed has been variously attributed to the country's Protestant heritage,[46] the intervention of the Stasi, and that of a celebrated conductor, not to mention more obvious influences such as the political culture of the civic groups, decisions taken by middle-ranking officials and – looming large in the background – the Kremlin.

The 'Protestant culture' explanation, at first blush, seems far-fetched. Even if the historical difficulty in linking protestantism with pacifism (most recently witnessed in the confessional adherence of the leaders of the contemporary world's most martial liberal democracies), the thesis must contend with the awkward fact that in its latter decades East Germany was among the most secular of societies. Within two generations the proportion of citizens who adhered to no religion had soared from 7 to 70 per cent. In the words of pastor Ehrhart Neubert, 'Protestant culture has collapsed as the dominant force in civil society'. This pre-ponderance of the godless was manifest in the turnout on 9 October: there was no difference in the rate of participation between Church members and the rest of the population.[47]

More persuasive is the narrower proposition that church-linked movements exerted a disproportionate influence upon the Leipzig protest culture, notably through the peace prayers. Thus, when asked why the revolution was largely peaceful, pastor Führer replied:

45 Tetzner, *Leipziger*, p. 17.
46 See, e.g., Sievers, *Revolution*, pp. 19, 63; Neubert, *Revolution*.
47 Pollack, 'Volkskirche', p. 271 and *passim*; Neubert, *Kommunikation*, p. 43; Opp *et al.*, *Origins*, ch. 8.

Through the peace prayers, definitely . . . Without the peace prayers things would have turned out very differently; it would have been awful, just like revolutions usually are. Without the Church there would have been violence, shooting, killing – that's why the peace prayers were decisive.

Protestant churches provided shelter for the peace movement and other dissident groups in the 1980s; these in turn provided the civic groups with what Karsten Timmer terms their core 'cognitive orientation', namely a commitment to civil liberties, dialogue and non-violence. On 9 October, activists from New Forum and from 'working groups' on 'justice', 'human rights' and 'environmental protection' distributed flyers appealing for non-violence to protestors and security forces alike. This input may have contributed to demonstrators' non-violence, although one suspects in the form of confirmation rather than conversion, for all were acutely aware that there were powerful figures and heavily armed forces itching for a pretext to crack down – simple prudence dictated that none be given.[48]

Yet, in accounting for the peaceful outcome on 9 October the roles of protestantism, prudence and political culture are necessarily of a secondary order. In revolutionary situations it is far more common that the authorities and counterrevolutionaries initiate and carry out violence than unarmed protestors.[49] For East Germans, Tiananmen Square served as a reminder of this historical law – all the more bracing, given that the leaders of their own 'peace state' had supported the Beijing butchery. The pacifism of protestors may have contributed to the restraint of the security forces but the critical factor to be explained is not the former but the latter and, by extension, the tactics of the regime.

For a military crackdown to work, reliable security forces are indispensable, yet in East Germany this was in doubt. The regime's weakness, the absence of a belief that Moscow would defend it to the hilt and the confident but pacific behaviour of demonstrators all bred uncertainty.[50] On 9 October, despite the efforts of officers and functionaries to pump up an atmosphere of impending civil war, sections of the security forces were in disarray. Already in preceding weeks police units, particularly in

48 Interview with Gideon Saunders, October 2004; Timmer, *Aufbruch*, p. 38; Mitter and Wolle, *Untergang*, p. 537.
49 For historical examples, and for discussion of the logic behind this, see Oberschall, *Social*, pp. 334–5.
50 On the impact of the demonstrators' behaviour on the security forces, see Leipzig Stasi report BVfS 136/89.

Saxony, had shown signs of disquiet and some officers were jailed for refusing to use force against protests. Even commanding officers had disobeyed orders in the first week of October, while police reservists, their superordinates observed with concern, showed serious signs of unreliability. In the army, conditions came close to mutiny when troops were ordered to prevent demonstrations. 'When their battalions were assembled, resistance broke out, especially amongst the soldiers', one military official reported. 'They spoke out openly, saying "we won't beat them up".' As regards the mobile police, around 10 per cent of its recruits had been purged in the run-up to 9 October; these were either deemed 'too unreliable politically to serve on Monday nights, or had been observed fraternizing with demonstrators'.[51] Of the remainder, some reportedly broke into tears upon hearing instructions that, 'if necessary', firearms should be used.

The greatest degree of unreliability was found in the factory militias. Alongside functionaries, these formations included many workers, and were sensitive to working-class opinion. Although workers were not the 'early risers' of the 1989 revolt, beneath the surface there were numerous signs of a process of politicisation and of individuals 'silently breaking' with the regime. In the summer and early autumn workplace morale declined, with a marked rise in reports of indiscipline and of workers expressing a wish to quit their job.[52] Growing numbers refused to accept functionaries' explanations of events or the denunciations of New Forum as enemies of the state.[53] This mood shift affected the militias. One militia member recalls, for example, that the electoral fraud of May 1989 provoked heated discussion. (That, he adds, 'was when we complained to the Party leadership that we wanted straightforward reporting, not gushing'.) In the summer an internal SED report raised concerns regarding both the diminishing number of workers who were signing up to the militias and the indiscipline that affected them. When autumn arrived many militiamen, including SED members, were reluctant to police the demonstrations and invented excuses to dodge deployment. Hundreds, possibly thousands, refused to train for street fighting, disobeyed orders or resigned from their units. There were numerous cases of mutiny, notably in the South, in units stationed along the route of the westward-bound 'emigration trains' or deployed to suppress demonstrations in Dresden and elsewhere. In Karl-Marx-Stadt one unit simply

51 Keithly, *Collapse*, p. 225; BDVP, 12 October 1989; Opp *et al.*, *Volkseigene*, p. 290; Pond, *Beyond*, p. 112.
52 Klenke, *Rationalisierung*; Mitter and Wolle, *Untergang*, p. 510.
53 See, e.g., Krone, *Briefe*, p. 55.

melted away. In Leipzig only a minority of factory militia units were up to strength in the autumn, and there were signs of mutiny on 2 October.[54]

These tendencies were heightened, according to a Stasi investigation at the time, by what is described in Stasi-speak as 'the effect of negative-enemy influence, such as solidarity with demands of the oppositional movement New Forum'. Many units, the report continues, 'were influenced by the curses of masses of demonstrators and passers-by, such as: "shame on you – workers against workers".' One officer recounted how his unit was given the order to proceed against the crowd using 'all possible means'. This, it was assumed, included live ammunition but his commander 'refused to issue weapons, and so did the commander of the district police'. He was ordered to prevent demonstrators – who would be 'only punks [and] anarchistic people' – from entering the city centre. Yet, when the crowds appeared,

> I saw no anarchists! Furthermore, what they were shouting to me, while hardly flattering, sounded about right. My group felt pretty much conned . . . The next day when we read in the paper that we had defended the city against punks and rowdies, we in our unit decided: if an order to move out comes down again, we would refuse. We would not go out again.

Members of another militia unit deployed to police the demonstration on 9 October have described how demoralisation set in already when its working-class members, having expected 'that the functionaries from the local and regional leaderships' would be with them as usual, noticed that 'none of these comrades were to be seen'. As demonstrators gathered, the militiamen witnessed the paralysis of the professional security forces. 'Police officers running hither and thither, without a clue what to do' – one of them even 'told us that we should just disappear, as quickly as possible'. The militia members were scared and confused. 'It was an apocalyptic mood', said one. To their surprise the 'enemy' before them consisted of fellow workers. 'We could see that it was ordinary folk who were shouting "We are the People!" ', another recalls, 'and we felt that we belonged to them too'. They found themselves in agreement with protest slogans and felt confused, or in some cases profoundly abused by the regime that they had hitherto defended with pride. In defiance of express orders many were persuaded to withdraw; others laid down

---

54 Bartee, *Time*, p. 161; Tetzner, *Leipziger*, p. 22; Pfaff, 'Revolution', pp. 323, 330–1; Liebsch, *Dresdner*, p. 19; Mitter and Wolle, *Befehle*, p. 221; Klein, *Visionen*, p. 459; Hertle, *Fall*, p. 413.

helmets, shields and truncheons and stepped forth to talk with 'the negative-enemy forces'.[55]

Even given these signs of vacillation within the security forces it would
still have been entirely conceivable, as the evening wore on, for a tense
or trigger-happy officer – with or without 'provocation' – to open fire.
The chances of this happening, however, were markedly attenuated
thanks to the actions of middle-level functionaries in Leipzig, in particular a group of three local SED chiefs. They were caught between two
powerful forces – orders from Berlin, and an impossibly large crowd of
Leipzigers on the streets before them. On the one hand, many of their
colleagues and friends counselled caution. The editor of the local newspaper had published a piece that morning calling for 'patient and open
dialogue'. Even the local Stasi chief, if his own account is to be believed,
advised that the security forces would be unable to prevent the demonstration. On the other hand, they were under instruction to suppress the
event, by 'any means necessary'. In an historic decision the three Leipzig
chiefs, led by hard-liner Hackenberg, ordered the security forces to
refrain from using weapons, and broadcast an appeal for non-violence
and 'dialogue' which three local luminaries had helped them to draft.[56]

Among historians of the East German revolution there is consensus
that these functionaries, supported by Leipzig police commanders, were
critical to the peaceful outcome. Their message, broadcast over loudspeakers to demonstrators and the security forces, has gone down in the
history books as a decisive intervention. Yet as to *why* these three functionaries contributed to a peaceful outcome, there is less agreement.

Of the 'Group of Six' functionaries and local dignitaries one in particular, the conductor of the Leipzig *Gewandhaus* Orchestra Kurt Masur,
has gained most plaudits. The conductor was a moderate; he was sharply
critical of regime hawks but also of the opposition ('You people from
New Forum scare me', he once said). He had excellent connections,
including to Honecker himself; as such, he was in a position to bring a
theologian and an actor together with SED functionaries to form the
'Six', who then prepared their entreaty for non-violence. In high school
history textbooks he is credited with prime responsibility for the lack of
violence. For Hubertus Knabe 'It was only a dramatic appeal by Kurt
Masur and several members of the SED district leadership that prevented
a bloodbath', while for US historian William Smyser it was the 'powerful figure' of Masur who made the critical difference: 'Masur's message

55 Mitter and Wolle, *Befehle*, p. 222; Bartee, *Time*, p. 162; Neues Forum
     Leipzig, *Jetzt*, pp. 90ff., 291.
56 Zwahr, *Selbstzerstörung*, p. 76; Riecker, *Stasi*, p. 218; *Oktober 1989*, p. 105.

and person carried the day.' However, one wonders whether these quotations do not derive their force from a desire to anoint heroes for a revolution in which such figures were noticeable by their absence.[57]

The Masur legend is not without foundation. Yet to explain the demonstrators' disciplined non-violence by reference to that appeal, as some accounts do,[58] is far-fetched, given that the temper of the demonstration was in any case pacific, that it had been peacefully underway long before most participants heard the appeal and, moreover, that the quality of the sound system was too poor for parts of the crowd to discern its content.[59] If Masur contributed to events it was by strengthening SED district leaders in their inclination – following in the footsteps of their counterparts in Plauen and Dresden – to talk rather than shoot. But to see why they were already leaning this way, one must look to wider social forces.

First, let us consider the stance of the SED leadership in Berlin. Here, again, it can be difficult to disentangle myth from reality. One theory holds that Politburo members Krenz, Herger, Schabowski and even Mielke were preparing a leadership and policy change, and so made sure that no orders to shoot live ammunition were issued lest their reform plans be drowned in blood; accordingly, the Stasi sent an envoy to Leipzig to ensure that the security forces exercised restraint. There is also reason to believe that when Honecker argued at the Politburo for the use of live ammunition, a narrow majority voted it down. Krenz identifies Politburo members, in particular his own calming influence, as the decisive factor in accounting for the absence of a bloodbath (and this view later received vocal backing from his successor as SED leader, Gregor Gysi). 'This must not lead to a new June 17', Krenz reconstructs his thoughts of the time: 'In this explosive period we must keep a cool head.' Already before the demonstration, he maintains, it was agreed at the highest level that the security organs would not attack. Elsewhere, he claims that he rescinded Honecker's order to shoot (although Honecker himself denies ever having issued that command). What is certain is that Hackenberg telephoned Krenz on 9 October to request guidance, and there are no grounds to doubt the SED leader's claim that, when he returned the call, he supported the Leipzig leaders in their decision to de-escalate. Yet the call came at 19:15, some 90 minutes after police had been ordered to hold back. Why Krenz delayed has been the subject of

57 Reuth and Bönte, *Komplott*, p. 131; Mögenburg, *Revolution*, p. 65; Knabe, *Aufbruch*, p. 16; Smyser, *Berlin*, pp. 338–9.
58 E.g. Pond, *Beyond*, p. 117.
59 Wielepp, 'Leipzig', p 72; Kuhn, *Entscheidung*, p. 129.

some speculation. Was his mind elsewhere, on the plot to oust Honecker? Perhaps so. But another possibility is that Krenz, recognising 9 October as a pivotal moment that would lead either to retrenchment or reform, opted to wait to see which way the wind was beginning to blow before giving his blessing to the Leipzig leadership. If so, this would have been entirely in character.[60]

If SED leaders bore some responsibility for the security forces' restraint this derived not from a brave decision to directly encourage their Leipzig subordinates to resist Honecker's hard line. It would be more accurate to say that the Politburo found itself insufficiently united to take a clear decision either way. As mentioned in chapter 1, uncertainty had been worming its way into leadership circles for some years. It had been exacerbated by the summer crisis, in which SED leaders showed uncharacteristic weakness (for instance, by granting embassy occupants permission to emigrate). Divisions then grew increasingly open and acrimonious. Sections of the media began to give space to conciliatory positions. *Junge Welt*, for example, conceded in mid-September that 'The fact that even younger citizens of our state are unable to stand the stress of the class struggle, that is a cause for sadness'. On 9 October the same newspaper published a critique of media policy by SED novelist Herrmann Kant.

As the pillars of the regime began to crack, spaces opened for initiative to be taken by middle-level officials. They sensed the paralysis of and divisions within the leadership, and were simultaneously under pressure from lower-level functionaries and SED members which, in turn, were exposed to an increasingly importunate and politicised public. As protests spread, officials felt pummelled by popular anger; 'accusations are hailing down on me', one lamented in her diary.[61] Although many remained stoic, and poured scorn on the demonstrations, others showed signs of independent thought and action. The Leipzig leadership – caught between a disunited, indecisive SED leadership and an inflamed citizenry – took the latter path.

The SED leadership's divisions and paralysis were, of course, bound up with the changes underway in the Soviet Union, and Gorbachev himself visited East Germany two days before the Leipzig watershed, to attend the anniversary ceremony and for talks with Honecker. The transcripts of their discussions reveal a stark contrast in substance and tone.

60 Prokop, *Unternehmen*, p. 48; Herger, in Riecker, *Stasi*, p. 123, see also pp. 207, 217; *Neues Deutschland*, 6 November 1989; Krenz, *Herbst*, p. 81 and *passim*; Reich, 'Reflections', p. 81; Wolle, *Diktatur*, p. 323; Timmer, *Aufbruch*, pp. 188–9. See also Krenz, *Wenn*, p. 138.
61 Liebsch, *Dresdner*, p. 50.

Honecker's contributions were wooden, and stacked with complacent platitudes, while the Soviet premier spoke with urgency, although often allusively, of severe social problems, of the need for rulers to listen to the public, and of the imperative of swift 'restructuring'. His words, Gorbachev later complained, fell on deaf ears – they had as much effect as 'throwing peas against a wall'.[62]

Nevertheless, several of Gorbachev's contributions, although ostensibly referring to the Soviet situation, were arguably intended to be open to wider interpretation and were certainly received in this way by some of those present.[63] The best-known of these was his warning of the costs of postponing change, as illustrated in a Russian adage: 'Those who arrive at the meal late must be content with the leftovers.'[64] According to political theorist Jon Elster, this utterance was the starter gun for the protest movement, which 'might not have taken place were it not for that speech'. In this, Elster is exaggerating Gorbachev's direct impact beyond all reason, and yet the importance of the Soviet position as a whole cannot be underestimated. As outlined in chapter 1, the lack of confidence within the SED leadership had much to do with its divergence from the Kremlin in the late 1980s, and the latter's presence loomed large behind the events of early October. On the one hand, Moscow was clearly worried that its grip on its German vassal might slip. 'The Soviet people will never forgive us for losing the GDR!', Gorbachev reportedly said. In his view, the prevention of that scenario required the SED regime to reform. On the other hand, the Soviet leadership was embroiled in domestic difficulties and in no position to push for further transformation among allied regimes. Already by the summer of 1989 perestroika had 'spun out of control', in David Remnick's phrase; (he cites working-class rebellion, national risings and economic dislocation as primary causes).[65] By autumn, the Kremlin's paramount concern was holding the line at home. Accordingly, Gorbachev did not directly speak out against Honecker but intervened behind the scenes. There is some evidence to suggest he gave tacit support to SED leaders who were plotting to oust Honecker,[66] and the Kremlin's gentle withdrawal of support was

62 Küchenmeister, *Honecker-Gorbatschow*.
63 Hertle, *Fall*, pp. 481, 463.
64 This was translated into German as 'life punishes those who arrive too late'. Von Plato, *Vereinigung*, pp. 61–2.
65 Elster, 'Introduction', p. 8; Maximytschew and Hertle, 'Maueröffnung', p. 1138; Remnick, *Lenin's*, p. 223.
66 For a brief summary of the evidence, see Stent, *Russia*, p. 89; also Simon, *Tischzeiten*, p. 132.

compounded by instructions to Soviet troops in East Germany that they remain in their barracks. Military intervention, Gorbachev's advisors were pointing out, 'would have catastrophic consequences, not only for the [Eastern European] countries and the entire system of East–West relations, but also for the policy of perestroika in the USSR'.[67] Indications that the Soviet army would not intervene to crush resistance, as it had done in 1953, not only gave succour to the regime's critics but also gave proponents of full-scale repression pause for thought.[68]

That the streets were blood-free on 9 October had much to do with the Soviet stance, the lack of confidence and cohesion at the top of the SED and the actions of middle-level officials. But what would have transpired if the crowds had been smaller? By early October the movement had spread far beyond the ranks of opposition activists and would-be emigrants and was drawing in wide layers of the population. Roland Woetzel, one of the Leipzig SED triumvirate, was later to admit that they were utterly confounded by this development – 'none of us had reckoned with these numbers'. Police were simply unable to apply their chosen tactics of splitting and encircling the demonstration. When the regional leadership capitulated, Tobias Hollitzer's research has shown, it was 'exclusively the result of the unexpectedly large crowds'. Others concur with his conclusion. 'It was not the appeal of the Six and certainly not Egon Krenz', argues Hans-Jürgen Sievers, 'but solely the enormous numbers of demonstrators that prevented an armed intervention by police'.[69]

It was not simply the numbers of citizens on the streets that counted but their courage and resourcefulness, their skills and tactics too. Protestors held firm in the face of truncheons. Even before 9 October, police brutality and mass arrests in Leipzig and elsewhere had provoked resilient displays of solidarity. Vigils had formed at churches, and witness statements and victims' testimonies were collated for publication. Letters of protest poured in to the authorities. 'In early October', Berlin activist Bert Konopatsky recalls, 'there were constant demonstrations and vigils – and even a rock concert – on behalf of those arrested. This gave you the confidence to demonstrate – the knowledge that there'd be a movement of support, should you land in prison.'

67 Leonhard, *DDR*, p. 212; Gedmin, *Hidden*, p. 102; Kuhn, *Entscheidung*, pp. 29–31; MccGwire, *Perestroika*, p. 358.
68 Although Gorbachev's comments were not released to the public, the knowledge vacuum was quickly filled by rumours, the most popular of which held that he had told bystanders 'if you really want democracy, then take it, and you will get it!'
69 Hollitzer, 'Verlauf', pp. 278, 249; Sievers, *Revolution*, p. 95.

Many of those who were arrested and mistreated by police were not intimidated but emerged from the experience strengthened. One who told me her tale was an SED member, Barbara Fuchs. On 7 October she was arrested in Berlin, not even for protesting but merely for taking photographs of the battle lines between demonstrators and police. Transported to the notorious Rummelsburg prison she discovered to her amazement that she and her fellow detainees 'were unbowed. It was a wonderful experience – how we managed to generate solidarity. For instance, we would all begin to hum together, or sing, or wink at one another – in the face of horrible intimidation by the police.' It was at that moment, she reflects, that 'I noticed this state was a gonner. I came out of Rummelsburg with more power.'

Conclusion

From its small beginnings, surrounded by security forces, the demonstration movement had grown to a point where police methods were unable to suppress it. This left the deployment of armed force as the only viable means of quelling the movement. That would require degrees of nerve and cohesion among the regime's leaders and apparatuses which were in short supply. This, combined with lack of support from Moscow, sapped the confidence of middle-level officials in Leipzig. But the critical factor in preventing the expected crackdown was that in those crucial weeks of late September and early October the numbers and determination of protestors had proved sufficient to intimidate the security forces and to boost the confidence of participants that they could withstand the repression. In the run-up to 9 October movement supporters signalled to potential protestors and government alike that they were not about to retreat. Solidarity events discouraged police and prosecutors from punishing protestors with long jail sentences, amplifying the fear in the corridors of power that a repressive response could backfire. In Plauen, Dresden and Leipzig a similar pattern could be seen: local officials and police commanders seek to prevent protest with a show of police force; thanks to the numbers and determination of demonstrators as well as the lack of resolve in sections of the security forces this plan falters; commanders and middle-level officials agree instead to rein in their forces and enter negotiations.

The success of the Leipzig demonstrators, according to LDPD leader Manfred Gerlach, 'horrified Honecker'. It exposed the impracticability of a hard-line stance, and encouraged protest to take off nationwide.[70]

70 Gerlach, *Mitverantwortlich*, p. 284; Przybylski, *Tatort 2*, pp. 121–33.

Despite a ban on Western journalists entering the GDR (which had been in place since early September) citizens were able to see images of the Leipzig demonstration on television that very evening, thanks to amateurs with a concealed video camera who had filmed it from a church tower and smuggled the cassette to West Germany. Peace prayers now mushroomed – in Neubrandenburg the first of these, on 11 October, brought 250 instead of the expected 30; a week later over 2,000 attended. Demonstrations too, despite their continued prohibition, were held in most major towns; for example, on 15 October in Plauen and Halle tens of thousands took to the streets. The 9 October demonstration was, visibly, a watershed.

3

Algebra of mobilisation

'Revolutions are very wordy occasions.' (Leon Trotsky)

If chapter 2 highlighted the importance of the numbers, tactics and stead-fastness of demonstrators to the success of 9 October, chapter 3 explores the question of *why* people took to the streets *en masse*. For it was far from obvious that they would. The threat of bloodshed was real, and there is no doubt but that Leipzigers were aware of the risks involved. Some older citizens, moreover, still carried wounds from previous battles; one recalls 'initially keeping my distance [from the public protests], because memories of the consequences of 17 June 1953 are still fresh'.[1] Anecdotal evidence of citizens' fears has been complemented by an important survey carried out by the sociologists Karl-Dieter Opp, Peter Voß and Christiane Gern in their *Origins of a Spontaneous Revolution*. They asked respondents to recall the sanctions that they expected demonstrators to face at and following protest events up to and including 9 October. The results are depicted in Table 2.

Given that expectations of sanctions were so widespread, one might wonder why any sane Leipziger would engage in protest at all. In *Origins* the anxiety experienced on 9 October is presented as a short-term spike within an overall trajectory of declining fear. As discussed in chapter 2, many East Germans were alert to changes in the political opportunity structure, including the diminishing prospect of Soviet intervention and the regime's trials in the face of liberalisation elsewhere in Eastern Europe (as highlighted by its inability to stem the summer exodus). With the regime visibly entering troubled waters confidence in the potential efficacy of collective action tended to grow and the perceived risks of protesting to diminish. The rising movement, moreover, tended to generate its own momentum, for, when individuals witnessed forms of action that had hitherto been inconceivable, or perceived others

1 Krone, *Briefe*, p. 123.

Table 2 Perceived risks of demonstrating[a]

	Probable (%)	Improbable (%)
Arrest	91	9
Injury by security forces	88	12
Sanctions at work	59	26
Sanctions for family members	65	21

Note: [a] From Opp *et al.*, 'Data', p. 6. See also Opp *et al.*, *Origins*, p. 140.

considering whether to participate, this itself encouraged them to re-evaluate their abstention and look afresh at the options.[2] As the ability of protestors to occupy public spaces, and the size of demonstrations, grew, the expected costs – such as the likelihood of arrest, or discrimination at work – fell. The movement's initial successes raised anticipations of political change. In these ways, the reforms in the Soviet Union and Eastern Europe set in motion cascades of what game theorists call 'assurance games' that culminated in the decisions of tens of thousands of East Germans to engage in protest.

With regard to participation specifically on 9 October, Opp, Voß and Gern advance three main arguments. First, reference to their survey data shows that not *everybody* feared that participation would entail high costs. Some reckoned the likelihood of large-scale arrests or injuries was low. One Leipziger present that day, for example, told me that despite being 'quite scared' he believed a 'Tiananmen solution was out of the question'.[3] Moreover, even some of the pessimists remained surprisingly sanguine, for the escalating scale of the movement seemed to reduce the likelihood of individuals facing sanctions. As Susanne Lohmann has pointed out, with vicarious stoicism:

> participants in the critical demonstration of 9 October, 1989, faced the very real possibility that their protest would end in a massacre; but even then they could reasonably expect that only a few dozen – in the worst case perhaps several hundreds – out of tens of thousands of participants would meet their death.

For any one demonstrator, she concludes, somewhat clinically, 'the implied probability of death is rather low.'[4]

Second, the rational calculation that the demonstration's expected size reduced the likelihood of personal injury (or worse) was complemented

2 James Rule, in Klandermans, 'Social', p. 86.
3 Mario Kessler.
4 Lohmann, 'Dynamics', p. 90, emphasis added.

by an emotional sense of strength in numbers. In Opp's survey, over a third of respondents who had demonstrated on or before 9 October endorsed the statement: 'I felt so secure with the many others around me that I thought nothing could happen.' Large majorities agreed with affirmations of collective action ('I felt that each individual was necessary for goals to be achieved') and the emotional charge of solidarity ('coming together with so many people who wanted the same thing was a wonderful feeling').[5] Here again, these findings tally with interview evidence. For example, the experience of the 9 October demonstration, Mario Kessler recalls, 'was a transformative experience; it kept my fears in check and alerted me to the power of working people in large numbers'.

Third, repression does not always reduce protest but can generate it, too. Heavy-handed police tactics in early October, *Origins* explains, increased levels of 'political dissatisfaction' with the regime, raised the 'moral incentive' to protest and spurred those who perceived the regime to be illegitimate or in need of reform to greater exertion. 'Social incentives' were strengthened, too: that objections to the regime's tactics were more widely and openly voiced encouraged potential participants to take action. In short, the intended 'deterrence effect' of repression was trumped by 'radicalising effects' that persuaded greater numbers to protest.[6] Here, too, the argument in *Origins* is convincing. In the early autumn, the regime's blundering reaction to the exodus followed by its ruthless attempts to crush dissent and to demonise public protest as the work of 'rowdies' was widely read as evidence of arrogance and incompetence. The disparity between the SED's complacent assurances that order reigned and the reality of deep crisis underlined this shift in mood. For some, savage policing dispelled the last vestiges of faith in the regime. Uwe Rottluf, a printer in the postal service, recalls that the behaviour of the security forces in early October provoked outrage among his colleagues. ' "That's not on!" they would say: "The police attacking our own people! And *these* demonstrators didn't even want to leave the country!" '[7] It was at this juncture, he adds, that 'criticism of the government exploded at my workplace'. The repression of early October delegitimised the regime in the eyes of many of its supporters and among the public; it also corroborated the arguments of those who framed the conflict as that of a non-violent citizenry against a barbarous, illegitimate elite.

5 Opp *et al.*, *Origins*, p. 141; Opp *et al.*, *Data*; also *Volkseigene*, pp. 68, 179.
6 Opp *et al.*, *Origins*, pp. 146–7.
7 See also Kuhn, *Entscheidung*, p. 76.

On the individualism of collective action

The analysis in *Origins* is designed to showcase Opp's 'rational actor' theory of collective action. A methodological-individualist approach, it holds that society is constituted by the individuals that comprise it, social behaviour is reducible to the actions of individuals and only these actors have real interests.[8] Each individual is assumed to be acting in order 'to maximize his or her utility' – to increase benefits and to minimise costs. The investigation of the calculus of mobilisation centres on the changing opportunities and constraints faced by individual actors. In explicit disavowal of 'micromobilisation' models (on which, see p. 41), *Origins* explains collective action as the outcome of individuals who share similar grievances and a common antagonism towards the regime perceiving changes to the political opportunity structure and, separately and spontaneously, calculating that resistance would be worth their while. This 'spontaneous coordination' of behaviour ('without arrangement, organization, or mobilization') is illustrated by analogy with Adam Smith's model of the market – a mechanism that ensures that the acts of individuals pursuing private ends, calculated in cost-benefit terms, result in advantages for all. At this theoretical level, the crux of the argument is summed up in Opp's proposition that 'revolutions are the result of individual decisions'.[9]

Although a species of rational choice theory, the approach in *Origins* deviates in significant respects from the orthodoxy. It does not presuppose stable structures of preferences upon which individual decisions are based, nor does it assume social behaviour to be that of *homo œconomicus*, reducible to material self-interest. Most importantly, the notion of 'selective incentives' to action is extended to include not only material ends but rewards of a normative and affective type, too – even including those that arise through collective action itself. Following norms that have been internalised or which are approved by peers, it argues, 'is associated with benefits: one has a good conscience, has done one's duty, and this provides feelings of joy and satisfaction'. Emotions and affections such as anger, indignation, sympathy and pride are not sidelined; rather, *Origins* presents them as co-sponsors of rational action.[10]

---

8 In *Origins*, a slippage occurs between methodology and ontology, with methodological individualism presented as the logical corollary of the sheer existence of acting individuals, as in, 'The protests of the population were the actions of many individuals. *Therefore*, in explaining these protests, the individual is our starting point', emphasis added.

9 Opp *et al.*, *Origins*, pp. 31–3, 42–3, 241.

10 Opp *et al.*, *Origins*, p. 81. Cf. also Hough 'Logic'.

Opp's modification of utilitarian theory sidesteps some of the difficulties that orthodox approaches confront, but is not without its own distinctive problems. By pressing manifold normative, emotional and material factors into the single mould of incentives – rather as the grandfather of rational choice theory, Jeremy Bentham, once proposed that money could function as the sole measure of utility – the specificity of modes of rationality and forms of action is obscured.[11] Although the flattening of heterogeneous actions into one dimension lends the model parsimony, this comes at the cost of an impoverished understanding of human nature and action. In behaviourist fashion the affects and emotions are viewed as one more set of incentives the desired satisfaction of which prompts individuals to act, ignoring the specific role played by emotions in shaping the assessment of the potential gains and costs involved in collective action.[12] Opp's model neglects the sense in which individuals' relations within social groups and within society as a whole enter not only into individuals' calculations of whether an act is rational, but condition the values, and the very sense of identity, that inform and shape that calculus.

Lest misunderstanding arise, the critique advanced here is not that Opp's rational actor model 'cannot deal with emotion'. Rather, it is that in so far as such 'non-rational' elements are incorporated they forfeit their specificity and the concept of incentive loses purchase. A similar point has been made by Mark Thompson, in a review of *Origins*, who observes that the 'radicalisation effect' identified by Opp and his colleagues, whereby repression amplifies the 'social incentive' to protest, 'is another way of saying that individual-utility maximization has been abandoned (particularly in regard to personal well-being) and that actors are engaging in unusual levels of risk-taking in pursuit of a "public good" '. The threat of repression contributes to protestors' belief that they are engaged in a Manichaean struggle, in the heat of which the 'rational' calculus of normal life yields to extraordinary and emotionally charged hopes.[13] If the concept of utility maximisation at the heart of rational actor theory is stretched to include such phenomena, Thompson argues, the model becomes tautological.

But the main charge that I would level against the rational actor model is that if fails to adequately theorise the social context and relational nature of *individual actions*. Preferences do not express *a priori*

11 On this question, for a suggestive argument that draws upon communitarian theory, see Thompson, 'Germans'.
12 See Aminzade and McAdam, 'Emotions', p. 17.
13 Thompson, 'Germans', p. 272

desires but are constructed within the field of social relations and norms in which the individual exists – we make decisions within a system of social interdependence, and our choice to participate (or not) in collective action is conditioned by expectations of the behaviour of others.[14] If this criticism can be summarised in a phrase, it is that Opp's maxim that 'revolutions are made by individual decisions' neglects the role of collective action in shaping those individual decisions. Our judgements of interest are deeply affected by our sense of identity; how we weigh up costs and benefits, what time-scale is deployed in the calculation, and how we act accordingly, are influenced by who we think we are – and this, in turn, is affected by the actions in which we engage.

Identity, in this usage, refers not to immutable characteristics of individuals that pre-date action but 'the process by which social actors recognize themselves – and are recognized by other actors – as part of broader groupings'. It is a relational concept: our state of identity is shaped through a 'circle of recognition' in which the self is constructed through relations to others. Identities are shaped in the course of the 'personal and political projects in which we participate', they are influenced by participation in collective action, in which feelings of belonging are reinforced or weakened. The allegiances, or collective identities, that result are vital aspects of collective action. They may be strong or weak, and may or may not entail a coherent world-view, but they necessarily comprise positive orientations to those participating in a certain group, negative attitudes to those who are actively opposed and also a relationship with those in a neutral position. In Colin Barker's words, collective identity refers to 'who we are in terms of our relations with others in our group, who we are as a group orienting to others, and who those others are in their orientations towards us'. Participation in social movements, he continues, 'entails envisaging the world as open to intervention and change and thus, commonly, to re-evaluation of the self and the group, and of the possible meanings of such terms as solidarity and community'.[15]

As this last quote suggests, collective identities are not only relational but dynamic constructs. They are not fixed at the moment of movement participation but evolve over time and are subject to continual renewal. In processes of collective action participants continually redefine their

14 Della Porta and Diani, *Movements*, p. 107.
15 Della Porta and Diani, *Movements*, p. 85; Pizzorno, 'Otherness', p. 366; Barker, 'Empowerment', p. 14; See also Barker and Lavalette, 'Strategizing', p. 142.

relations to others, their interests and identities. Barker also draws attention to the sense of collective *obligation* that arises in social movements, which 'permits the costs of action to be re-evaluated on the basis of a calculus revised by considerations of mutuality'. This revised calculus, he goes on, 'depends on emergent shared evaluations: cognitively, of the character of the situation, morally, of both the problem requiring action and of the movement; and, pragmatically, of the practicality of collective action itself'. Other social movement theorists have described how the sense of collective obligation enables the open-ended and sometimes risky outcomes of collective action to be faced in a way that individualist utilitarians could not. Donnatella della Porta and Mario Diani put it this way:

> Feeling part of a shared endeavour and identifying one's own interests not only at an individual level but also at the collective level makes costs and risks more acceptable than they would otherwise have been, if considered from the point of view of the maximization of individual utility over a short period.[16]

In the pages that follow, these ideas are developed through an examination of protest dynamics in 1989.

Micromobilisation and the creation of solidarity

It is not inconceivable that many East Germans who shared similar grievances and a common antagonism towards the regime decided, separately and individually, that participating in protest was worthwhile, but Opp's 'spontaneous coordination' model addresses only the experience in Leipzig, and even there it offers at best a partial explanation. In respect of the experience at least of the participants whom I interviewed, a better guide is provided by a model towards which *Origins* is at best ambiguous, that of 'micromobilisation', with its focus upon rudimentary organisation and will-formation in small-group settings. For them, the decision to protest was typically taken with reference to others – the same groups with whom, over preceding days and months, they had shared grievances and evaluated the crisis. At work, or among friends and family members, individuals would discuss the unfolding political drama, deliberate over whether to take part and in many cases proceed together to the demonstration. Among groups of friends and colleagues it became 'fashionable', as one interviewee from Dresden put it, to say 'there's a demo

16 Rule, *Theories*, p. 40; Della Porta and Diani, *Movements*, pp. 104–8; Barker, 'Introduction'; also McAdam *et al.*, *Dynamics of Contention*, p. 57.

taking place: let's go!'[17] Another reported that 'seventy to eighty per cent of staff, typically the younger ones, would go to demonstrations *together*'. That the norm of solidarity gained ground in these circumstances cannot be adequately explained in terms of discrete individuals altering their calculations as to how to achieve goals 'cost effectively'. For many, the decision to participate was itself a collective process, one that developed within existing networks in which solidarity and cognate values of cooperation and obligation were already present.[18]

Even for those whose decision to demonstrate was taken in relative isolation, the experience of collective protest would catalyse change in their perceived capacities and goals. Consider the story of a functionary's son in Leipzig.[19] Although normally a conformist, patriotic sort of chap, he decided – like so many, out of sheer curiosity – to venture into the city centre to observe a demonstration. He wished to see for himself what all the fuss was about. Upon arrival he was confronted by ranks of police and dogs, a menacing spectacle. Facing them, a huge crowd had gathered. On this side the atmosphere was exuberant. Heads were held high. The presence of the protestors, their demeanour and demands, formed a stark contrast to the amassed forces of the state. The young man began to re-evaluate his views; thoughts of a regime-loyal kind receded, while those with a critical aspect came to the fore. Eventually he joined the demonstration, and in the process experienced a slight but significant identity shift: he now was, and perceived himself to be, a movement participant.

This scenario is far from uncommon in collective action situations, not least during confrontations between crowds and security forces. In East Germany, participation in the mass demonstrations generated confidence; protestors, 'in coming together in collective action experienced their own power and simultaneously the impotence of the powerful'. One Leipziger describes how, on 9 October, she

> met up with friends, and we gave one another courage. Some cried, and some wanted to leave. But, we said, we are going to stand our ground together. And then we moved towards the church, and could hardly believe how many people were amassing there . . . we looked around, furtively, nervously, and realised to our surprise that we could no longer see the state's forces . . . And suddenly a feeling arose, an incredible feeling of solidarity.

17 Interviews with Ollie, Antje and Gabi Engelhardt; see also Neues Forum Leipzig, *Jetzt*, p. 139; Zwahr, *Selbstzerstörung*, p. 45.
18 For a similar argument, see Pfaff, 'Collective'.
19 Königsdorf, *Adieu*, p. 69ff.

Even where the security forces appear highly threatening, demonstrators' sense of solidarity can grow, as the perception of a threatening 'them' heightens the sense of a necessary 'us'. Police attempts to contain protests, psychologist Steve Reicher has shown, tend to have 'the effect of uniting crowd members and hence empowering them in resisting police action'. This exemplifies a crucial theoretical point: that context and subjectivity are not external to one another. If a situation involves collective and confrontational experiences, these will impinge upon the values and norms, the beliefs and behaviour, of participants. As Rick Fantasia has shown in his influential study of a wildcat strike, a sense of solidarity is generated when individuals experience collective action in connection with perceived mutual interests and aims.[20] In short, although decisions to engage in collective action self-evidently involve weighing up costs and benefits, they cannot be reduced to such calculations. They also involve shifts in actors' preferences, perceptions and identity. This tends to elude rational choice theory. It is based upon the simple premise that people make decisions, but this conception should be reconstructed to recognise that decisions also make people.

On the streets of East Germany, the generation of solidarity was not simply a matter of rational individuals calculating that greater numbers would lessen the likelihood that they themselves would escape death in the event of a massacre. Nor was it an automatic consequence of participation in collective action and confrontation with the security forces. It was also consciously and collectively produced. People learned to vanquish their fears, in an interactive and often creative process. Demonstrators encouraged others – friends, colleagues, strangers – to join in, or to come next week. 'We need everybody!', they would shout. 'Get out! Join us!', they called to bus and tram passengers and other onlookers. Such methods were often crucial to persuading the uncertain, the curious, or random bystanders to become participants. After attending peace prayers in Leipzig on 9 October, Sybille Freitag recalls that although initially she milled around outside the church, 'still wavering', over and again 'the demonstrators shouted "join in!" – until we spontaneously followed their appeal'.[21] From mid-October this mobilisation technique became formalised, with demonstrators chanting alternately 'We're here again next Monday!' and 'Each of us, bring a friend along!' In these ways, protestors generated moral incentives and imperatives to participate and mobilise; what Fantasia terms 'cultures of solidarity'

20 Baule, 'Politische', p. 43; Kuhn, *Entscheidung*, p. 128; Reicher, 'Collective', p. 11; Fantasia, *Cultures*, p. 88.
21 Neues Forum Leipzig, *Jetzt*, p. 85.

flourished. The demonstrations were not only embedded in pre-existing moral economies of discussion and dissent, but were themselves productive of new norms and values. These included, not least, the worth and necessity of protest itself, as expressed in banners such as 'The street is the tribune of the people' and 'We must keep on the street, If the state is to retreat'.

The propagation of solidarity was a product of instrumental calculation but not of that alone. There was an affective component, too. The recognition of belonging to an alliance forming around shared goals, and the perception that the world was being 'turned upside down', elicited strong emotions. All my interviewees recalled their experiences in just such terms. Many spoke of their enjoyment of the occasion, as contrasted with official parades. 'The atmosphere on the streets was so open, so honest', Ollie from Dresden reflected. 'There were no pompous speeches, no spin.' The sense of shared risks and fears deepened bonds of solidarity. One young man described his first demonstration as a 'fundamentally liberating experience' – 'At last the great community which I and my friends had been longing for was discovering collective action; at last we had begun to overcome those feelings of impotence.' Another characterised the mood as 'euphoric'. Her sense of timidity yielded to a realisation of strength in numbers and common purpose. 'For me', she recalls,

> the best moment was when I walked into the crowd – completely alone – and cried, at first quietly and then ever louder, 'We are the people! We are the people!' . . . I saw police but felt no fear. I felt strong, raised my arms in the air, and shouted at the top of my voice.[22]

At the time, this trumping of anxieties by solidarity was a widely noted phenomenon. The Leipzig sociologist Hartmut Zwahr described it well: 'how people in a crowd demanding justice gained the ability to mount resistance, overcome fear and muster the courage to meet force with force.'[23] Up and down the country, protestors were able to craft rituals and cultivate emotional responses that helped to strengthen their commitment to face down the security forces. In my own experience the sense of impotence evaporating was witnessed at the very first public gathering of Potsdam New Forum. It was a cold evening, 4 October. Although the meeting had of necessity to be publicised by 'whisper propaganda', with only limited support from nocturnal leafleting and flyposting, the church filled to the rafters and so many thousands still remained outside that two or three 'sittings' had to be held before the last of the crowds

22 Bahr, *Sieben*, p. 101; Lindner and Grüneberger, *Demonteure*, p. 51
23 Zwahr, *Selbstzerstörung*, p. 45.

eventually trickled out of the churchyard.[24] Within, the atmosphere was thick with feelings of hope but also fear and trepidation. Was the person sitting beside you a Stasi employee or informant? Had your face been recognised and would your details be passed to the authorities or to your employer? The meeting had been called by a Church group and began with a prayer, the message of which made a good deal of sense even to the many atheists present: 'God enjoins the weak to find solidarity, for only thus will they be able to assert themselves in these times.' There followed a brief period of singing – *We Shall Overcome*, if I recall correctly, and *Dona Nobis Pacem*. Something about the chemistry in the hall was transformed by this musical prologue. The atmosphere changed palpably; its oppressive density was dispelled. The audience relaxed. Fear subsided. It was not so much the words themselves, nor the religious temper of the songs, but the sense that the thousands within were no longer individuals anxious at the prospect of sanctions but participants in a common cause that, although lacking precise definition, found symbolic expression in our collective, musical voice – and the Stasi members present were welcome to sing from *our* hymnsheet or risk attracting attention by refusing so to do.

'The people' versus the 'People's Police'

If processes of mobilisation and solidarity creation were not automatic and individualistic but conscious, collective and dialogical, so too were those of grievance interpretation and the formulation of demands. The banners on marches were directed expressions, intended to be seen by co-participants and observers both on the streets or watching on television. The chants did not arise automatically, via the aggregation of individual demands, but were elaborated in collective, sometimes conflictual, processes. Broad areas of consensus notwithstanding, a polyphony of interests and issues intersected; the demonstrations were sites of disagreement and contest. Slogans were rejected or taken up, played with and revised. One protestor recalls that his chant demanding 'Visa-free travel to Czechoslovakia!' was picked up by others but refashioned to 'Visa-free travel to China!'[25] Another related how,

24 Cf. Stasi reports in Meinel and Wernicke, *Tschekistischem*, pp. 142–8. At a similar event in Karl-Marx-Stadt, Ramona Hübner recalls, 'The church overflowed and the meeting, it was clear, would have to be repeated, more than once. The organisers said "go home for a while!" They were worried, due to the police presence. But nobody left. We stood there, outside, for three hours!'
25 Lindner and Grüneberger, *Demonteure*, p. 303.

Individuals shouted many different things. But clear choices were made. By no means all chants were taken up by the crowd . . . the various chants were discussed. Someone might shout something which was then countered with 'Don't shout that here! You're on the wrong demonstration!' or the like.[26]

A salient example is recalled by Ramona Hübner, a hotel worker from Karl-Marx-Stadt. 'Mid-way through the demonstration one man started shouting "Hang them!" But as soon as he did, others approached him, arguing that there should be "no aggression", or simply telling him to shut up.'

As this incident suggests, consensus was established around certain slogans and tactics. In the first phase of the uprising protestors adopted non-confrontational tactics, and chants and songs that emphasised the legitimacy of their movement. On the streets of Leipzig and other towns, chants of 'No violence!' framed their collective identity as a peaceable one. The *Internationale* was sung in this phase, too. The choice reflected the socialist bent of many, probably a majority, of demonstrators;[27] they could identify with the lyrics, with their burning claims for justice and rights. Belonging to the SED's repertoire, the song also served to blur lines of conflict between protestors and regime; police officers would have to think twice before clubbing a section of the crowd that was belting out 'comrades come rally. . .'. It also signalled an impertinent and ironic appropriation of the regime's symbols as the movement's own, in an implicit denial of the SED's monopoly of emblems of socialist solidarity.

The slogan that seemed to encapsulate the movement's early phase was 'We are the people!' It was a rallying cry, expressing the new-forged alliance of the powerless and signalling the desire for democratic change. It spoke of ordinary people seizing the political agenda and insisting upon their right to be heard and represented in the public sphere. It asserted protestors' belief that their basic aims were shared by the bulk of society, and that this majority should determine the political process. Invocation of 'the people' challenged the Party's claims to a power monopoly; as one banner put it, 'The people should have the leading role!' (a play on the SED's claim that it should take the 'leading role' in society).

'We are the people!' expressed a sense of unity that is commonly found during the first stages of revolutions, when the working and middling layers unite against the old regime. It bore the imprint of the classic republican framing of political conflict whereby a patriotic 'people'

26 Bahr, *Sieben*, p. 97.
27 In the survey by Opp *et al.*, 58 per cent of respondents reported that one of their aims in demonstrating was to achieve 'democratic socialism'.

unites against a dynasty or elite that is defined as illegitimate and, implicitly, alien. 'The GDR belongs to the People, not to the SED', banners proclaimed. Such slogans possessed an ironic charge because, in line with Communist orthodoxy since the 'People's Front' phase of the 1930s, the regime itself laid claim to republican discourse. So 'The People' found itself pitted against a 'People's Democracy', fronted by the 'People's Police' and 'People's Army'. 'We are the people!' thus signified both a claim to popular legitimacy on the part of protestors and a denial of the ruling class's definition of its collective identity in republican terms. In a context in which demonstrators were vilified in the official media as dangerous deviants, reappropriating the concept of 'the people' – particularly when conjoined with other slogans such as 'Prison for Stasi officers' – suggested that the deviants were in fact to be found in uniforms or wearing SED badges.

Honecker's moustache

The above descriptions of solidarity at demonstrations, singing in a Potsdam church, placard-making in a Leipzig hospital and the sounds of 'We are the people!' on the streets give a glimpse of what was an intoxicating atmosphere. Possibilities for meaningful intervention in the political process were opening up to millions who had become accustomed to exclusion from public affairs. The country was awash with excitement, fear and the desire for change. The heightened experiences that are observed at revolutionary times cannot be readily conveyed in the normal lexica of the social sciences. Writers who have explored this subject, such as Emile Durkheim, V. I. Lenin and Aristide Zolberg, use evocative phrases such as 'collective effervescence', 'festive energies', and 'moments of madness'.[28] What is it about a revolutionary situation that seems to foster 'effervescence'?

As a first cut, consider the phenomenology of political crisis: its drama, its impact upon citizens. In modernity, according to Jürgen Habermas, there is a sense in which history 'is experienced as a crisis-ridden process, the present as a sudden critical branching, and the future as the pressure of unsolved problems'; this generates 'an existentially sharpened consciousness of the danger of *missed decisions* and *neglected* interventions'.[29] If this is a pervasive quality of modern life, how much more so

28 For discussion of these authors and of the theme in general, see Barker, 'Empowerment'.
29 Habermas, *Theory*, p. 58, emphasis in original. See also Habermas, *Legitimationsprobleme*.

during periods of political crisis, in which we experience the irruption of
the extraordinary into the routine and the course of history appears
about to enter a period of dramatic change. The radical indeterminacy
of such times is captured in Theodor Shanin's concept of 'alternativity',
which Colin Barker paraphrases thus:

> Quite long periods of time pass when life appears bound to cycles of simple
> reproduction. Fundamental change seems improbable, the dominant
> images in society are of repetition and stability, and what [Shanin] nicely
> terms 'the alternativity of history' is low. Then, relatively occasionally but
> often suddenly, there occurs an 'axial' stage,

in which established institutions are rocked, old habits are broken,
common sense stereotypes overturned and 'all bets are off.'[30]

Political crises involve clashes, typically involving states, political
parties (or factions), and social movements. At such times, the relations
among them become illuminated; political alliances and enmities are
brought into the open, tested, strengthened or broken. 'This mutual discovery', writes Régis Debray in his inimitably romantic idiom, 'reveals to
each of the forces involved its own identity, by revealing to it the resistance and nature of the opposing force'. Crisis seems to crystallise under-
lying social contradictions, yet the actors involved experience and
mediate these in their own ways. They propose different interpretations
of why the crisis is occurring and advocate diverse strategies for its resolution. So while a crisis highlights the existence of structural contradictions and its resolution may carry the aura of inevitability, equally striking
is the role of human agency in determining which of many possible roads
is taken – in Debray's phrase, crises are 'objectively over-determined,
while subjectively indeterminate'. In a situation of expanding 'alternativity', the outcome appears as radically open and critically influenced by the
decisions of the collective and individual actors involved. 'One mistake,
one false step, one error that would not normally matter at all', Debray
reflects, 'may become irreparable in a time of crisis'. The heightened sense
of historical openness and the salience of human agency in such situations
are not lost on citizens; the feeling grows that 'anything might happen'
and 'everything is possible', that 'what is at stake' is about to be determined within a peculiarly 'condensed' period of time; that 'it is "now or
never" . . . "one thing or the other" '.[31]

The clash of forces and ideas; uncertainty, trepidation, excitement and
fear; a sense of alternativity, of momentous events about to unfold; a

30 Barker, 'Cycle', p. 13.
31 Debray, *Prison*, pp. 104, 114–15, 121; see also Hay, *Re-Stating*.

profound rupturing of routine behaviour, and the visible importance of human agency; these all may contribute to the 'feverish' qualities observed in revolutionary situations. Yet all are common to political crises in general – recent examples being the run-up to the 1994 genocide in Rwanda,[32] or to the US–UK 'coalition's' 2003 war on Iraq. To explain the element of 'festive energy', other factors must be involved. Here, the work of American political scientist James C. Scott is relevant, especially to societies such as East Germany in which the political views of subaltern classes are systematically suppressed.

The focus of Scott's work is on the intersect between power relations and discourse, especially as these are manifest in the differentiation between the 'public transcript' of official political life – the account of the world as rulers would like it to appear – and 'hidden transcripts' that circulate below decks, a nether world in which grievances are voiced, bosses and officials lampooned and critical and oppositional views aired. The latter is a world of local, low-key and disguised acts of everyday resistance, or 'infrapolitics', Scott's term for 'the veiled cultural struggle and political expression of subordinate groups who have ample reason to fear venturing their unguarded opinion'.[33] In East Germany perhaps the most developed – and certainly the most famous – form of infrapolitical discourse was political humour. Its prevailing modes were black, and blunt.[34] Given that humour often pivots on two contrasting perspectives it was, arguably, suited in its very form to carrying criticisms of a regime that sought to impose a single 'line' on so many issues.

At the interface between the infrapolitical and public spheres lies a zone in which members (or movements) of subordinate classes venture forth to test the limits of the permissible, probing for fissures in the facade of power, for the faltering of bosses or functionaries. Here, heads raised above the parapet are invariably slapped down; insubordination is nipped in the bud. Subversive students or unruly workers are punished, to deter others and to assert the authority of the established order. Yet there are times when a head is raised . . . and nothing happens. A pregnant silence fills the air where the sound of a slap is expected. In East Germany this was a common 'infrapolitical' phenomenon in the early phase of the rising.

32 See Prunier, *Rwanda*, p. 210.
33 Scott, *Domination*, p. 184
34 A typical example, one of dozens that I jotted down in 1989, is the following. 'Honecker, Krenz and Mittag are standing at the top of East Berlin's television tower. All three jump off. Which of them hits the ground first?' To the reply that one cannot guess comes the response: 'Who cares – so long as they all jump.'

By way of illustration, consider some stories, from October. The first is related by Jens Steiner, a Berlin school student.

> On 6 October we were asked to line the Schönhauser Allee for 'Honni und Gorbi'. I don't know why some of my classmates suddenly decided to make some placards. They had never done that before. A day after the 7 October there was a big flag-raising ceremony in the schoolyard, on the occasion of the state's fortieth anniversary. The headmistress, a dogmatic Czech who taught citizenship, was unable to finish her speech because she couldn't stop crying . . . A couple of days later the portrait of Erich Honecker that had always hung in the secretary's office was chucked out into the schoolyard. Everybody wanted to have a kick at it. I did too, even though I had waved to him at a May Day parade on Karl-Marx-Allee just a couple of years before.[35]

Another Berlin school student, Olaf Klenke, noticed one day in early autumn that some joker had drawn a moustache on one of the portraits of Honecker that hung on the school walls. 'Yet nothing happened! That would never even have been conceivable before. The headmaster – no question at all – would have combed every last class until the culprit was found . . . but that simply didn't happen on this occasion.' A similar tale was recounted by Ollie, an eighteen year-old apprentice from Dresden: 'We realised that we could pin things up on the works noticeboard that we would never have dared before – a caricature of the company director, for example.' Jens, also an apprentice (in a fishing firm), described himself as 'loyal to the state and the SED', yet he savours the memory of how 'discipline crumbled at our lessons. We stopped wearing our sailors' uniforms! We were punished of course, but with such tiny fines. Before long, teachers just had to accept it.' Teachers themselves were not simply authority figures but were situated within wider relations of subordination. Petra was a Russian and German teacher in Berlin. On 7 October, the FDJ ordered school students to the city centre to cheer Honecker and Gorbachev. She and her colleagues refused to insist that their students follow FDJ instructions and so, as expected, an official paid them a visit. 'Yet he didn't threaten us at all!', she recalls, with surprise and satisfaction in equal measure.[36]

These stories evince a number of features that contributed to the rising's 'effervescence'. To begin with a general observation, each involved changing perceptions of *what exists* and *what is possible*. Factual judgements of this sort are as vital to processes of political norm change as are value judgements (*what is good* and *what is right*). What

35 http://de.indymedia.org, posted 13 August 2004.
36 Interviews with Olaf Klenke, Ollie, Jens König and Petra N.

we deem a desirable end is conditioned by judgements about what is feasible. In practice, conceptions of the possible and the desirable are interwoven. As the well-rehearsed scripts of social life disintegrated, people were obliged to improvise – and here we reach a crucial insight into 'effervescence': when individuals step out of their normal roles, states of heightened consciousness are more likely. (Indeed, 'stepping out' is the root of the term 'ecstasy'). When constellations of power and political identity are in flux, individuals begin to relate to others, not least their immediate 'superiors', in radically different ways. With society in upheaval, new possibilities can be descried and new hopes formulated. Recalibrated perceptions of possible behaviour catalyse reconsideration of the questions 'what is this society?' and 'what can we do to change it?' As Barker observes, these 'processes are simultaneously affective and cognitive, for there is a potential pleasure-shock in the intellectual appreciation of a new situation'. Participants in collective action, he continues,

> regularly report that they 'discover' aspects of their selves, and their capacities, which they had not previously tested. Heightened and re-focused energy and attention, the formation of new relationships, the undertaking of new tasks, the emergence of new forms of understanding, the affective shock of treating one's self and one's fellows as centres of significant decision and action, promotes a new sense of dignity and a new 'status order' – even if only temporarily.[37]

Alongside the changing relations of force on the streets of Leipzig and elsewhere, relations of consent and the 'status order' altered, too. Even the initial small triumphs over the state's ban on collective action turned a host of convictions on their heads. Attitudes of resignation and deference, rooted in the seeming omnipotence of the ruling class, were cast aside. Injustices hitherto accepted as inevitable were reinterpreted as subject to human intervention. People vowed to bury the bitter experiences of humiliation, those years spent stooping to authority figures and speaking their hackneyed phrases through gritted teeth. In a million infrapolitical moments ordinary citizens relished extraordinary sensations of freedom and self-respect. An example that can stand for many was captured on film, on one of the 'emigration trains' from Prague in early October. In order to uphold the official pretence that emigrants were being expatriated, Stasi officers entered each compartment,

---

37 Barker, 'Muck', p. 17; 'Empowerment', pp. 10–11. On the connections between the emergence and organisational form of social movements, and participants' redefinition of their identity and interests, see also Therborn, *Ideology*, p. 108; Clemens, 'Organizational'.

demanding that passengers return their ID cards to their rightful owner (the state), and in so doing affirming the sovereign's authority over its borders. By the simple device of chucking their documents onto the floor, the ritual was completely subverted. 'There's your card!', said one emigrant, 'you can't threaten me any more'. With the Stasi officers obliged to bend down and pick up the cards an elementary but emphatic point was made: the tables have been turned! 'I found it all so very satisfying', one emigrant enthused to a journalist at the scene.[38]

For me, this scene exemplifies what Scott has termed 'those rare moments of political electricity' in which 'the hidden transcript is spoken directly and publicly in the teeth of power'. The electricity, he suggests, is generated in part by 'the release of the tension generated by constant vigilance and self-censorship', and also from the shock of unexpected revolt. 'Social scientists, not to mention ruling elites', he goes on,

> are often taken by surprise by the rapidity with which an apparently defer-ential, quiescent, and loyal subordinate group is catapulted into mass defi-ance. That ruling elites should be taken unaware by social eruptions of this kind is due, in part, to the fact that they have been lulled into a false sense of security by the normal posing of the powerless.

In my experience of East Germany, the powerless themselves are just as surprised, and this may provide a further clue as to the causes of 'effer-vescence'. Not only did each week bring news of impossible develop-ments actually occurring, from the dethronement of Honecker to the fall of the Wall, but much of the population received additional 'pleasure-shocks' as hidden transcripts emerged into full, public view. People who for years had vented their grievances and criticisms in closed circles of trusted friends and colleagues could now turn on their televisions to see vast crowds giving voice to similar concerns – and with such wit and style, too. The dissolution of the culture of fear that had restrained indi-viduals from engaging in public life was an emotional phenomenon, as was the sense among hitherto powerless people that their political opin-ions now mattered, that there were immediate and pressing reasons to deliberate, voice and act upon them. Above all, these explosive changes were coming about through collective action. As Ronald Aminzade and Doug McAdam have noted, the 'palpable sense of "we-ness" that defines peak moments of collective action is among the most emotionally intox-icating and socially connective experiences one can have'. In East Germany, one psychologist even suggested that the 'power of collective

38 CNN, Cold War television series, episode 23.

uprising and the surprise at the creativity of the protest brought about a therapeutic liberation'.[39]

The autumn months of 1989, anecdotal evidence and opinion surveys show, were characterised by a remarkable process of politicisation.[40] Discussion and argument abounded, not least in regard to acts of protest themselves. Collective action was a novelty, its forms and norms had to be constructed and elaborated, its goals considered and debated, its tactics put to the test of practice. Curiosity for public affairs blossomed in workplaces and neighbourhoods; at one point I recall looking out of my window to see knots of people on the street, in conversation. Among friends and colleagues question piled upon question: What should be the wording of our work brigade's letter to the trade union organisation (FDGB)? Should we go to the demonstration? What slogans should we write on placards? Practical deliberations of this sort necessitated and nourished wider-ranging discussion. Was the analysis in this newspaper article correct? What is the nature of this or that aspect of society? Should it be so? Can it be changed? If so, how do we get there? Is German uni-fication a possible and desirable goal? And so on.

Ordinary people had collectively hijacked the political agenda, in the process revealing hitherto hidden potentials and this underlay an experi-ence of 'cognitive liberation', McAdam's term for processes whereby oppression and injustice become redefined as 'subject to change'.[41] To the irritation of party loyalists and other conservatives,[42] the country became a cauldron of discussion – on street corners, in cafés, after theatre per-formances. 'There was discussion about something new every single day', one interviewee (Petra) recalled. Media organs and state institutions were

39 Scott, *Domination*, pp. xiii, 213; Aminzade and McAdam, 'Emotions', p. 43; Schneider, *Revolution*, p. 132.
40 See, e.g., Opp *et al.*, 'Data', p. 21.
41 McAdam, *Political*, p. 34.
42 For an example of a conservative citizen's irritation at the 'debating club' atmosphere, consider this letter in which an 'anonymous correspondent' rebukes New Forum Leader, Bärbel Bohley: 'And where are the children; have you stopped to consider what children do at a time like this? At school, at home and everywhere they are being overwhelmed by a flood of discus-sion of proportions that not all of them will be able to deal with. What will become of them – morally and physically? There is tumult in the schools. It will no doubt reach the stage when teachers will have to ask pupils "what are your wishes, how should I structure today's class?" We're almost there already.' The letter concludes with a flourish 'And one other thing. Was it also your intention that people at work now engage only in discussion, rather than working properly?', Krone, *Briefe*, pp. 214–15.

bombarded with letters and resolutions. Channels of communication among neighbours, demonstrators and colleagues sprang up or deepened. A West German journalist observed that 'The GDR has become a debating club', while an East German sociologist described it in these terms: 'All of a sudden, people were talking to one another about politics, conditions at work, about their hopes and fears. They confided in one another. The outburst of emotions welled up out of a deeply felt sense of humiliation.' Discovering and thinking through new questions and debating old ones afresh stimulated a formidable thirst for learning and reading. Marianne Pienitz wrote to a friend in Britain: 'Can you believe that I read *four* GDR newspapers every day???!!' In a subsequent letter, she returned to the theme: 'It strikes me that we have learned more in the past four weeks than in the last forty years.' Another interviewee, Antje Neubauer, recalls that: 'Even opening the newspaper or listening to the news was such a *pleasurable* experience; it all felt like a step towards freedom.'[43]

Summary

This chapter began with a brief examination of *Origins of a Spontaneous Revolution*, the most systematic attempt to put social movement-theoretic concepts to the service of explaining mobilisation in East Germany, and found it insightful but flawed. *Origins* is at its strongest when exploring how individuals interpreted changes to the political opportunity structure in such a way that large numbers came to see public protest as rational. But rational choice theory is ill-equipped to account for the diffusion of the norm of solidarity, as this developed through the collective experience of movement building. The positing of the individual's interests, capacities and preferences as given attributes that are logically prior to social structures leads to a lack of regard for the manner in which the conceptions of preference-satisfaction that actors adopt are affected by their resources and social circumstances. Although it departs from the narrow assumptions of orthodox rational choice theory, Opp's model nonetheless reduces norm-following behaviour and perceptions of legitimacy to a single dimension of personally experienced incentives. The manner in which norms, values and collective identities develop through processes of discussion, negotiation, collective practice and confrontation with the forces and discourses of the state are touched upon in *Origins*, but in reducing these multi-faceted

43 Fehr, *Unabhängige*, p. 249; Menge, *Ohne*, p. 175; Marianne Pienitz to Geoff Brown and Judy Paskell, 25 and 29 October 1989.

and interactive processes to their effects on individuals' cost-benefit calculations, integral aspects of the protest dynamic are neglected. Many 'goods', such as the sense of solidarity or the creation and refashioning of collective identities, are generated in the process of collective action itself, and this is difficult to conceive in rational actor terms. Opp's approach, in short, lacks a developed sense of humans' capacities to link their interests to those of others or to abstract principles that transcend self-interest. An alternative, outlined in this chapter, is to conceive of the interests and values that motivate protest as simultaneously individual and collective, developing interactively and dialogically.

The changes described in this chapter and chapter 2 – the defeat of the security forces in Leipzig and elsewhere, the discovery by the formally powerless of a new-found sense of power, the prising open of opportunities and the galvanising of new forms of action and consciousness – had all developed to a significant degree by mid-October. From the perspective of the regime, its hard-line strategy had been put to the test and failed. It had failed as a result of lack of support from Moscow, vacillation in its own ranks and the growing popular protest manifested in public meetings, letters and resolutions that flooded in to the authorities, and above all the mass demonstrations. Unable to vanquish this movement, the regime now had to address the question of how to contain it.

4

The *Wende* and protest upswing

How smoothly they donned the mantle of reform and put on their nicest glinting smile. 'Outwardly everything must look like democracy, but behind the scenes we keep the reins firmly in our hands!' (Sarah Kirsch, novelist) [1]

The protests in Leipzig and other Saxon cities broke the pattern of repression. They revealed the limits of a strategy based upon police methods, undermined its authors and showed that senior security-force commanders and middle-level functionaries were willing to improvise alternative tactics. These developments, compounded by reports of vacillation in the SED and security forces, of strike threats and of a rising torrent of criticism of the government's obdurate position and haughty tone, prompted a few senior functionaries, cautiously at first, to dissent from the prevailing line. New phrases, such as 'honest dialogue with all citizens', could be heard. Several regional Party secretaries voiced dissent over the handling of the crisis. One, Hans Modrow, made an outspoken plea for 'renewal' – albeit with the proviso that its impetus and content must come 'from us, from the Party . . . and not from the people on the streets or in the Church!' [2] A number of top functionaries, including Harry Tisch and Wolfgang Vogel, sensed which way the wind was turning and proposed modest reforms, such as the decriminalisation of illegal emigration. The FDJ leadership wrote to Honecker, informing him that the majority of youth were critical of the 'inadequate dialogue between the Party leadership and the population' and urging that action be taken to remedy the situation. [3]

Meeting on 10 October, the Politburo engaged in its first serious discussion of the crisis. Honecker reminded the gathering of the armed

1 Kirsch, 'Kleine', p. 80.
2 Stephan, *Vorwärts*, p. 160.
3 At this, the General Secretary is said to have recoiled, spluttering that 'this is the first time in the history of the GDR that the FDJ leadership has made a concerted attack on the policies of the Party and its Central Committee'. Przybylski, *Tatort 2*, p. 122.

might of the state, Günther Mittag proposed austerity measures and the whipping up of a 'fighting spirit', while others continued to place their faith in orchestrating media philippics against West German revanchism. Yet such hawkish tones were no longer monolithic. A surprising number of contributors worried openly that the Party's power was at stake. Some drew attention to the domestic roots of the crisis, and one member even floated the idea of a public 'dialogue' about the nature of 'socialist democracy'. Although the Politburo's official statements remained complacent, bombastic and laced with vitriolic denunciations of emigrants and protestors, they also betrayed the first small signs of tactical reconsideration as well as hints of disunity. Media organs were instructed to soften their propaganda a little and television news even acknowledged that East German 'socialism' must be made more attractive. The need for 'renewal', including 'sober dialogue', was conceded although the latter, it was emphasised, would be a privilege granted only to citizens who accepted the constitutional order.[4]

In the week that followed, East Germany see-sawed between repression and liberalisation. While police brutally attacked demonstrators in Halle on 10 October, a vigil in Berlin was left in peace. Two days later, travel to Czechoslovakia was restricted still further, yet on the following day detained demonstrators were released. On 13 October the SED leadership reaffirmed its acceptance of the need for 'dialogue' but only in the vaguest terms and without the slightest indication that New Forum would be legalised, yet on the very next day local officials in Karl-Marx-Stadt, Leipzig and Potsdam admitted to contacts with New Forum representatives. Signs of differentiation appeared in the media, too. Whereas *Neues Deutschland* remained implacable in substance and bellicose in tone, the FDJ daily (*Junge Welt*) carried reformist commentaries and the LDPD's *Der Morgen* published a critique of the SED's media policy.

Despite these cautious openings the road towards a military crackdown was not yet closed. It was now clear that nobody would authorise a deliberate and planned massacre, but the option of inciting or even organising a 'provocation' that would then justify the use of live ammunition remained available. As late as 14 October, Honecker decreed that the next Monday demonstration in Leipzig be prevented at all costs. Appeals to protestors to stay away were distributed by teachers and priests, and by local radio broadcasts. Army units were put on stand-by, and Honecker even proposed that a tank regiment be sent through Leipzig. In the event, local officials backed by Politburo members ensured that the tanks were kept away and bloodshed was avoided.

4 Hertle, *Fall*; Keithly, *Collapse*, p. 160.

(According to one general, they were dissuaded by the argument that a large proportion of demonstrators, being young men of conscription age, had received training in anti-tank combat.)[5]

Proponents of a tactical retreat now acted to remove Honecker from his post. Although initially a rather confused process, with Schabowski and Krenz tentatively sounding out their colleagues, in its dénouement at a Politburo meeting on 17 October the coup unfolded smoothly. Even Honecker's otherwise staunch allies Mittag and Mielke turned against him. The SED leader himself resisted at first, but quickly bowed to the inevitable and accepted Schürer's proposal that he retire 'honourably', on grounds of ill health. He even voted in favour of his own resignation, although soured the occasion with a prophecy that his dismissal would set a bad precedent: by showing the public that 'we can be blackmailed', he cautioned, it would only aggravate the SED's predicament.[6]

On the following day Honecker's 'voluntary resignation' was presented to the Central Committee for ratification. Confirming the impression that little had changed at the top of the SED, serious debate as to the nature of the crisis or the merits of alternative candidates for the vacant post was absent. Some contributions from the floor, notably an oration in praise of Honecker's patronage of competitive sports, were almost surreal in their apparent obliviousness to the political storm that was raging outside the walls of the Central Committee's *Große Haus*.[7] Peculiar too was the General Secretary's valedictory, in which he recommended the already-appointed Egon Krenz as his successor. If intended as a blessing, this was of the back-handed (or perhaps cack-handed) kind.

Krenz's accession to the top job did not mark a comprehensive break with the past. The rest of the leadership, apart from the two most unpopular hawks, media boss Joachim Herrmann and economics tsar Mittag, remained at their posts. Krenz himself had long been seen as Honecker's crown prince; he had, one worker said, 'been fed the same shit, he *was*, in fact, the same old shit. Nothing, absolutely nothing, was possible with him.'[8] Nevertheless, this was a major turning point, coming as it did after eighteen years of continuity at the top. And it was utterly unexpected, not to say thrilling, for the public. I was in a café at Alexanderplatz when the news broke. Looking up, I noticed somebody hurry in and speak to guests near the entrance. The word then passed from table to table.

5 Hollitzer, 'Verlauf', pp. 282–3; Schabowski, *Absturz*, p. 23; Przybylski, *Tatort 2*, p. 130; Hertle, *Fall*, pp. 129–30.
6 Fricke, 'Honecker's'; Hertle, *Fall*, p. 436.
7 Hertle and Stephan, *Ende*, p. 121.
8 Philipsen, *People*, p. 285, emphasis in original.

Animated exchanges followed: 'Could it really be true?', people asked; 'After this miracle, what on earth will happen now?' For activists, too, it was a moment of high drama. Gabi Englehart, of Karl-Marx-Stadt United Left, recalled that she even 'burst out crying when Honecker was deposed' – but, she added, these were 'tears not of sadness but of excitement and joy. "Now it's really going to kick off", I thought.'

Krenz's *Wende*: a holding operation

The regime's failure to quell the protests brought to an end the immediate dilemma of whether or not to unleash armed force, but new questions and quandaries appeared in its place. If the movement could not be directly suppressed, how could it be contained? How could the seemingly intractable problems of the continuing exodus and economic crisis be resolved? To what extent should domestic political structures be reformed, and what degree of personnel reshuffle ought to take place? The new leadership was uncertain as to how to confront these urgent and concurrent problems. It recognised the need to reform but feared the 'Tocquevillian predicament': that reforms introduced by an authoritarian government are likely to fuel rather than dampen protest.

Krenz was a cautious and conservative figure; he did not favour a sweeping review of policy or personnel. In his inaugural speech he did promise that the SED 'will introduce a *Wende* [turnaround], with immediate effect'. But the intention was to carry it through 'with minimal sacrifice'. Indeed, *Wende* suggests a steering correction rather than a transformation. Oddly enough, it later entered common usage as the term to describe the events of 1989 as a whole – to the chagrin of Krenz's critics. One of these, Jens Reich, has written of how, 'with one sentence – "At this [Central Committee] meeting we shall initiate a *Wende*" – Krenz became the author of an historical definition'. For the entire decade since then 'it has irritated me that of all formulations' that could have been adopted – such as revolution or upheaval – it was this one, connoting 'a change of horses, a little turn, resurfacing after a dive into cold water', that came to signify what was in fact a momentous historical transformation and one, moreover, that was the achievement of a spontaneous movement from below. 'Redolent as it is of wise and insightful measures initiated from above', the term, he laments, 'diminishes these events'.[9]

In its public aspect, the *Wende* appeared as a piecemeal assortment of concessions and promises of reforms. The media began to change relatively quickly; critical letters appeared in the press, the Leipzig

9 Reich, 'Freiheit', pp. 210–11.

Mondays were covered on television news and the 'ordinary' people interviewed for news programmes were no longer pre-selected stooges. The regular publication of ecological data was promised, too. However, even these modest concessions were granted, Schabowski recalls, 'not voluntarily but under duress'.[10] The SED leadership was committed to reforming as little and as late as possible.

The *Wende* also involved a search for new methods of suppressing protest. This was no easy task, for the usual military options were ruled out. Interior Minister Friedrich Dickel professed himself at a loss as to how to tackle the movement:

> What should we do? I'll just put it as a rhetorical question. Should we march in there, amongst 20,000, 30,000, 40,000 people? Do you know what that would mean? We would send armoured cars or tanks through. But we know that in the current situation, with all these changes, that is impossible.[11]

This was not necessarily his personal preference, the frustrated minister hastened to add. In his own view, he admitted to a gathering of his 'dear comrades', the 'simplest solution would be to open fire, and to deploy tanks in front of the district headquarters and the Central Committee. But it is such a complicated situation . . .'

To the disappointment of Dickel and others of his ilk, the 'complicated situation' precluded military solutions. Behind the scenes, nonetheless, the security agencies were still plotting repressive measures for the 'Roll Back of Anti-Socialist Movements'.[12] Local commanders were instructed to prepare their forces to take 'offensive measures to block and disrupt conspiratorial assembly'. Plans for emergency rule remained live at least until 31 October, and army divisions were mobilised around Leipzig and Berlin as late as 11 November.[13]

In the meantime the Stasi's tactics were evolving. It was instructed to 'prevent an escalation of events', to 'avoid confrontation' with demonstrators and to contain oppositional activities 'by political means'. In effect, as Modrow later admitted, its remit was to destroy the civic groups from within.[14] The techniques were familiar ones, notably to 'exploit the open situation' of the civic groups in order to infiltrate them with agents whose instructions were to 'prevent/inform of activities that

10 Schabowski, *Politbüro*, p. 110.
11 At a meeting on 21 October. In Hollitzer, 'Verlauf', p. 286.
12 Adomeit, *Imperial*, p. 418.
13 Hollitzer, 'Verlauf', p. 287; Hertle, *Chronik*.
14 *Die Andere*, 50, 1991, p. 11.

are hostile to the state'.[15] On 21 October Mielke told his generals that the civic groups would be still more systematically infiltrated, with greater reliance placed on informal agents such as Wolfgang Schnur and Ibrahim Böhme, leading members of Democratic Awakening (DA) and the SDP, respectively. The plan was carried out with some success, at least in terms of the degree of penetration achieved. Modrow's Dresden district, for instance, reported that 'we have succeeded in infiltrating 80–100 informal agents into the new movements, both in leadership positions and as members. This will enable us to improve the detection and manipulation of anti-constitutional activity.'[16]

These tactics generally escaped public attention, but in other instances the deployment of old techniques showed through. In Berlin, SED leaders attempted to obstruct a church-initiated inquiry into security-force violence. In Schwerin, the organisers of a pro-regime rally set up loud-speaker trucks, provided by the army, in order to broadcast supplementary applause. In Gera, police ordered a batch of metal-toothed attachments for their vans, intended for use against demonstrators – a plan that failed when the workers assigned to produce them, guessing their intended purpose, refused to deliver them and demanded instead that police representatives be summoned to the factory to explain themselves.[17]

The dominant trend, however, was away from repressive tactics and towards alliances with extra-regime forces. The *Wende* inaugurated closer cooperation with the Protestant Church; it is significant that one of Krenz's first engagements, immediately after acceding to the SED leadership, was with Church leaders. The transcript of the meeting reveals that the country's temporal and spiritual guardians were disposed towards friendly relations. Bishop Leich informed Krenz that 'Sunday after Sunday', clergy offered prayers for state functionaries, in good Protestant tradition.[18] To this benefaction the SED leader responded with an unusual request: 'that the police and Stasi officers of Leipzig be included in your prayers, as their job – having to face such hate-filled people – is not an easy one'. It is unlikely that Krenz was simply being mischievous, or that he was making a serious plea for divine intervention (much as he may have wished for it). Rather, he was reminding the bishops of a diagnosis that they and he shared: that the street protests threatened the stability of

---

15 I am grateful to Uwe Bastian for providing a copy of this document, from Hauptabteilung XVIII, 24 October 1989.
16 Wolle, *Diktatur*, p. 339; Mitter and Wolle, *Untergang*, p. 533.
17 Neubert, *Opposition*, p. 866; *Der Spiegel*, 48, 1989, p. 28.
18 Gespräch Krenz mit Dr. W. Leich, 19 October 1989, in BA-SAPMO, SED Parteiarchiv.

the existing order and made the re-establishment of social peace a matter of urgency.

For their appeals to citizens to keep away from street demonstrations and prevent 'trouble' in workplaces, Church leaders would be rewarded with greater freedoms and responsibilities, including invitations to clergy and laiety to participate in a variety of SED front organisations. Krenz also dangled the promise of significant political reform, including free elections (at an unspecified future date). The question of travel to the 'non-socialist abroad' would be examined, he promised, although whether the economic cost could be met by the state was unclear. Krenz therefore agreed with Stolpe's suggestion that the Protestant Church 'discretely' engage in diplomacy with state and Church officials in West Germany, in the hope that Bonn would meet the expense of this particular reform. In his memoirs Krenz appears satisfied with the outcome of this meeting, for the Church leaders responded positively to his appeal that the country required order, not protests, and pledged their goodwill, for example in the staging of public 'dialogues' in churches (more on which on p. 63).[19]

In sum, Krenz's *Wende* involved the renunciation of overt armed force in favour of conspiratorial techniques of countersubversion coupled with modest concessions and promises of further reform. It was expected that these measures, together with enhanced cooperation with the Church, would boost the government's credibility and enable the movement to be contained. Whereas repression had provoked protest, SED leaders believed, concessions would appease it. They assumed that a breathing space of several months would be gained, in which to retrench and restructure.[20] Having won time and re-established stability, the administration would then be in a position to consider, in a suitably dignified manner, how to proceed with more substantial reform. In this sense, the *Wende* was, in intention at least, a holding operation, providing a framework within which the *nomenklatura* could begin to restructure itself in an orderly fashion.

Early indications were that these designs might succeed. Hardly had Krenz entered office than several Church representatives expressed satisfaction that the *Wende* was already successfully complete.[21] It quickly became apparent, however, that this was a minority reaction. Amongst the public at large the dominant response only highlighted the 'Tocquevillian dangers', for the *Wende* reforms reduced the costs of

19 Stephan, *Vorwärts*, p. 177; Krenz, *Herbst*, p. 138.
20 Schabowski, *Politbüro*, p. 111.
21 Neubert, *Opposition*, p. 868.

collective action and raised the expected benefits. More civilised policing, and the granting of official permission to demonstrate (from 30
October) reduced the risks of protest, while concessions and promised
reforms were widely interpreted as a victory for collective action. The
change of leadership and strategy, being forced, sudden and unplanned,
had exposed the regime's weaknesses – as Honecker had foretold.
Moreover, some concessions, notably the loosening of its control over the
media, directly undermined the regime, for example through the reporting of corruption amongst senior functionaries. Despite intentions, the
Wende encouraged protest; the perception that the movement had forced
the regime to reform fuelled its further growth.

   At the same time the persistence of 'old tricks', combined with the government's dilatory attitude to reform, sparked fears that the concessions
might yet be rescinded. Krenz's government was, after all, widely
regarded as a coven of hypocrites: the same politicians who had defended
tyranny now posed as champions of democratic reform. Krenz in particular was not credible in reformist guise. He had headed the commission
that had manipulated the May election results and had loudly applauded
the Tiananmen massacre. As chief of the security forces he bore responsibility for the violence of preceding weeks. Even after announcing the
Wende he continued to defend Honecker's legacy, including the building
of the Wall. Little wonder that, no sooner had Krenz acceded to office
than the prolific banner designers got to work, expressing their amuse-
ment or outrage at the spectacle of this dyed-in-the-wool authoritarian
presenting himself as a kindly democrat. 'Egon, what big teeth you have!'
read one of several banners which drew witty links between Krenz's most
identifiable feature and his presumed intentions. 'A *Wende* is not a loop-
the-loop', another admonished.[22] More forthright slogans appeared too:
'Egon Krenz, don't get settled in, we won't forget China, May elections,
police violence!'; 'Egon Krenz, no license'; 'Against Ego(n)ism'; and,
perhaps the neatest of snubs, 'eGOn!'.

The 'dialogues': private parleys and public tribunals

Of the various initiatives begun under Krenz it was 'dialogues' that made
the most immediate impression. In the sense of negotiation, dialogue had
already taken place, in the talks between demonstrators and officials in
Plauen and, in Dresden, with the meetings between the 'Group of
Twenty' and local leaders (Modrow and Berghofer). In those leaders'
view, the selection of a group of random citizens as negotiating partner

22 Schneider, *Demontagebuch*.

was a crafty ruse: it enabled the authorities to appear forthcoming whilst ignoring the civic groups. Reporting to the Central Committee on 16 October, Berghofer recommended that the Dresden model be applied more widely. Thus, the concept was already in the air during Honecker's final week in office. But it was picked up by Krenz in his debut speeches as SED General Secretary.[23]

For the new leadership, dialogue promised to serve several ends. It would appease protestors by slaking the popular thirst for 'voice', and could fragment the movement. Listening to the *vox populi* would refresh the Party, enabling it to gain a more realistic understanding of society. Above all, the tactic would redirect the popular desire for political discussion from opposition-influenced mass demonstrations into small spaces controlled by 'progressive forces' – universities, factories and town halls. Debate would take place behind closed doors, with only limited media access. Dialogue partners would be recognised not as legitimate representatives of wider groupings but as individuals. 'Temperate' voices would be privileged, as would local issues. In so far as wider political topics were broached, discussion could be diverted towards abstract questions (such as 'conceptions of socialist democracy'). As such, Krenz and Modrow emphasised, the tactic offered a controlled alternative to the 'actually existing dialogue' that was filling the streets. It encouraged grievances to be voiced, but quietly, without anger or impatience; as Berghofer put it, dialogue was an exercise in 'listening and introspection'. It also offered a lever with which to press citizens to refrain from street protests; at one point, the mayor of Halle threatened a group delegated from a demonstration – in the symptomatic but false assumption that it could control the mass of protestors – that dialogue would be broken off if demonstrations continued.[24]

In handling dialogue *qua* focus group session or negotiations with small groups, the regime was acting well within its capacities. The tactic entailed a broadening and modification of, but not a challenge to, established clientelist techniques. Yet it was also a game the rules of which, not to mention the players, were far from clear. How could meaningful dialogue be institutionalised? Who should take the role of dialogue partner? If the SED occupied one corner at the negotiating table, who should sit at the others? Here the absence of institutions intermediate between regime and populace became all too apparent. Although the

23 Richter and Sobeslavsky, *Gruppe*, p. 332.
24 Timmer, *Aufbruch*, pp. 228, 245; Richter and Sobeslavsky, *Gruppe*, p. 402; Links and Bahrmann, *Volk*, p. 59.

SED had long maintained that the mass organisations (FDGB, FDJ, etc.) and the bloc parties played this role, the rise of protests entirely external to these organisations revealed this to be wishful thinking. The regime faced a mass movement without significant buffers in between.

An alternative would have been to invite opposition representatives to negotiations. They were, after all, passionate advocates of dialogue – and indeed, in a form that was compatible with that proposed by the SED. In late September, a New Forum leader, Jens Reich, insisted that he 'strongly rejects any hostility to the SED and to its State' and that his 'vision' was of 'cooperation with those who govern':

> We do not want power and are not calling for the Party to give up its leading role. *We only want the Party to seek dialogue with the population, with us, New Forum* . . . This society needs constructive dialogue like in the Soviet Union. Otherwise people will demonstrate in the streets and flee across the border like rabbits.[25]

Several days later, Wolfgang Ullmann of Democracy Now (DJ) made a similar appeal for dialogue, in the form of talks between SED, the Churches and opposition.

Yet Reich and Ullmann presided over organisations that were still illegal and considered 'negative-enemy forces' by their would-be dialogue partners. At a dialogue held at Leipzig University, SED district chief Roland Wötzel refused to debate with New Forum, for one doesn't sit at the same table as enemies of the state. At another, on 19 October, a New Forum representative was refused entry. The dialogue tactic, after all, was designed to enable the Party to reach out to the majority of the movement, defined as 'vacillating and led astray', while *isolating* them from the 'enemy oppositionists'. The tactic was spelled out in a Politburo document on 'Measures against anti-socialist movements'. While advocating an ideological offensive against the civic groups, it proposed that those who 'are interested in solving the problems which confront the further progress of socialism in the GDR . . . including many who disagree with our perspectives . . . are to be welcomed into all arenas of social dialogue and cooperation'. Individuals whose criticisms were directed against particular policies were to be treated leniently and encouraged to 'engage constructively within the existing framework of social structures', while harsher measures were reserved for radicals. Even many of society's critical spirits could be

25 *Die Zeit*, 29 September 1989; *Financial Times*, 3 October 1989, emphasis added.

coopted in this way, it was thought, and the 'enemies of socialism exposed'.[26]

The regime did its utmost to keep the boundaries of dialogue under tight control, while the public sought to expand them. The first dialogues took place, not coincidentally, in towns where demonstrations had occurred and were viewed as a concession wrested from a weak regime; one interviewee from Chemnitz recalls with glee 'that the mayor was *forced* to come and talk with the likes of us!'[27] Although initiated as forums for anodyne exchange they were open to reinterpretation as opportunities for impassioned debate, the broaching of taboo themes, verbal confrontation and accusation. In form as well as content they became sites of contest. In the context of a rising movement they were subject to a logic of escalation, with demonstrators pressuring the authorities to hold dialogues in larger venues or even in public squares. Where 'the rulers hoped for controlled and private parleys, the crowds demanded public exchanges', as Maier has put it.[28]

Nowhere was this dynamic more conspicuous than in Dresden. In the first formal dialogues, the SED appeared to have found the ideal negotiating partner. Because drawn at random from a street demonstration, the 'Group of Twenty' (G20), Berghofer insisted, lacked legitimation. But one of their number, Friedrich Boltz, interpreted the mayor's rebuff as a challenge. 'That's why', he recalls, 'I suggested the One-Mark Initiative': all citizens who supported the G20 should donate just 1 Mark to a bank account set up in its name. 'After three or four days', he continues,

> I received a letter from the Post Office, saying that I should contact them immediately, that this initiative had completely paralysed post office operations. The giro centre was doing nothing but dealing with payments into this account. After three or four weeks, well over 100,000 Marks had been paid into it.[29]

The first negotiations between the G20 and Berghofer, on 9 October, took place behind closed doors, but G20 delegates then made their way to city centre churches where some 20,000 people listened to their reports on the proceedings and mandated them to attend further meetings. A week later, when Berghofer again met with the G20, crowds

26 Liebold, 'Machtwechsel', p. 455; Neues Forum Leipzig, *Jetzt*, p. 134; Timmer, *Aufbruch*, p. 256; Stephan, *Vorwärts*, pp. 175–7; See also Mitter and Wolle, *Befehle*.
27 Ramona Hübner.
28 Maier, *Dissolution*, p. 176.
29 Lindner, *Revolution*, p. 78; Richter and Sobeslavsky, *Gruppe*, esp. p. 65.

outside the town hall demanded that a microphone connection be installed to enable them to listen in. An increasingly confident G20 successfully pressed the SED to hold the next dialogue in public. Some 10,000 Dresdeners attended; they chanted their desire to participate, to talk to the mayor, and called for loudspeakers to be brought so that the proceedings within could be transmitted to them live. Fearing that the crowds would otherwise 'become completely uncontrollable', Berghofer agreed. But even this event was dwarfed by the next dialogue, on 26 October, to which 100,000 turned up. During this extraordinary dialogue *cum* mass meeting, which lasted several hours, microphones were distributed around the square, enabling protestors to call the SED leaders to account on a range of issues including housing, privileges, travel, the environment and the right to demonstrate. In these ways, Dresdeners transformed the regime's offer of limited dialogue into a form of movement activity. Designed as a mechanism to undermine demonstrations, dialogue was converted into the precise opposite.[30]

The capturing of dialogues 'from below' went furthest in Dresden, but similar processes occurred in many other towns. At one, in Prenzlau, the chairperson had just introduced the seventeen (!) speakers and was on the point of inviting the first to commence when a middle-aged man walked up to the podium and took the microphone. 'My name's Dirk Weise. I'm a worker and would like to have a few questions answered.' He had recently resigned from the SED, he explained, and was 'a little nervous and fearful. Nervous, because under this regime I haven't been able to learn to speak. And fearful, because of an organ of power that goes by the name of State Security.' Why, he wished to know, had Krenz taken *both* positions at the top of the power hierarchy. Why had there been no referendum on this? And why was New Forum outlawed?[31]

As this vignette indicates, members of the audience did not always read from the allotted script. For their part, functionaries, unpractised in open debate and unaccustomed to being on the defensive, performed poorly. As recent converts to the cause of transparency and reform they possessed little credibility. One did the cause of SED-led reform no favours by bringing his handgun along. Elsewhere, opposition supporters succeeded in putting their case from the floor, forcing regime spokespeople onto the back foot and setting the agenda. In Mühlhausen, an eyewitness recalls: 'We'd never seen the like, our functionaries being laughed and whistled at. It feels like an explosion of feelings, that everyone is able for the first time to freely release their frustrations in this way.' At a dialogue

30 Maier, *Dissolution*, p. 176; Timmer, *Aufbruch*, pp. 248–9.
31 Villain, *Revolution*, p. 225

in Sömmerda, attended by over 600, local leaders were roundly booed and were perturbed to see that even SED members in the audience were not prepared to rally to their defence. At the other end of the country, in Rostock, one dialogue included the following exchange between a New Forum supporter and the city's SED chief, recounted by Lothar Probst. 'I'm initiating dialogue with you', the oppositionist began. 'I have a question. What do you understand by the dictatorship of the proletariat?' To this, the functionary could muster no more than a feeble 'Ah . . . ah . . .' before breaking into a stutter. The audience erupted in laughter, prompting the hapless official to cry out: 'Hang on! First I'll have to look up what Lenin said.' Meanwhile, his interlocutor produced a New Forum banner, got onto the podium and unfurled it before seating himself alongside the functionary. By this point, Probst tells us, 'the audience had lost all respect for the most powerful man in Rostock'.[32]

By the end of October, regime forces in some parts had entirely lost control of the dialogues, for these were swept up in the wider process of radicalisation. The strategy was backfiring, with SED speakers subjected to chants of 'You're to blame!' and 'Too late! Too late!' Karsten Timmer has related one example, from Zwickau, where the National Front (SED and bloc parties) had organised a rally *cum* dialogue at which their representatives were to address the people:

> Against the organisers' expectations it was not only Party-loyal citizens who turned up at Zwickau's Hauptmarkt but also critical ones, who accompanied the speeches with whistles, boos and chants. In the face of the critical echo from the crowd, control of the rally visibly slipped from the organisers' grasp, and they eventually lost it completely when some citizens found their way into the town hall and thence to the speakers' balcony, where they put an end to the monologues. With the help of the crowd, which supported the speakers' spontaneous addresses with applause, the rally was taken over and turned into a people's gathering. The organisers were not even able to succeed in their attempt to terminate the rally, so had no choice but to passively look on, while ever more speakers used the platform to denounce SED rule. Finally, the city mayor was obliged to accept an application for legalisation by New Forum, accompanied by applause from the crowd, which then left the square and marched into the town centre.[33]

The wave of radicalisation to which these examples testify prompted the regime to rethink its strategy towards the civic groups. The more it

---

32 Hertle, *Fall*, p. 136; Langer, *Norden*; Timmer, *Aufbruch*, p. 262; Remy, 'Letzten', p. 63; Probst, 'Vereinigung', p. 52.
33 Timmer, *Aufbruch*, p. 261.

was driven to respond to popular pressure, the more it sought representatives with whom to negotiate, and here, in practice, there were few alternatives to the organised opposition. Although still outlawed, the civic groups gradually won *de facto* recognition.

For Krenz and his colleagues greater toleration, even legalisation, of opposition groups would have been an acceptable price to pay for the achievement of the key objective of appeasing public disquiet. On this front, however, no progress was made – except briefly in Karl-Marx-Stadt, where demonstrations were suspended for one week. The attempt to present dialogue as an alternative to demonstrations floundered – sometimes in comical fashion, as in Leipzig on 16 October where university professors distributed leaflets amongst a crowd of at least 120,000 that enjoined 'Don't demonstrate! Dialogue, moderation, compromise – that is the proper way!'[34] (The advice, needless to say, fell on deaf ears.) Where local officials and dignitaries faced the public at mass dialogues they could use the occasion to broadcast appeals for moderation, but at the price of affirming the legitimacy of what were in effect mass demonstrations.

The problems with mass dialogue were not lost on senior functionaries. 'These debates are less like dialogue and more like tribunals directed against our Party and its leading personalities', one Central Committee member complained. 'We must put a stop to these mass dialogues', an SED district secretary enjoined, 'for the opponent is in command of them right from the start, and the emotionally charged masses are putting our representatives through the wringer'. An alternative to mass dialogues was to offer masses *of* dialogues, in the form of small-scale public discussions and debates. A pioneer, once again, was the Dresden region, where Modrow announced that over 500 committees would be set up to organise dialogues between representatives of state, the Churches and the public. Being smaller, these events were more amenable to control by 'moderate forces'. However, for precisely this reason they were unlikely to form a magnet capable of pulling large numbers away from the streets. And indeed, attendance figures were low. 'The people don't even want dialogue', one SED member complained in late October; 'that's shown by the fact that, out of the twenty dialogue meetings on offer, a total of only one hundred people attended'.[35]

As time passed, ever fewer citizens took the 'dialogue' offer at face value. Already on 17 October Leipzig SED secretary Hackenberg telegraphed

34 Neubert, *Opposition*, p. 864.
35 Hertle and Stephan, *Ende*, p. 139; Hertle, *Chronik*, p. 88; Liebsch, *Dresdner*, p. 96.

Berlin to warn that citizens were beginning 'to see dialogue as a delaying tactic'. A week later the *Leipziger Volkszeitung* lamented that 'many of the chants and slogans [on the Monday demonstration] showed hardly any inclination to take a serious part in the open dialogue about society's problems that is currently underway'.[36] The slogans to which the piece referred included:

- 'Dialogue is good but deeds are better!'
- 'Enough talking, let's see action!'
- 'No dialogue with Party bosses!'
- 'Those who've tricked us for years now say they want to treaty!'[37]
- 'Dialogue is now cliché, so on the streets we shall stay!'

By the first week of November a journalist at the Leipzig Monday demonstration could report that 'the anger has increased; the only people still talking of dialogue are representatives of the SED'.[38]

Whether the crowds reshaped the dialogues into their own events or dismissed them as focus groups staged to divert attention from the stalling of real reform, the strategy was fruitless. The basic problem, a postal worker interviewed on Leipzig radio pointed out, was that 'the majority of the population is not content that things remain at the level of talking; they are asking instead for clear signals from the government'. After 9 October, one study has summarised, 'there was no shortage of attempts to bring people off the streets by offers of "dialogue": the streets should not be the forum for debate. In vain. The attempts failed.' Far from deserting the streets, protestors began to formulate more radical demands. If the monological character of political discourse was giving way, they asked, what about the monopolistic framework of power? And where would the SED – with or without its dialogues – be then?[39]

A short autumn of utopia

Although the reforms announced in the three weeks since Honecker's ouster equalled those passed in Gorbachev's Russia in as many years,

---

36 Schneider, *Demontagebuch*, p. 59.
37 'Die uns jahrelang betrogen kommen jetzt mit Dialogen.' Banner slogans are from Lang, *Wendehals*, p. 47; *Tribüne*, 31 October 1989; *Die Welt*, 8 November 1989; Schüddekopf, *Volk*.
38 *die tageszeitung* Journal 1, p. 88.
39 Neues Forum Leipzig, *Jetzt*, p. 112; Dönert and Rummelt, 'Montagsdemonstration', p. 154.

such was the continued growth of popular protest that even these concessions were too little and too late. They failed to dampen the street
protests. To the contrary, numbers climbed exponentially. In the third
week of October at least twenty-four demonstrations took place, with
attendances including 35,000 in Plauen and 125,000 or more in Leipzig
(population 530,000). The following week saw well in excess of half
a million citizens attend over 130 demonstrations.[40] The movement
reached into small communities – Ueckermünde, a town of some 12,000
souls, saw 5,000 take to the streets – while, at the other end of the scale,
at least half a million demonstrated in Berlin on 4 November and two
days later a similar number braved sleet and rain in Leipzig. That same
day saw several hundred thousand gather in Dresden, its biggest demonstration so far, as well as 60,000 in Halle and in Karl-Marx-Stadt.

The autumn drama was not only played out on the streets but in living
rooms, bars and workplaces. 'All normal activity came to a halt', recalls
one Dresdener, 'you couldn't even celebrate a birthday or sit down and
read a book. There was just too much going on.' In early November a
journalist recorded in her diary that 'Everyone is roused. Everyone wants
to talk. Everyone is engaged. There is only one theme: the revolution in
the land. Whether at the bakery, on a tram or at a birthday party – the
only talk is of the social transformation.'[41] One after another, sealed
areas of state control were prised open. As censorship evaporated, outlawed films began to be shown at cinemas, banned books were lined up
for publication and former dissidents such as Walter Janka, Rudolf
Bahro and Wolf Biermann spoke and sang to crowded galleries. 'An
incredible range of possibilities and necessities suddenly opened up', one
interviewee recalled.[42] In ever-expanding areas of life, orders were
opened up to challenge and traditional habits scrutinised. As individuals
perceived that they could 'make a difference', both within their immediate environment and on the national political stage, the new-found
democratic space was exploited, and with relish. Throughout the land,
what might be called the 'balance of class confidence' was shifting: as the
strength of powerholders melted away the powerless gained heart and
old forms of deference and self-censorship dissolved.

Wolfgang Biermann – not the rebel poet but the country's most powerful company director – experienced this process from the wrong end,
at a mass rally in Jena in early October. Such was the pressure from the
crowd that the chairperson felt obliged to take the microphone from him.

40 Mitter and Wolle, *Untergang*, p. 537.
41 Dyke, *Dresden*, p. 220; Lindner, *Revolution*, p. 102.
42 Marianne Pienitz, Leipzig.

Biermann was used to being at the centre of events but not, in the words of his personal assistant, 'in the manner of this occasion. *Commands and authoritarian gestures got you nowhere now, and certainly could not silence anyone.*' At the same spot a few weeks later his words 'were drowned by an uproarious tumult and a concert of whistles.'[43]

Biermann and his ilk had previously 'owned' the political and economic decision-making process. To ordinary folk it was the exclusive fief of distant, powerful figures and seemed only remotely related to their life experience. But now they felt that they could exert some influence. Political questions that had once seemed impossibly abstract now appeared concrete and urgent. Individuals began to test the newly won room for manoeuvre; the public sphere filled with a tumult of demands. 'Wall newspapers' were transformed into hives of information exchange and comment – in one factory it extended to several hundred metres. Peter Marcuse has described the wall newspaper at his college: 'It takes half an hour to go down the corridor, just looking at the new pages that have been pinned up since the previous day.'[44]

In colleges and workplaces meetings were called where myriad long-suppressed grievances were aired and redress demanded. One interviewee recounts his experience as a student at an art and craft college:

> We began by boycotting Marxism–Leninism classes, and demanded the Director resign – which he did. Our goal was to establish democracy within the college, so we set up an independent student council, and invited teachers onto it too. The immediate aims were transparency in college life and co-determination by students both in the structure of the courses and in the appointment of new staff. The managers lacked confidence at that time, so a lot was possible. For example, student representatives were invited onto interview panels.[45]

At my own college I attended one student gathering at which discussion variously raged and meandered for hours, covering a riot of issues. I noted some thirty-two demands that were raised, a flavour of which may be given by this selection: for independent student councils, student co-determination in university decisions, the establishment of partner universities and student exchanges, an end to Saturday classes, the abolition of military training in schools and of military service, more pianos, improved heating, an end to obligatory courses in Marxism–Leninism and a public investigation into the 'blank spots' in official SED historiography.

43 Klenke, *Rationalisierung*, emphasis in original.
44 *Ibid.*; Marcuse, *Revolution*, p. 54.
45 Marcus Bahr.

It would be an exaggeration to say that civil society was being invented anew – under the old regime people had been involved in clubs, self-help groups, citizens' initiatives and the like. Nevertheless, autumn 1989 witnessed an extraordinary eruption of civic activity. Opportunities were opening up for all manner of projects that had been illegal, or indeed still were. Every day two–three applications to register new associations reached the interior ministry. By mid-January, 247 had been granted a licence; they included: 'Initiatives, associations, organisations and movements of both local and regional nature. There were civic rights groups, democratic, liberal, liberal-conservative and conservative ones; left-democratic, Marxist, Trotskyist, anarchist and many more.'[46] A civic initiative to change the name of Karl-Marx-Stadt to Chemnitz was established. Committees were formed to launch investigations into brutality by the security forces. Houses were squatted, in some of which art galleries and bars were opened. Students created independent unions; feminists and their fellow travellers set up women's centres, cafés and libraries.[47]

Some of these multitudinous initiatives were responses of the moment; others were the realisation of long-harboured visions for which the opportunity had suddenly arrived. The Independent Historians' Association which Mario Kessler, an interviewee from Leipzig, helped to initiate belonged to the latter category, as did the organisation that another interviewee, Marianne Pienitz, founded. A psychotherapist in a Leipzig hospital, Marianne was thrilled to discover that the autumn's events had ameliorated the condition of her charges: 'Suddenly, with the *Wende*, we had no more patients. Although we all kept our jobs, we only had two patients for the next two years!' Released from the normal stresses of work, her surplus energies were devoted to the long-cherished dream of setting up projects for disadvantaged youth.[48]

Protest diffusion and radicalisation

Between the fall of Honecker and the fall of the Wall East Germany experienced a protest upswing, a phase of the 'cycle of protest' that typically includes two features: a rapid diffusion of collective action from more

46 Müller-Mertens, *Politische*, p. 52.
47 Schäfer, 'Revolution', p. 28.
48 'It was wonderful', she added, and remarked that 'some former patients would come in to show us how well they were'. After German unification, however, this was to change: 'Now that the [social and economic] collapse has arrived, the ward has filled up once again.'

'mobilised sectors' of the population – in this case, oppositionists and emigration applicants – to wider layers, and the development of new or transformed 'collective action frames'.[49] In their essentials, the dynamics of the upswing can readily be grasped. The regime was perceptibly weakening, the risks associated with protest were falling, and the force of the demonstrations was visibly impacting upon the decisions made by politicians, functionaries and managers. Having failed to stop the movement in its tracks the regime opted to introduce reforms and, in the process, events hitherto considered inconceivable suddenly materialised. 'That Honecker could be deposed was unthinkable', Ramona Hübner recalls; 'previously, we had harboured vague hopes that he'd go, but that was all'. Yet if the SED chief could be overthrown, she now thought, why not his loyal lieutenant Krenz? And if the border to Czechoslovakia could be re-opened (as occurred on 27 October), what about that other, more famous one with its dogs and landmines? If such an apparently stable regime could be toppled, why acquiesce to new limits? Like a hill climber reaching successive ridges, each concession wrung from the regime spurred further momentum towards new horizons, new goals.

In their spirit the demonstrations in this phase differed from those of the previous and subsequent periods. In the early autumn public protest had carried high risks. Courage was required and the prevailing mood, although far from joyless, bore a sober edge. Demands raised had been present-oriented; the focus was on creating a public space for protest in the here-and-now. Typical slogans were 'We're staying here!' and 'We are the people!' From mid-October, the movement became Janus-faced. On the one hand, protestors looked backward, with relief; the mood reflected the blessings of the recent past. With repression relaxed and early victories posted, tones of celebration and festivity could be heard. It was in this phase that the culture of political humour previously concealed within hidden transcripts burst into the open in the form of satirical slogans emblazoned on myriad home-made banners.[50] Re-reading them

49 In social movement theory, a frame is 'an interpretive schema that signifies and condenses the "world out there" by selectively punctuating and encoding objects, situations, events, experiences and sequences of action in one's present or past environment'. Frames serve as 'accenting devices that either underscore and embellish the seriousness and injustice of a social condition or redefine as unjust and immoral what was previously seen as unfortunate but perhaps tolerable'. Steinberg, 'Tilting', p. 845; Snow *et al.* 'Frame', p. 477; Snow and Benford, 'Master'. On protest cycles, see Tarrow, *Power*, p. 153, also Koopmans, 'Protest'; Barker, 'Cycle'; Barker and Dale, 'Protest'.
50 See Lang, *Wendehals*; Jackson, *DDR*.

now, one is struck by the breathtaking range of issues addressed as well as by the extraordinary care taken, and spark displayed, in the slogans. Language was reinvented, words and songs reclaimed, irony and ebullient wit flourished. Propaganda slogans were parodied and refashioned, as in the banners 'As we demonstrate today, so shall we live tomorrow!' (from the SED's 'As we toil today, so shall we live tomorrow') and 'Democracy, its strength will last; it shan't be slowed by ox nor ass!' (in which 'democracy' replaces the word 'socialism' in a recent homily by Erich Honecker). On the other hand, the future began to loom larger. Questions concerning the nature and direction of the movement gained a sharper edge. What change do we now want?, demonstrators were asking. What, concretely, should we be demanding? Who is in a position to implement reform and can they be helped? Are the reformists in the SED our allies or enemies? And the civic groups, what are their goals? Can we trust them? Should we support them, or pin our hopes on intervention from Bonn?

The period under study in this chapter may be thought of as a transitional one. A sense of unity prevailed. The rallying cry 'We are the people!' continued to symbolise the movement's breadth, including as it did young and old, Prussian and Saxon, white- and blue-collar worker, Communist and anti-Communist.[51] However, a process of differentiation was underway. Alongside the major issues of the day a profusion of subsidiary demands appeared. Opposition was expressed to all manner of evils – from fascism to nuclear power to school classes on Saturdays. Banners proclaimed the need for longer holidays, equal opportunities in education, a reduction in police numbers and the legalisation of busking. There were slogans calling for pollution controls, rights for disabled people, independence for Saxony, 'filter installation at the Espenhain power station', 'freedom for the conscientious objectors of Schwedt', solidarity with the victims of police violence in Prague, and so forth.

The movement's evolution in this phase was also shaped by its diffusion from opposition activists and emigration applicants to wider layers,

---

51 One survey found that 35 per cent of Communist respondents had participated in demonstrations, as against 48 per cent of non-Communists (McFalls, *Communism's*, p. 121). Contradicting widespread conceptions about the background and values of the SED's membership, the same survey found that SED members who took part in demonstrations were *more* likely than the average non-SED respondent 'to disapprove of the GDR's universal day-care system; to be offspring of fathers who had belonged to the Nazi Party; to have a telephone in their home; and to be sympathetic to famous Germans not generally revered in the GDR', such as Otto von Bismarck and Konrad Adenauer or (West German) soccer star Franz Beckenbauer.

notably white-collar and manual workers. Although the pivotal moments of 1989 did not occur in workplaces it was not entirely a 'leisure time revolution'. There were small strike waves, notably in the Erzgebirge region in early October, and in multifarious ways the movement on the streets, on the one hand, and workplace discussion, protest activities and FDGB meetings, on the other, intertwined. Demands raised in workplaces tended to echo those on the streets: 'No more bureaucratic impositions!', 'Abolish all privileges!', 'SED out of the factory'. Marianne Pienitz worked in a Leipzig hospital. She recalls that already in mid-October employees at her workplace were strongly supportive of oppositional initiatives; and 'when my colleagues and I drafted a collective letter to the FDGB it made us pretty popular at work'. Each Monday, she continues,

> after locking the doors to keep management out, we would paint placards. We – the staff on my ward, that is – would take an hour or so to discuss what slogans to write. At first we wrote things like 'For alternatives to military service!' Later, the slogans changed to, for example, 'For free trade unions!'

In such ways, workplaces functioned as 'relay stations' of protest. In some, colleagues would gather after work to walk to a demonstration – and when workers at one factory were told that they would be barred from taking part in a local demonstration they replied that they would leave by climbing over the fence.[52]

As the movement upswing continued its working-class element grew, and this infusion influenced the agenda. 'Workers were especially attuned to economic and material issues', Uwe Rottluf explains. 'They would ask: "What can the country afford?"; "Should so much money be spent on arms, or on aid for the Third World?"; and "Am I on a decent wage?"' On the streets questions of economic organisation, exploitation and social justice came to the fore. Some banners called for market reform. Some addressed terms and conditions of work, calling for a forty-hour working week or declaiming 'It's outrageous – your prices, our wages!' Other chants and banners broached questions of economic priorities and class relations, such as:

- 'Functionaries onto the shop floor!'
- 'Bosses out!'
- 'Millions in hard currency spent on sport. Why?'
- 'Evict the Stasi from their quarters – make nice homes for our sons and daughters!'

52 Marianne Pienitz to Geoff Brown and Judy Paskell, 18 October 1989; Weil, 'Wirtschaftliche', p. 536; Grix, *Collapse*, p. 111.

- 'Minimum pension for the Central Committee!'
- 'Sacks of cement instead of concrete heads!'[53]

Within this strand, a sub-genre parodied SED propaganda, with slogans including 'Privileged of the world, abdicate!' and 'Expropriate the privileged!'

The content and tone of demonstration banners and slogans testified to a process of radicalisation. Those that had prevailed in September and early October tended to demand civil liberties, toleration of diverse opinions in the media and that citizens be granted an influence upon government. Combative slogans such as 'Stasi out!' had been restricted to specific occasions when demonstrators were under attack, and those that targeted members or institutions of the regime had been light-hearted, such as 'SED = Agony!' That now began to change. 'We are the people!' gave way to 'All power to the people and not the SED'. On at least one demonstration an image of Honecker was carried aloft, as if on an official May Day parade except that his visage was montaged onto a figure in prison clothing. One protestor, recalling the mood immediately following Krenz's inauguration, describes how he 'was forced to realise that other demonstrators were miles ahead of me, for they were attacking Krenz head on for shoring up the old system'.[54] Other slogans that were characteristic of the late October radicalisation included, alongside the ubiquitous 'Stasi out!':

- 'Disband the factory battalions!'
- 'Bring the election fraudsters to justice!'
- 'Get all those arses off their seats!'

53 'Concrete heads' was a popular pejorative term for functionaries.
54 Lindner and Grüneberger, *Demonteure*, p. 93.

5

'Evolution slipped out of our hands': radicalisation and the fall of the Wall

Even a fortnight into Krenz's reign, the continued growth and radicalisation of protest ensured that his preferred tactics of gradual reform and dialogue were not producing the desired results. In public, Krenz welcomed the demonstrations. He proclaimed that 'In contrast to similar mass events in the West, after which absolutely nothing changes, the Party and state leadership in the GDR is receptive to every idea.' In his diary, in the same week, he wrote the opposite.

> Our problem is that, in contrast to the Soviet Union, the transition has been initiated not 'from above' but by a broad popular movement. Ultimately, everything boils down to two issues: On the one hand, we have no time to develop our policies. On the other, the demands of the demonstrators go beyond the point at which I'd be prepared to take them up.

The crisis brought a thicket of thorny questions. Should reforms be made to Party, polity and economy? If so, what exactly should be attempted, and at what pace? The Party was far from united over its response. 'I am under immense pressure', Krenz complained; 'Many comrades are saying: Don't give in to it! Others see me as a man of indecision.'[1] Not enough time! Too much pressure! Too conservative for the reformers, too reformist for the conservatives! These are the stock complaints of rulers in revolutionary situations. In this chapter we examine how constraints upon Krenz's government – with regard to the economy, border regime, protest movement and the SED – reduced its room for manoeuvre and led to its notorious blunder when attempting to effect a controlled opening of the Berlin Wall.

Economy and Party in crisis

I have analysed the political economy of 1989 in detail in *Between State Capitalism and Globalisation*, and need not dwell on it here. For present

---

1 *Junge Welt*, 2 November 1989; Krenz, *Herbst*, pp. 232, 234.

purposes it suffices to say that the economy was in grave crisis. Exports were stagnant despite booming world demand, and the perpetual under-achievement of export targets was aggravated by the exodus of workers and professionals. Foreign debt was spiralling out of control; although the figures had long been kept hidden from all but a few top functionaries, in early November they were divulged to the Central Committee, prompting some uncharacteristic expressions of shock and outrage from otherwise taciturn members.[2]

Of the economic strategies that offered themselves to the beleaguered regime, none held out much promise. One, the imposition of austerity in the form of price rises and cutbacks in government expenditure, was hardly an attractive option in the context of mass protests and ferment in the workplace. Another was to expedite cooperation with West Germany, in the hope that further loans would be forthcoming. This would be contingent upon significant political liberalisation and concessions on East Germans' freedom to travel, which would accelerate the exodus. It would also necessitate market reform, including introduction of a bankruptcy mechanism and opening to world market competition, a course which threatened to spark large-scale industrial action as well as pitching a weakening and liberalising GDR into ever-greater reliance upon its 'enemy' to the West.

Confronted by intractable problems on the economic front, wracked by internal divisions and with no sign of the storm on the streets abating, the SED leadership now faced tumult within the Party, too. Discontent had risen throughout the summer, not least in response to the leadership's clumsy and arrogant handling of the exodus. Many SED members had greeted Krenz's accession to the post of General Secretary with disbelief, and had been astounded and dismayed when, only days later, he also took over Honecker's positions as Prime Minister and Chair of the National Security Council. This act was protested by a spontaneous gathering of some 13,000, including many SED members.

That 'Krenz, of all people, was chosen as Honecker's replacement came as a terrible shock', in the words of Lily M., a junior official in a government ministry. Lily tore up her party card in early November. 'I had never really felt deeply connected with the Party', she told me:

> The ideal of a just distribution of wealth was not bad, but in reality this is impossible. And anyway those ideas were spoilt; the leadership got the main slice of the cake – they lived life as Communism should be, but that

2 In fact, the figures released were overestimates. East Germany was not, as it appeared, bankrupt. Nevertheless, its ability to repay foreign debt was in steep decline. Steiner, *Plan*, pp. 224–5.

wasn't possible for the rest of us. We – myself and colleagues [who were also Party members] – reckoned that unemployment would be necessary in order to boost labour discipline, and that subsidies on basic goods would have to be cut.

Lily typified a wide layer who belonged to the SED essentially because membership was a career requirement or brought other sorts of personal advantage. They were the type, often labelled 'opportunist', about whom the joke went: 'there are three good reasons why I'm in the Party: my spouse and two kids.' As long as the SED controlled the life chances of such individuals it could count on their support. Now that its grip was relaxing, they began to exit the Party (and even, in a surprising number of cases, the country). In the weeks following Honecker's ouster, the stream of resignations became a flood. It drew from all echelons of society, including top managers, Stasi employees and police officers, but was heavily concentrated among workers, who comprised around 70 per cent of resignations in this period. The percentage of blue-collar workers in the SED plummeted from 33 in late 1989 to only 8 in spring 1990.[3]

While many turned their backs on the SED, others voiced discontent. Some members were opposed to the incipient market reforms, others to the sluggishness with which democratic reform was proceeding. In late October, a report prepared for the Politburo noted with concern that although 'a large section of comrades' supported Krenz's 'course of renewal', others, including many functionaries, had misgivings or were in a condition of 'profound shock' in the face of the leadership's inept-ness and 'lack of collectivity'. Many had 'completely abandoned the posi-tions' of the SED, while some even espoused 'policies and demands that are similar to those of New Forum'. As a result, the report warned, SED loyalists 'are frequently left to fight alone. At public meetings other Party members stab them in the back, leading to ever more conflicts between comrades breaking out in public.'[4]

Probably the biggest single threat to the SED's credibility began to emerge in Krenz's second week in office, when revelations of the high life enjoyed by senior functionaries began to appear in the press. Some 'concrete heads' refused to believe the reports, and smelt a conspiracy organised by the comparatively doveish Günther Schabowski, but a far more prevalent reaction was outrage. Already after the first reports appeared – and these were relatively mild compared to what was to

3 Kowalczuk, 'Artikulationsformen'; *die tageszeitung* 27 November 1989; Nakath, *Kreml*, p. 138; Bahrmann and Links, *Chronik 1*, p. 164; Menge, *Ohne*, p. 117; Stolle, *Aufstand*, p. 117; Pfaff, 'Revolution', p. 663.
4 Stephan, *Vorwärts*, p. 189.

come – the Politburo was apprised of the darkening mood among the rank and file:

> Impatient and sometimes very aggressive discussions concerning the privileges of leading Party and state functionaries have increased dramatically. Their special shops, sojourns in the non-socialist world, private use of jets for holidays, remuneration in and ownership of hard currency, and, above all, the privileges granted to the children, grandchildren and relatives of members of the Politburo and government are the subjects of repeated and ubiquitous criticism.

Numerous local branches, including some in the army, passed resolutions criticising the leadership and calling for open debate. Party members raised their concerns at the 'dialogues' and even organised their own demonstration, at the Central Committee's headquarters in Berlin, at which thousands voiced their lack of confidence in the leadership. Chanting 'We are the Party!' (in echo of 'We are the people!') they demanded a special Party congress be convened to enable ordinary members to exert a direct influence upon the formation of policy and upon the appointment of a new leadership. Central Committee members were obliged to admit that the leadership had suffered a double blow to its legitimacy: from the Party ranks as well as the general public.[5]

With the crisis deepening, Krenz travelled to Moscow to seek advice. The Kremlin, he found, shared some of his fears. 'These processes are very dynamic and could accelerate still further', Gorbachev warned. 'The Party leadership must react appropriately. It would be most unfortunate if these processes were to gain in spontaneity, or if political orientation were lost. If that happens, a hopeless situation could arise.' The Soviet leader offered little in the way of practical assistance, but recommended further turnover at the top. 'The populace has arisen and is speaking its mind openly', he said. It will 'continue to raise questions of responsibility for the situation, and for this reason fundamental personnel changes are necessary'.

These were in any case underway. FDGB leader Harry Tisch was one of the next to step down, in the face of protest letters, strike threats and mass resignations from his organisation. He was quickly followed by the Education Secretary, Margot Honecker, the leaders of the CDU and the German National-Democratic Party (NDPD), and a host of district-level SED and FDGB leaders and city mayors. Encapsulating the popular response to these waves of resignations were the chants of 'Encore!

5 Weinert, 'Massenorganisationen', p. 140; Stephan, *Vorwärts*, p. 190; Hertle and Stephan, *Ende*, p. 71.

Encore!' at a demonstration in Gera when the mayor announced that the region's SED leader had resigned.[6]

As the SED disintegrated, notes of bitterness and recrimination began to enter even discussions at the Central Committee. Its meeting of 8–10 November witnessed angry scenes, and indictments of the leadership. Speakers had to confront heckles, even insults. One delegate was aghast that the Politburo had attempted to blame its inactivity in the face of the exodus upon Erich Honecker's absence through illness. Another charged that the reforms being introduced, even those that had been in the pipeline for some time, now appeared as nothing but desperate responses to pressure from the streets. A third accused the leadership of lying to the country, and declared in favour of media freedoms. Against this, conservative delegates, including Krenz, launched diatribes against journalists and sniped at the bloc parties for scapegoating the SED as culprit for the country's plight.[7]

The SED's fracturing and fraying vitiated the regime's capacity to control events. Having shifted emphasis from military to political methods of crisis management, the SED leadership was *more* reliant on the efforts of 'progressive forces', above all its own rank and file, to counter the protests. Until about 25 October, 'progressive forces' were exhorted to 'be resolute and allow oppositional forces no room for manoeuvre'. Yet, as reports prepared by the Stasi and by the Central Committee repeatedly warned, they had become unreliable, even 'spineless'. To the consternation of the SED leadership, its members and other 'progressive forces', when faced by oppositionists or other critics of the regime, tended either to sympathise with them or to practise evasion. At a student gathering in Berlin, for example, 'progressive forces were all but totally ineffectual'.[8]

Recognising its failure to weld its supporters into a force capable of containing the movement, the regime changed tack. From mid-October, and more so from the end of the month, individuals and institutions of the old regime wrapped themselves in reformist clothing, proclaiming the *Wende* to be their own and celebrating it as already accomplished. LDPD leader Manfred Gerlach, who had belonged to the GDR's political elite since its foundation, led the way, followed by Krenz and Schabowski. Some organisations, such as the FDJ, announced that they

6 Hertle and Stephan, *Ende*, p. 64; Stephan, *Vorwärts*, p. 221; Simon, *Tischzeiten*, p. 139; Haug, *Perestrojka-Journal*, p. 107; Gehrke, ' "Wende"-Streiks', p. 253; Hall, *Fernseh-Kritik*, p. 111.
7 Hertle and Stephan, *Ende*, pp. 135–437, esp. pp. 245–59.
8 Mitter and Wolle, *Befehle*, p. 223.

had transformed themselves, as if 'born again'. The SED, bloc parties and mass organisations all appropriated the language of radical change, presented themselves as instigators of a 'movement for socialist renewal' and sought to blur the distinction between demands for far-reaching change that were raised on the streets and the promises of limited reform that issued from Berlin. SED members were instructed to join demonstrations and seek to inject moderate ('socialist') content. The highpoint of this manoeuvre came at a mass rally in Berlin on 4 November that was addressed not only by Gerlach but also by Mielke's former deputy, Markus Wolf, and by Schabowski. The latter, Krenz insisted, must be among the speakers, 'in order to ensure that the demonstration is not dominated by oppositionists'.[9]

However, few were convinced by these attempts by figures and institutions of the old regime to reinvent themselves as pioneers of change. Functionaries were unable to persuade the public of their 'genuine' belief in reform. In Erfurt, for example, when the hard-line district SED chief, Gerhard Müller, attempted to convince a crowd that the *Wende* had been initiated by Krenz, and that he was its most avid supporter, a voice from the crowd heckled: 'The *Wende* wasn't initiated by you and the Party, but the people on the streets.'[10] As a public relations exercise, the tactic had little traction; a fresh approach was clearly required.

Of cabbages and Coca-Cola

The failure of the dialogues and the 'movement for socialist renewal' to contain protest prompted SED leaders to develop a new strategy, of 'constructive engagement with the friends of socialism'. The formula that had been adopted in the first weeks of Krenz's administration, whereby 'enemy oppositionists' were to be spurned while the 'vacillating and misled' were courted, proved open to adaptation. Some sections of the opposition, such as Magdeburg New Forum, with its 'demand for the abolition of the Party's leading role' and for a referendum on the issue, retained 'enemy' status.[11] Others, however, could be redescribed as 'socialist reformists' – people with whom the authorities could work.[12]

The new initiative was spawned in the public dialogues. As detailed in chapter 4, these had necessitated locating representatives with whom the authorities could talk, and here the civic groups could not easily be ruled

9 Gerlach, *Mitverantwortlich*, pp. 10, 316; Stephan, *Vorwärts*, p. 218.
10 Dornheim, *Politischer* p. 16.
11 Stephan, *Vorwärts*, p. 218; Mitter and Wolle, *Befehle*, p. 246.
12 Krenz's gloss on this strategic turn may be found in *Herbst*, p. 151.

out. The dialogues, one historian has observed, 'became an entry point, through which the movement, initially at municipal level, penetrated the political system'. In embryo, this process had begun already in mid-October, at the local level. Dresden region led the way, with permission granted for a New Forum meeting in Zittau, cooperation of managers and Party officials with a New Forum workplace group at Dresden's Mühlenbau works, and invitations to opposition representatives to speak at public dialogues in the city. Other districts followed suit, although some lagged behind – in Gera, as late as 8 November, the mayor was still insisting that podium places at a public dialogue be restricted to a regime representative and a priest. By this stage, opposition representatives elsewhere were being admitted into official politics at the local level. In late October, the G20 were granted speaking rights at a Dresden city council meeting, and New Forum took part in town council committees in Weimar, Neubrandenburg, Rostock and Gera. Shortly afterwards, the first of many local 'round tables' was established, and talks were held between the SED and New Forum at the national level, too.[13]

The creeping toleration of New Forum inevitably drew attention to the vexed question of its legal status. The SED faced a dilemma, which was expressed sharply in a letter from Roland Wötzel to Wolfgang Herger, the Central Committee member in charge of security, in late October. 'If we legalise New Forum we are legalising opposition', the Leipzig chief began, and warned that this could lead to 'a Polish-type scenario, with New Forum becoming our Solidarność. The potential consequences are impossible to calculate.' And yet, he added, 'if we outlaw them, we are courting our defeat on the streets'. Wötzel's preferred option was to stall for as long as possible, and Krenz – who naturally inclined to prevarication – seems to have shared this position.

On his visit to Russia, on 1 November, Krenz admitted to Gorbachev that no decision had yet been taken with regard to New Forum. The Russian leader advised action. Speaking of the relation of ruling Communist parties to social movements in general, he counselled against 'throwing good and bad together into one pot'. One should tackle 'anti-socialist and criminal elements' head on, he argued, while seeking to pull others into the 'socialist' camp. If the friendlier sections are not 'bound into the Party's activities' then a process of polarisation could ensue in which they would end up 'on the wrong side of the barricades'.[14]

Following Krenz's return from Moscow, the legalisation of New Forum was expedited. At the Central Committee's next plenum, a number of

13 Krone, *Briefe*, p. 163; Hall, *Fernseh-Kritik*, p. 111; Timmer, *Aufbruch*, p. 250.
14 Stephan, *Vorwärts*, p. 218.

delegates spoke in favour of the new tactic. 'A situation has arisen in which we must approach certain representatives of "New Forum" in a constructive way', argued Lorenz, 'particularly *those who seek to prevent chaos*, who show clearly, and in public, a willingness to exert a calming influence'. Another Party notable, Otto Reinhold, came up with the canny argument that negotiations with the opposition would, paradoxically, provide the best means of 'demonstrating, in practice, our power and our leading position'. Gerhard Schürer went further, proposing that a transitional government be formed, with Lorenz as premier but with the inclusion of opposition representatives such as Eppelmann and New Forum leader Bärbel Bohley. Along similar lines, Leipzig's SED chief ventured that the Party should aim to form a coalition government which would include the civic groups, while Potsdam's Party boss Günther Jahn even advocated that New Forum be incorporated into the National Front.[15]

That Politburo members were making overtures to a movement that they had regarded hitherto as public enemy number one attested to an extraordinarily rapid tactical shift. How, though, would the 'enemy' react? These unaccustomed approaches by regime institutions presented the civic groups with the first in a series of strategic choices. Would they interpret the Party's offers as a genuine offer of friendship? Or would they spurn the outstretched hand as the desperate attempt of an illegitimate government to avoid drowning? Should they follow the Magdeburg New Forum leaders Hans-Jochen Tschiche and Erika Drees, who proposed that cooperation with the authorities be used as a bargaining chip, with negotiations to proceed only if the opposition groups were legalised and elections promised? Or should the radicals, who urged non-cooperation and demanded instead the resignation of the government, be heeded? These included the United Left (VL), for whom Krenz's *Wende* confronted the opposition with the choice of cooperation or of 'supporting all forms of self-organisation of the demonstrating masses', a course that would involve 'replacing the question of dialogue with the question of power'. In this scenario, the opposition would press the government to resign, to be replaced by a transitional government following elections to a constituent assembly.[16]

In reaching their decision, opposition leaders had to take two major developments into account: the ongoing collapse of government authority and the radicalisation of the movement. As outlined above, the street demonstrations, having begun with calls for reform, now rang to demands

15 Hertle and Stephan, *Ende*, pp. 199, 336, emphasis added; Przybylski, *Tatort 2*, p. 333; Stolle, *Aufstand*, p. 184; Pfaff, 'Revolution', p. 451.
16 Timmer, *Aufbruch*, p. 275; Klein, *Visionen*, p. 235.

that threatened the regime at its foundations: for freedom of travel, for corrupt officials to be brought to justice, for the sacking of SED leaders and for the dissolution of the Stasi. On the streets, the *Wende* reforms and dialogues were dismissed as too little and too late. 'There is always a hard core of demonstrators', Stasi informants reported, 'who attempt to delay the dispersal of the demonstrations and to direct them instead towards offices of the SED, state apparatus and State Security'. In the workplaces, SED organisations were being forced to shut up shop. The potential for the movement to begin the process of prising the SED from power was becoming more apparent each day.[17]

An additional factor to be considered was the condition of the civic groups themselves. They had only been in existence for a few months; most of them counted their membership in thousands, at a time when millions were attending demonstrations. According to one journalist reporting from Leipzig in late October, with a throng of 420,000 on the streets, 'the little group of "New Forum" with their two megaphones made about as much impression as a few Jehovah's Witnesses on the margins of roaring crowds at a football cup final'.[18] Yet the civic groups' influence, actual and potential, was markedly greater than this image suggests. Within the wider movement's exponential growth, they had been expanding steadily. Their meetings attracted large numbers: 100,000 in the week of 16–22 October (including one in a Potsdam church, attended by over 6000, that required five separate sittings!). A fortnight later the figure had soared to 300,000. Organisational networks were developing, too. Already by the time of Honecker's departure, New Forum groups existed in every district of Berlin and in all major towns. Although its active core was not enormous, New Forum's list of supporters numbered some 200,000. Its influence was extending into workplaces and 'to a substantial degree', according to Stasi reports, into the army.[19] It was the subject of discussion at kitchen tables and bars throughout the country, and 'Legalise New Forum' was chanted on the marches. Unlike Jehovah's Witnesses in a stadium, the civic groups were perceived as a vital part of the movement.

For Klaus Wolfram, a member of New Forum's national steering committee, his organisation's growing popularity raised the question of how to build upon that support: 'What do we do with this ever-growing mass base that we now have? What demands should we raise that can give

17 Mitter and Wolle, *Befehle*, p. 250.
18 Hartung, *Neunzehnhundertneunundachtzig*, p. 50.
19 Hertle, *Chronik*, p. 195. See also the letters from conscript soldiers published in Krone, *Briefe*.

structure to the civic movement and to the people's movement while also pushing the ruling powers further into a corner?' It was rapidly becoming apparent, he concluded, that 'far greater opportunities were arising, and far larger questions were being thrown up, than we had expected'. But for other New Forum leaders these opportunities weighed heavily; a 'certain helplessness and hesitancy' began to enter their thoughts and deeds. According to Stasi insiders, New Forum's national leadership 'did not wish for a "power vacuum" to arise, and thus had no interest in seeing a sharpening of social contradictions in the GDR or in questioning the SED's leading role'. Continued SED power appeared as a lesser evil if the alternative were 'anarchy'. As Jens Reich saw it, there was at the time 'no alternative' to the SED: if it were overthrown, the country would 'fall into chaos'.[20]

The combative approach advocated by the VL and other leftists was emphatically rejected by New Forum spokespeople.[21] They advised that the regime's advances be treated with respect, and the other groups adopted similar positions. At its inaugural meeting in late October, DA vigorously debated its attitude towards the SED. Of candidates for election to the party's chair, the advocates of a confrontational approach, Edelbert Richter and Rainer Eppelman, shared the votes of only thirty-six delegates while the lawyer and Stasi agent Wolfgang Schnur, who favoured cooperation, was elected with 108 votes. As for the SDP, its leader (and Stasi agent) Ibrahim Böhme, assured the SED that it had no intention of seeking confrontation – a stance which also received the influential support of West Berlin's SPD chief, Walter Momper.

This phase of the uprising witnessed a divergence of 'two streams of protest', as Charles Maier has put it: 'the one emanating from dissident groups and the church-oriented; the other based on the . . . working class, fed up with urban overcrowding and material and ecological privation.' These two tendencies responded in divergent ways to the *Wende*. A primary purpose of the Krenz regime's *Wende* strategy, as Tschiche warned at the time, had been to 'fragment the "critical potential"', and in this it partially succeeded. Divisions grew between civic groups and the crowds. Whereas the latter turned increasingly against Krenz and his government, opposition leaders pleaded 'Give Krenz a chance!' Nor did opposition spokespeople lend their voices to the calls from the streets for punishment of corrupt officials and the sacking of SED and Stasi functionaries. While demonstrators were pressing for the freedom to travel,

20 Wolfram, interview; Mitter and Wolle, *Befehle*, p. 247; *Financial Times*, 8 November 1989.
21 Klein, *Visionen*, p. 225.

New Forum leaders rejected this as unrealistic, an issue of secondary importance, while New Forum's keynote speaker at a Leipzig demonstration in late October warned the crowds not to 'let yourselves be bought off by higher consumption and the freedom to travel!' At the gigantic rally in Berlin on November 4, *not a single speaker* broached the issue of travel rights, even though the Berlin Wall was within spitting distance. Moreover, 'none of the speakers' at that event, Klaus Hartung has written with incredulity bordering on exasperation, 'tried to mobilise, to give out battle orders'. Quite the opposite. The agenda, for them, was conciliation. Pastor Schorlemmer (DA) summed it up with his call to 'rebuild our country together with the SED'. In a gesture that spoke volumes, when Schabowski was subjected to a chorus of booing at the Berlin rally, the pastor from DA patted him on the back. In such ways, Hartung continues,

> it was clear that the opposition's process of organisation lagged behind the masses. By [mid-October] at the latest, the process should have been given direction through the propagation of an action programme aimed at taking over government. Instead, New Forum's proclaimed purpose was to offer the masses grassroots democracy as an alternative form of political engagement. This was little but an exercise in political pedagogy.[22]

The divergence was underlined on 8 November, when leaders of all of the mainstream groups,[23] along with Kurt Masur, signed a statement, read out on radio and television by the author Christa Wolf, that urged a halt to further emigration and a renewal of socialism. It contained the telling phrase, 'What can we promise you? No easy life, but a useful one. No quick prosperity, but participation in a great transformation.' This was an extraordinary message, not least for its candour, and for the Calvinist (or orthodox Communist) overtones in the conjoining of a temporal ethic of work and abstemiousness with promised paradise. Yet in counterposing prosperity to 'participation' in a nebulous democratic experiment – a dichotomy which drew upon and echoed that between consumption and 'free communication' (to be discussed in chapter 6) – the statement cut against the mass movement. Here were found hosts of ordinary people who championed 'communication', participation and democracy but

22 Maier, *Dissolution*, p. 374; Mitter and Wolle, *Befehle*, p. 233; Hawkes, *Tearing*, p. 80; Rein, *Opposition*, p. 26; Mosler, 'Klassenkämpfe'; *die tageszeitung* Journal 1, p. 84; Schüddekopf, *Volk*, p. 212; Schabowski, *Absturz*, p. 283; Hartung, *Neunzehnhundertneunundachtzig*, p. 60.
23 New Forum (NF), DA, SDP, DJ and Initiative for Peace and Human Relations (IFM).

were *also* giving thought to the means by which living standards could be increased – whether by automation, market reform, cutting corruption or reducing funds spent on the security forces.[24] Whatever the merits of these proposals for escaping crisis or redistributing wealth, the point is that few outside the civic groups believed that they should be obliged to *choose* between material gain and democratisation.

The dichotomy between participatory democracy and consumption was a leitmotif for all the civic groups. A New Forum poster presented East Germans with this perplexing choice: 'Don't drink yourselves to death on Coca-Cola; pull together in the municipality instead!' Democracy Now declared that it would be 'criminal to aspire to consume at West German levels', while the VL scoffed at those who coveted West German living standards.[25] These examples represent a strand in the opposition discourse that lacked empathy with ordinary people and tended to self-righteousness and condescension. Lest the reader be under any illusion, the average East German consumer was hardly at risk of overdosing on Coca-Cola, or on much else for that matter. Even basic goods such as fresh fruit and vegetables, not to mention cars or telephones, were frequently out of stock and of poor quality. 'Only cabbage in the vegetable section, always only cabbage, and perhaps a few cucumbers or the like', was a typical shopper's refrain.[26] With the GDR's supermarkets in such a sorry state (as those of us who depended upon them knew only too well) one can imagine the popular response towards civic groups' announcements that higher living standards were not on their agenda.

As the movement on the streets edged towards direct confrontation with the regime, and with the borders of the SED-state, the civic groups moved in the opposite direction and commenced, cautiously at first, to dialogue and duet with the SED leadership. In this process, as Timmer has noted, their importance 'increased to the extent that they were recognised as people's representatives not only by the population but now by the powerholders too'. But their policy proposals were resonating less with the public. The streets were ringing to demands that were either outside the scope of, or even in direct contradiction to, those of the

24 In one factory, workers demanded 'an end to the production of bicycle locks'. Although an intentionally humorous slogan, it contained a serious criticism of the decree whereby each *Kombinat* was obliged to develop sidelines in consumer goods, a notoriously inefficient procedure. Gehrke and Hürtgen, *Aufbruch*, p. 43.
25 *Märkische Volksstimme*, 7 and 10 February 1990, p. 3.
26 *die tageszeitung*, 28 August 1989.

opposition. The latter, Jens Reich has written, went through a 'Sorcerer's apprentice' experience. 'We had not wanted, had not expected' events to radicalise in this way: 'Evolution, reform and reason slipped out of our hands and towards revolution.'[27]

The fall of the Berlin Wall

Evolution was slipping from Krenz's hands, too. 'The CC has lost its footing', he noted in his diary in early November: 'It's overstretched in this situation.' Similar feelings applied lower down the hierarchy, as evinced in the following excerpts from memos sent to Schwerin district headquarters from local SED offices:

> Party secretaries are reporting: We can hardly endure the pressure any more; overwhelmed by the dimensions [of crisis]; functionaries and cadre showing signs of paralysis, great worries as to whether the Party can withstand the pressure . . . The Party showing signs of disintegration . . . a great wave of resignations in the large factories. Party secretaries here are talking of an avalanche.

An element of disarray entered the behaviour of SED and government leaders, but this should not be confused with headlong retreat. Signs of desperation notwithstanding, the regime restructured and regrouped as best it could.

Some measures were destructive. Stasi officers had already been busy eradicating some of their more incriminating materials, but on an ad hoc basis; now, in early November, Mielke ordered that shredding proceed systematically. His command unleashed 'a veritable orgy of destruction in the offices of the Ministry of State Security'.[28] All manner of documents were destined for the shredders: those that named western agents, involved fatalities, exposed the degree to which Stasi and SED were intertwined, bore directly upon the organisation's tactics during the autumn, or simply revealed the extent of its surveillance operations.

Other measures were constructive. Further reforms were announced. A law on media reform was prepared, and legal proceedings commenced against officers of the security forces accused of mistreatment of demonstrators. Compulsory military training in schools was ended, conscientious objection recognised and a constitutional court promised. Although Krenz continued to invoke the oxymoronic formula whereby pluralism

27 Timmer, *Aufbruch*, p. 252; Reich, *Abschied*, p. 23.
28 Krenz, *Herbst*, p. 232; Langer, *Norden*, p. 178; Richter, *Staatssicherheit*,
    p. 36.

was said to exist thanks to the SED's 'leading role', he nonetheless propounded reforms – including greater independence for the bloc parties and for parliament, and the dissociation of Party and state – that would inexorably undermine the latter part of the formula.

Of the many problems besetting Krenz's administration, the least tractable was the question of the country's border regime. Already from mid-October, the streets, especially in Leipzig, had resounded to chants of 'The Wall must go!' If his new leadership was to be at all credible, major concessions on travel rights were unavoidable. If, argued an editor of the *Berliner Zeitung*, extensive freedoms were granted, if the Wall were removed as a meaningful barrier, this 'could win time for concepts to be worked out, and time . . . is what Krenz lacks'.[29] The issue rapidly rose to the top of the policy agenda.

The SED leadership was clear about one thing: it had to remain in control of the border; an uncontrolled mass exit could not be contemplated. 'Measures must be taken to prevent any attempt at a mass breakthrough across the Wall', Krenz told Gorbachev of his fears in advance of the 4 November demonstration in Berlin. 'That would be dreadful, because then the police would have to intervene [with force] and elements of a state of emergency would have to be introduced.' But the task of drafting new travel regulations, begun in late October, was far from straightforward. Only if travel to the West were permitted, officials were aware, would a sufficient number of citizens retain the reserves of hope and courage necessary to fashion 'a strong and attractive socialism'. Yet a full opening of the border would have 'uncontrollable consequences' and would, in addition, generate an urgent need for scarce hard currency. To the extent that a compromise was possible, it entailed a controlled opening of borders, with travel permitted only to those in possession of valid documents. Journeying to the West would proceed in an orderly fashion, with the state maintaining symbolic control over its borders as well as the real sanction of withholding passports or visas. 'Overhasty decisions', Krenz insisted, 'must be avoided'. The new law, it was envisaged, would come into effect in December.[30]

Even as officials were drafting it, the border regime was changing, and shifted the ground under their feet. It was announced that, from 1 November, visa-free travel to Czechoslovakia would be permitted (as it had been until early October). Yet, East Germans still could not exit that country to the west and so, as in the summer, would-be emigrants

29 Greenwald, *Berlin*, p. 217.
30 Fulbrook, *Anatomy*, p. 260; Stephan, *Vorwärts*, pp. 195–6; Krenz, *Wenn*, p. 180.

proceeded to occupy West Germany's embassy in Prague. Czechoslovak Party leader Miloš Jakeš told Krenz that East Berlin must find a way of solving its emigration issue without involving his country. Lest their brazen defiance of the authorities encourage domestic protests, Jakeš' government permitted East Germans to emigrate across its western border on 3 November, and over the next five days one arrived in West Germany every 9 seconds on average. Both Prague and East Berlin considered re-sealing their mutual border but decided against. That would be courting disaster, senior GDR functionaries admitted.[31]

On 6 November, the draft travel law was duly published. It had perforce been prepared in haste. 'We would certainly have been capable of producing a better draft', Krenz fretted; 'We allowed ourselves to be put under pressure. Our political credibility is slipping further.'[32] Promising the right to travel for every citizen, the law would have been inconceivable even a month earlier, and yet such had been the pace of change that its restrictive clauses elicited outrage. These included a range of grounds upon which applications could be denied, a thirty-day limit on time spent abroad and a maximum of 15 Deutschmarks to be exchanged at the official rate. Given the GDR Mark's plummeting black market exchange rate, this effectively put travel to the 'non-socialist abroad' beyond the reach of all but high earners and those with generous Western relatives.

The publication of the draft law was met by a hurricane of disapproval. Banners appeared on the streets with slogans such as:

- '30 days and no cash, Egon you are trash!'
- 'Real freedom of travel: with hard currency!'
- 'Visas but no proper money; the whole world finds that funny.'
- 'Alu-chips[33] buy nothing on this earth; we need money that's got real worth!'
- 'Alu-chips abroad? No way!; We need hard currency right away!'

I was alerted to the storm's force when one of my students, a shy woman who was generally supportive of the government, requested that class be given over to writing protest letters over the travel law. But the most vehement reaction was found in workplaces. In factories, 'workers, who

---

31 Nakath and Stephan, *Countdown*, p. 226; Hertle, *Fall*, pp. 208–12; Krenz, *Herbst*, p. 226.
32 Krenz, *Herbst*, p. 224.
33 East Germans' derogatory description for their non-convertible currency, with its aluminium coinage. For this and other demonstration slogans, see Jackson, *DDR*.

felt discriminated against by the planned law, because it didn't envisage hard currency for them, spontaneously downed tools'. The strength of working-class sentiment was conveyed to New Forum by correspondents who wrote, for example:

> In this case freedom of travel will hardly help us common people (workers). It will only serve the so-called 'new rich' and Party and state functionaries. Unlike our sort, these folk have enough money to buy sufficient D-Marks to travel all over the world.

Public indignation was accompanied by criticisms of the bill's restrictive clauses in media organs such as *Junge Welt* and *Tribüne*, and by sharp words from the leaders of the mass organisations (FDJ and FDGB) as well as SED reformists such as Gregor Gysi. Even professors at the arch-conservative College of State Jurisprudence joined the chorus. In the context of this crescendo of censure, parliament – in an unprecedented display of independence – rejected the bill, prompting both government and Politburo to tender their collective resignations. Authority figures were coming to resemble skittles, an impression that was underlined when four of the new faces on the Politburo were notified that their local SED organisations, under pressure from strike threats, were withdrawing their support.[34]

The travel law had been rejected, yet a swift resolution of this issue remained imperative. 'This border stands, and this border will be defended', Dickel declared to loud applause at a Central Committee plenary, and castigated those who were calling for the Wall to be brought down. Yet, even as he spoke, the leaks in border defences were becoming a flood. In effect, the surge of emigrants through Czechoslovakia, backed by the street protests and strike threats, had already forced the border open. Several days before the Wall's actual fall, adventurous residents of the border areas managed to take day trips to West Germany, via Czechoslovakia, even without passports. One sharp-eyed reporter concluded on 6 November that 'the revolutionary movement has deprived the Wall of its existence'.[35]

Having ruled out a closure of the GDR–Czech border, officials realised that they had little choice but to drop all restrictions on permanent emigration. Foreign Minister Oskar Fischer proposed that a border crossing point be opened between East and West Germany, obviating an

34 Görtemaker, 'Zusammenbruch', p. 23; Krone, *Briefe*, pp. 235–6; Hertle, *Fall*, p. 204; *Chronik*, p. 116.
35 Hertle and Stephan, *Ende*, p. 297; Küttler, 'Wende,' pp. 125–7; *die tageszeitung*, 7 November 1989.

embarrassing feud with Prague (and sparing emigrants and day-trippers the detour through Czechoslovakia). But this was rejected. To grant *emigrants* a right that was denied GDR citizens who wished simply to visit West Germany would be tantamount to political suicide. It would also be nigh impossible to enforce: already, scores of citizens who had ostensibly emigrated in recent weeks were returning; others were popping back into East Germany to collect possessions – furniture, for example – that they had been unable to take with them previously. Could these people be allowed to come and go as they pleased? Or be expatriated for good?

At this critical juncture, confusion reigned. Some functionaries sought to pass difficult decisions down the chain of command. Others were unclear as to the difference between travel and emigration. Despite obvious implications for the Soviet presence in Germany, the Kremlin was not informed of the momentous changes that were about to occur. 'Whatever way we do it will be wrong', Krenz admitted to the Central Committee.

The fateful regulation, announced on 9 November, aimed to modify but not demolish the state's control of its borders. It allowed freedom of travel, but only to passport holders. If a surge of citizens were to occur, this would be at police stations and offices, not at the border; population movements to the West would be staggered. And although this, regulated, border liberalisation would appear as yet another concession to popular pressure, by presenting it as a positive reform on the part of a well-intentioned leadership, Krenz's new Politburo, it was hoped, would gain a modicum of credit (as well as actual credits, in billions of Deutschmarks, from Bonn).[36]

However, SED leaders were uncertain over their decision and blind to its consequences. Krenz's earlier insistence that hasty measures not be taken proved to be wishful thinking. The new regulation was not even perused and approved by the Council of Ministers. The Central Committee was informed, but its members were too focused on other unfolding catastrophes to give it sufficient attention. Some functionaries did fret that 'the GDR will bleed away if we adopt this measure', but, according to Lorenz, its full import was not grasped.[37] Even Schabowski, charged with announcing the measure at a televised press conference, was patently unsure of the details – indeed, he had not even been in attendance when the measure was announced to the Central Committee. The decree permitted passport holders alone to apply for visas, from the following morning, with the promise that their documents would be

36 Hertle, *Fall*, pp. 226–7, 349; Hertle and Stephan, *Ende*, p. 303.
37 Hertle, *Fall*, p. 350; Hertle, *Chronik*, p. 133.

processed 'quickly and unbureaucratically'. But when asked by a jour-nalist to specify the time frame, Schabowski's erroneous reply – 'with immediate effect' – was as momentous in consequence as it was indeci-sive in tone.

Schabowski's gaffe has become an iconic moment in the story of 1989, but it makes little sense when abstracted from its context. It was a forced error. The travel decree had been introduced hastily, by an administra-tion that was under enormous pressure, and with the normal processes of deliberation suspended. The SED leadership was not so much chart-ing new territory as on a forced march through it, enveloped by the 'fog of revolution'. Only given the dizzying twists and turns of recent events could the decision to open the Wall appear so thinkable and actionable for Schabowski – even a month earlier he would have responded to the journalist's question with greater care.

The second set of actors involved in the Wall's fall, ordinary citizens, were initially stunned by the announcement. For them, the Wall had long been felt as a force of nature. A typical reaction to Schabowski's announcement are these words from a Dresdener: 'someone said to me, "Hey! The Wall is going to be opened tonight!" I couldn't believe it! Imagine if someone said to you, "Hey! Tomorrow the sun will rise in the west!"' A month or two earlier, Schabowski's statement would have prompted askance looks; viewers would not have acted upon what they heard. Even now, many reacted with disbelief. Andrea Vogt, from Berlin, told me: 'I heard reports of Schabowski's announcement on the radio news and thought, "that can't be true, they're talking rubbish", so switched it off and went back to reading my book.' It was only a wilfully optimistic interpretation of the press conference by citizens who pos-sessed a degree of curiosity, impatience, confidence and/or political nous that can explain what ensued. Thanks to the movement's recent suc-cesses, these qualities were present in critical mass. When the news was heard, pubs emptied out and columns of people filed out of Berlin's housing estates, all heading towards the border crossing points.[38]

The third set of actors were the border guards at the Wall. No less than Schabowski and the crowds, their behaviour was conditioned by the events of previous days and weeks. Morale was low. Their *esprit de corps* had wilted, as political developments rendered their role ever less central to 'national security'. Their instructions were simple: passport holders were to be allowed through, from 10 November, full stop. Accordingly, they instructed the first groups of people that began to cluster at the gates on the evening of 9 November to turn back, insisting that they attend the

38 Dyke, *Dresden*, p. 232; Sarotte, *Devil*, p. 280; Hertle, *Fall*, p. 180.

proper office and return on the next day with the requisite documents. The crowds, it appeared to them, were in error. And so, when someone produced a communication from the official news agency confirming that Schabowski had indeed uttered the word 'forthwith', the guards were confounded. At least one senior officer regarded the Politburo member's statement as 'nonsense', a case of 'mental diarrhoea'.[39]

Refusing to leave, and emboldened by their swelling numbers, the crowds began to chorus that the Wall must be opened. At the Bornholmer Strasse crossing, officials had allowed some citizens through, on the assumption that they were emigrating: the intention was to open a safety valve, not the floodgates, and their visas were stamped as invalid for return. Yet this was perceived by others as both a concession and an injustice to themselves; they pushed against the fence and chanted 'open the gate!' all the louder. The critical moment came, at around 9.30, when officers decided that the crowds could no longer be controlled without the use of violence, and that this would pose a risk to their own lives. 'If we had shot at the masses as they pushed forward', one guard said, 'we'd now be hanging from that flagpole over there'. A number of them decided that the crowds must be permitted free passage, regardless of either their purpose (emigration or otherwise) or possession of the requisite documents. Shortly afterwards, guards at nearby Checkpoint Charlie, fearing a pincer movement by crowds that had gathered on both sides, opened the gates there too. By midnight, people were converging on the Wall from all directions. At the Brandenburg Gate,

> Hundreds of East Berliners broke through the police cordon, saying that they wanted only to walk through the gate without even going to West Berlin . . . Once at the concrete barriers, the young pulled themselves and each other up. As a final touch, some used the empty water hoses of the police as climbing ropes.[40]

The opening of the Wall had occurred in precisely the opposite manner than intended. The border guards, in Schabowski's words, had been 'overwhelmed by the masses'.[41] The gates had been opened prematurely, hastily and to all citizens. Passport control had, temporarily, been torn out of the state's hands. As thousands of East Germans poured across the borders into West Berlin and the FRG, numerous additional exit points had to be opened. Rather than gaining credit, the country's maladroit leadership suffered only humiliation. It was not a reform but a rout.

---

39 Hertle, *Fall*, p. 183.
40 *Ibid.*, pp. 186–91; Smyser, *Berlin*, p. 345.
41 Allen, *Germany*, p. 189. See also Hertle, *Chronik*, pp. 163–83.

Jubilation and despair

Reactions to the fall of the Wall were diverse, and not altogether pre-dictable. One group with an especially intense response consisted of military leaders and officials with operational responsibility for security. When notified of Schabowski's error and of the storming of the Wall that ensued, they raised the security forces' alert level to red. In this, their motivation is not entirely clear. According to Hans-Hermann Hertle, who has documented the event in meticulous detail, the intention was to keep all options open; a terrible error had clearly been made and any attempt to reverse it would require a massive military presence at the border. Hertle's interviewees in the security forces claim otherwise. In their view, it was a panic reflex reaction, a measure taken to ensure adequate preparedness in the event that an already unstable security situation degenerated further.[42]

The response of political leaders was less immediate. Although, newly appointed Politburo member Hans Modrow recalls, 'we were all aware that something had happened which did not correspond to our intentions', the scale of the previous night's cataclysm only dawned slowly. The Central Committee plenum on 10 November commenced with an address by Krenz that did not even mention it. Nor did contributors to the ensuing debate. Only belatedly, over the course of that morning, was the full import of events recognised. At that point, a 'wild tumult broke out', that later yielded to 'impotence and resignation' as the realisation sank in that the government had lost control of the border regime (and, for some shrewder functionaries, that the prospect of 'selling' border liberalisation to Bonn, in exchange for billions of Deutschmarks in new loans, had vanished).[43]

For the general public, the news came as a bolt from the blue. Some reacted with incredulity, others with caution. The mood ranged from intoxication to wide-eyed wonder, but if there was a dominant sentiment it was jubilation. On 10 November, many workplaces in Berlin and Potsdam (including my own) were deserted, as employees queued for visas and crossed into West Berlin for the day, or even just for lunch.[44] Subsequent weekends witnessed unprecedented traffic jams on East Germany's normally unclogged roads as millions took their first trip to West Germany. Within a fortnight, over two-thirds of the population had travelled west.

42 Hertle, *Fall*, pp. 362–97.
43 Hertle, *Chronik*, p. 7; Steiner, *Plan*, p. 224; Krenz, *Herbst*, p. 263; Hertle and Stephan, *Ende*, p. 73.
44 Schabowski, *Politbüro*, p. 140; Hertle, *Chronik*, p. 209.

Not all sections of the populace exulted at the Wall's fall. A negative reaction, John Torpey tells us, 'was widespread among East German intellectuals'. Of those who had welcomed the protests of September and October, many concluded that, with the border opening, the revolution was careering off the rails. A famous expression of this view came from Stefan Heym's pen, in his essay 'Ash Wednesday in the GDR':

> The people who, after decades of submission and flight, had taken their fate into their own hands and had seemed only yesterday to be striving towards a radiant future were now transformed into a rabid mob which, crowded together, stampeded into western department stores in pursuit of glittering kitsch.

Heym's essay on the evils of consumerism, the former East German author Monika Maron sniped, netted him over 3,000 Deutschmarks and was his latest in a series of three. Its tone brought to mind 'the arrogance of the man with a full stomach, disgusted by the table manners of the starving'. But Heym's fear that the opening of the Wall would derail the revolution struck a chord among many oppositionists. Although these had, of course, been among the Wall's most vociferous critics, few had advocated its *immediate* removal. For that, one veteran oppositionist had warned in June, could undermine international order.[45]

When the Wall did fall, opposition supporters worried about the threat of instability, social and geopolitical, but their prime concern was the meretricious allures of western materialism. They would throw up their hands at the sight of their compatriots returning from shopping sprees in the West weighed down with plastic bags. The masses, they believed, would renounce revolt in favour of travel; the pursuit of consumption would usurp that of 'free communication'. Opposition leaders were ambivalent, too. Marianne Birthler of IFM, while 'very happy' to hear of the border breakthrough, 'was, equally, concerned that the power that we had felt only days earlier, at the huge demonstration of 4 November' would dissipate. 'We worried that the incredible energy and the powerful will for change, to democratise this country, would now be diverted, with people wanting only to travel West.'[46] Bohley felt similarly. She knew the West well, having lived in Britain and regularly visited West Germany, but did not rate a general right to such delights as of immediate and paramount concern. Rather, her response was guided by presentiments of the evils – such as North Atlantic Treaty Organisation (NATO) membership

45 Torpey, *Intellectuals*, p. 164; Heym, 'Aschermittwoch,' pp. 71–2; Maron, 'Writers', p. 37; Schorlemmer, *Träume*, p. 84.
46 Findeis *et al.*, *Entzauberung*, p. 44.

and mass unemployment – that might march through the country's wide-open gates. On hearing the news she 'made a stiff drink, went to bed and pulled the covers up over her head'.[47]

Birthler and Bohley were not lone voices. Sebastian Pflugbeil experienced 'the very same physical reaction' to the fall of the Wall as he had at its construction. Irene Kukutz, a co-founder of 'Women for Peace', a pioneering opposition group of the 1980s, and of New Forum, 'was sick for three days, lying down with a terrible headache', for she saw the border opening as 'an outrageous betrayal'. Wolfgang Ullmann, a leading figure in Democracy Now, even floated the idea that the civic groups call for the border to be re-sealed – for, he inquired of friends in DA and the SDP, if it were to remain open would it not lead to economic ruin? At least one DA leader, Friedrich Schorlemmer, agreed, insisting that 'the Wall should stay for a while'. Similarly, Werner Fischer of IFM felt 'extreme rage' at the 'mean and undignified' decision to open the border on the fifty-first anniversary of *Kristallnacht*, a response that betrayed a bewildering lack of awareness of the pressures forcing the government's hand.[48]

Most of these spokespeople wisely kept their counsel but some did not. Leipzig New Forum issued a communiqué claiming that the border opening was a ruse designed to divert the public from protest, to re-establish 'order' and to subdue the streets. Bohley issued a public statement lamenting that 'The people have gone crazy and the government has lost its head.' Such phrases bore an unfortunate resemblance to the SED's justification for having built the Wall. In Jens Reich's words, they 'had devastating consequences [and marked] the watershed in our popularity curve'. A West Berlin newspaper reported that 'if one inquires about Bohley anywhere in East Germany, one soon hears the comment: "people will never forgive her for what she said about the opening of the Wall".' Similarly, Ehrhart Neubert (DA) reported that 'at that moment, a saying began to circulate among the people: "We wouldn't even let Bohley paint us, let alone govern us".'[49]

New Forum rushed out a statement seeking to repair the damage wreaked by Bohley's remarks:

> We have been waiting almost thirty years for this moment! Wall-sick, we have been rattling at the bars of the cage. Young people have grown up with

47 Andrews, 'Criticism', p. 132.
48 *Ibid.*; Joppke, *Dissidents*, pp. 159–60; Neubert, *Opposition*, p. 877.
49 Timmer, *Aufbruch* p. 287; *die tageszeitung*, 13 November 1989; Reich, *Rückkehr*, p. 201; *die tageszeitung* Journal 2, p. 60; Neubert, *Revolution*, p. 94.

the dream of being free one day, able to explore the world. This dream will now be realised: it is a day of celebration for us all!

Yet, despite this introduction, it also reinforced the impression that the opposition was ambivalent towards free travel. East Germans, it continued, will inevitably 'remain poor for a long period, but we do not want to see a society in which profiteers and "elbow types" lap up the cream'. The communiqué appealed to the pride that citizens had come to know through successful collective action. 'You are the heroes of a political revolution', it began, and then appealed to the (presumably somewhat naïve) heroes 'not to allow yourselves to be neutralised by travel and by debt-exacerbating consumerism'. This was a characteristic formula of the civic groups; was it a manifestation of the Ghandian asceticism that had prevailed in the 1980s opposition milieu, or a call for austerity by a government-in-waiting?[50]

The days surrounding the fall of the Wall were a pivotal moment for the civic groups. Their legalisation on 8 November marked a highpoint, the fall of the Wall a challenge. The national question now appeared on the political agenda, dividing the civic groups and reinforcing trends that separated them from the wider movement. These developments will be narrated in chapters 7–10, but first the genesis and morphology of the opposition will be explored. Chapter 6 examines its origins, ideals, frames and strategy. It inquires into its relationship with the mass movement, and asks whether the civic groups played an important mobilising role, or whether 1989 was a 'revolution without revolutionaries'.

50 Reich, *Rückkehr*, p. 203.

6

Of raisins and yeast: civic groups and mass movement

The danger of conceiving democratic life as dialogue is that we may forget that its primary reality remains strife. (Perry Anderson) [1]

Opposition platforms and street protests arose contemporaneously, in the late summer and early autumn of 1989, but the nature of the connection between them has been the subject of some controversy. Were they simply two facets of a single movement, or are they better characterised as distinct streams within the same movement delta? Did the demonstrations push the opposition activists into the limelight, or is it more accurate to say, with Reinfried Musch, that 'the civic groups brought the people onto the streets'?[2]

The first half of this chapter examines two contrasting interpretations of these issues, and finds both wanting. An alternative interpretation, drawing upon recent innovations in frame theory, is tendered. The latter half explores the civic groups' 'master frames', as well as their organisational structure and political culture.

Did opposition activists play the role of 'movement organisers'?

A widely held view of the role of the civic groups in 1989 is that they created focal points at which resistance gathered; they brought the people onto the streets and formed the 'organised core of the masses'. For Mary Fulbrook, it was the 'leaven of dissident groups' which 'began to raise the bread of the largely subordinate masses'. The civic groups were, in Timmer's words, a 'mobilising force'; they 'offered many thousands of people the opportunity to get involved constructively, they tapped into the ubiquitous sentiment that something must be done'. For Klaus von Beyme, the revolution was 'basically the work of intellectuals and their followers in ad hoc demonstrations'. However, others see things very differently. For Pfaff and

1 Anderson, 'Power', p. 43.
2 Musch, 'Linke', p. 97.

Kim, the civic groups remained 'out of step with popular demands' throughout the protest cycle. Mark Thompson proposes that 'would-be emigrants started the protests, mass emigration ignited further demonstrations, and demands for unification were the culmination of the revolution'. The 'real revolutionaries' of 1989 were not opposition supporters but 'exiters, would-be exiters, and those who demanded reunification'.[3]

The most systematic criticism of the 'dissidents as leaven' thesis is offered by Opp and his colleagues, in their *Origins of a Spontaneous Revolution*. In their judgement, organised oppositionists contributed little, if anything, to the emergence and mobilisation of the demonstration movement in Leipzig. Their survey data shows that, although members of the civic groups were much more likely to have participated in 'general protests' in the early autumn than were respondents who belonged to no such group, they were only slightly more likely to have demonstrated.[4] Alluding to a 'well-known snowball effect, in which a small number of revolutionaries sparks a mass movement', they contend that in 1989 protest developed quite differently: '[t]he few "revolutionaries" in fact remained among themselves'; far from playing an outstanding role they remained marginal to events; their success in 'getting others to protest or of providing incentives for protest [was] very minor'. Moreover, they failed to encourage those outside their milieu to become 'professional revolutionaries'. On this point they quote Jochen Läßig, a leading member of Leipzig New Forum:

> People came to me and wanted to become members of New Forum. But I could get very few of them to really embark on political work. [They] signed up as members and were willing to take part in some evening activities, but nobody really wanted to take a personal risk by saying, 'Yes, we will invest our energy. We'll forget our professions for a while and invest time in a new organization'.[5]

Opp's conclusion is that East Germany in 1989 was a 'revolution with no head', a 'revolution without revolutionaries'.[6] The crucial demonstrations

3 Bruckmeier, 'Bürgerbewegungen', p. 42; Fulbrook, *Anatomy*, pp. 246–7; Timmer, *Aufbruch*, p. 210; von Beyme, *Transition*, p. 41; Pfaff and Kim, 'Exit-Voice'; Thompson, *Democratic*, pp. 53, 58.
4 Opp *et al.*, 'Data'; also *volkseigene*, pp. 150, 207. My own impression was that oppositionists were considerably more likely to attend demonstrations than others, but Opp and his colleagues' conclusion is based upon extensive research the accuracy of which I have no reason to doubt.
5 Opp *et al.*, *Origins*, pp. 156–66, 104.
6 Opp *et al.*, *volkseigene*, p. 213. This finding is generalised to show that 'resourceful' social movement activists are not necessary ingredients of successful large-scale collective action.

were the products of a 'silent coordination of behaviour', whereby large numbers of isolated individuals who shared similar grievances 'spontaneously' made the same rational choice, to demonstrate.[7] It was a 'spontaneous revolution', and if New Forum was prominent this was not because 'it initiated the mass protests but rather the converse: the masses got their own movement going and pushed New Forum to the fore'.[8]

Opp and his colleagues show convincingly that the civic groups were in an embryonic stage of development in the early autumn and bore little direct responsibility for mobilising individuals to the demonstrations of early October. If any were needed, additional evidence can be adduced in support of this finding. In Leipzig, Detlef Pollack has pointed out,

> the leading representatives of New Forum and the other civic groups met on 24 September 1989 and agreed to meet next on 22 October – by which time the main phases of the upheaval, such as the replacement of Honecker by Krenz, had already taken place. This indicates that the civic groups not only did not organise the mass protests, but to a considerable extent did not even recognise the urgency of the situation.

Evidence from studies elsewhere in East Germany suggests that these experiences in Leipzig were not unusual. One study of the northern town of Schwerin inquired into the source of the initial impulse for the first mass demonstration on 23 October and discovered that

> although the New Forum group *organised* the event, they did not *initiate* it. Instead, pressure from within the factories and workplaces throughout the district . . . forced the small New Forum group to act . . . One of their number recalled 'I can still remember how M. came to me and said: "the workers at the Plastmaschinenwerk, they're off, no matter what your group does. The demonstration is now to take place on Monday" '[9]

Of protest participants whom I interviewed, several recall that in October they were merely aware of New Forum's existence and largely ignorant of its goals. Others described their stance towards the civic groups as 'sceptical'. One young Berliner, who described herself as 'kind of Christian', 'never had a good feeling about New Forum. It seemed so vague, expressing no clear position. It gathered together such a disparate bunch of different people that it couldn't give any clear political direction'. In the survey of over 200 randomly selected individuals conducted by Lawrence McFalls, a large minority of respondents – 45 per cent – had

7 Opp *et al.*, *volkseigene*, p. 211.
8 Detlef Pollack, quoted in Opp *et al.*, *volkseigene*, p. 33.
9 Pollack, 'Bedingungen', p. 311; Grix, *Collapse*, p. 111, emphasis added.

taken part in at least one demonstration, but only 5.5 per cent belonged to an opposition organisation.[10] In concord with Opp *et al.*, McFalls concludes that 'the masses got their own movement going and pushed New Forum to the fore'. He illustrates the point with a felicitous metaphor from a Greifswald demonstrator's questionnaire response: 'The civic groups were like the raisins that happen to sit atop a risen bread dough, exclaiming "Look what I have done!"'[11]

Yet even this image may flatter some of the 'raisins', for there are grounds for doubting whether they all felt pleasure and pride as the dough rose. Those opposition representatives who conceived of their role primarily as a think-tank of reform policies to be implemented, ideally, through negotiation between themselves and the government saw the demonstrations as a potential threat. 'The groups are not seeking to accelerate the rapid dynamic by openly supporting or even calling for demonstrations', West Berlin's *tageszeitung* reported; 'the fear of an uncontrolled situation lies deep'. When New Forum declared itself to be an umbrella organisation for all critical forces, one of its members told western journalists that the move was 'rather unfortunate' because it could be construed as declaring the organisation to be a political opposition. One opposition leader confessed to fearing the 'force of the population', and warned that 'we may no longer be able to restrain the demonstrations'.[12] 'We look at these demonstrations with a very critical eye', added New Forum's Sebastian Pflugbeil; 'They have no form and contours. This worries the security forces and we well understand their concerns.'[13] In early October, with the fate of the revolution still in the balance, Eppelmann (DA) called on citizens to stay away from demonstrations and for protests to be suspended for a fortnight to allow 'constructive dialogue' to take place.[14]

10 '[A]nd several of these', he adds, 'entered the sample only because friends or neighbours had transmitted to them my request for survey participation'. McFalls, *Communism's*, p. 65. As indicated by this comment, the survey evinced a degree of bias towards civic group members and probably also to participants in protest in general. See also p. 15.
11 McFalls, *Communism's*, p. 65.
12 Renken, 'Oppositionsgruppen'; *Guardian*, 26 September 1989; Rein, *Opposition*, p. 24.
13 Joppke, *Dissidents*, p. 156. See also p. 238: 'On the eve of the GDR's 40th anniversary celebration, New Forum leaders even urged their fellow citizens not to demonstrate, in fear of a violent clash with security forces.'
14 Reuth and Bönte, *Komplott*, p. 110; *die tageszeitung*, 18 October 1989.

A spontaneous revolution?

The thesis that the civic groups were the crucial agents of mobilisation is clearly flawed, yet the alternative advanced by Opp, Voß and Gern is far from immune to criticism. Their case rests upon two claims, both of which are highly problematic. The first is that civic group members 'did not organize the protests; rather, the protests occurred spontaneously' – and the Monday demonstrations in Leipzig were not organised *at all*.[15] The second is that the civic groups did not act as a 'reference group'.

The first of these claims is not without foundation. It is well known that part of the magic of the Leipzig demonstrations was that they emerged from regular Monday 'peace prayers' in the Nikolai Church, an event which appeared to be 'unorganised' or 'spontaneous', and as such presented the authorities with an intractable problem. As one Stasi Lieutenant General complained, 'these "peace prayers" don't need to be organised any longer; over months they have become such a customary gathering for these people that they go there completely autonomously'. Note, however, those two words: 'any longer.' The Nikolai Church had not 'spontaneously' become a meeting place for oppositionists but had been actively created as such, by 'movement organisers' over the course of the 1980s. Radical pastors, notably Christoph Wonneberger and Christian Führer, had stood up to the church authorities, and even braved death threats, in order to maintain their church as a site at which criticism could be voiced. Opposition activists had politicised the peace prayers, even when pastors Wonneberger and Führer had counselled caution. And when Führer and church superintendent Friedrich Magirius eventually succumbed to pressure to cancel the prayers (in 1988), oppositionists had resisted. Admittedly, it was not opposition activists but emigration applicants who then, in early 1989, converted Monday political prayers into Monday *protests*. But they had only begun to arrive at the peace prayers in large numbers when they observed that *opposition-ists* in Berlin had been expelled from the country as a result of so-called anti-state activity. Moreover, it was from within the opposition milieu that the impetus came to transform emigrant-led protests in support of their exit from the country into demonstrations for political change. As Wayne Bartee has shown, political opposition groups in the 1980s not only 'kept opposition alive in Leipzig, their persistent, public acts eventually created a sort of threshold of safety for the general public as they also began to attend the prayer meetings and finally to march'. If one attends to the origins of the Monday demonstrations it appears that

15 Opp *et al.*, *Origins*, pp. 23, 118.

organised oppositionists exploiting external resources – the Nikolai Church – were indispensable. It was these same individuals who later went on to found Leipzig New Forum.[16]

Outside Leipzig, the contribution of oppositionists to organising the protests was outstanding. One researcher, Carsten Johnson, has systematically recorded protest activities in East Germany throughout 1989 and 1990. His findings show that the great majority, at least until October, were organised by 'political groups' and that only in the last three months of 1989 were the bulk of such events initiated by the 'populace'.[17] In short, the mass movement – in Leipzig and elsewhere – emerged from a culture of peace prayers, church meetings and small demonstrations in the 1980s, all of which were strongly influenced, and in many cases instigated, by opposition activists.

The second problematic claim advanced by Opp, Voß and Gern concerns the relations between civic groups and demonstrators. In their view, the former did not act as a 'reference group' – a term they use to designate organisations 'that contributed to the development of protest simply by means of their existence'. They could not play this role, because 'most GDR citizens were unaware of the exact goals and activities of the opposition groups'.

The evidence provided to substantiate this claim is thin,[18] but if the word 'exact' is taken literally, it is irrefutable. What I would take issue with is the ensuing conclusion: that, by virtue of their *partial* ignorance, East Germans 'could not identify with these groups'. Why identification with a group should depend upon cognisance of its *exact* goals and activities is not spelled out. Indeed, a few pages later the authors cheerfully employ much looser criteria. Discussing survey respondents' attitudes to the Church, they find that despite the ambivalent and sometimes hostile attitude of Church leaders towards opposition and protest, '[m]any GDR citizens have probably identified with the goals of the Protestant Church because of its somewhat critical stance toward the SED regime'.[19] The Church was too fractured for any clear (let alone 'exact') picture of its goals and activities to be drawn, yet Opp, Voß and Gern nonetheless feel

16 Zwahr, *Selbstzerstörung*, p. 20; Bartee, *Time*, p. 141; Fehr, *Unabhängige*, p. 232. On the history of the peace prayers, see Wagner, *Freunde*, especially the introduction; also Pfaff, 'Politics'; Schwabe, 'Entwicklung'.
17 Johnson, 'Massenmobilisierung', p. 89, also Johnson, 'Data'.
18 The largest body of evidence refers to the period *prior to* May 1989; another is the recollection of one interviewee who had heard of New Forum but did not 'really know what it was'. Opp, et al., *Origins*, p. 105.
19 Opp et al., *Origins*, pp. 118, 135.

that an unambiguous conclusion is warranted: 'This identification [of East Germans with the Church] promoted participation in the protests.' Compare this with their refusal to acknowledge that ordinary citizens identified with the civic groups. It is hard to avoid the conclusion that double standards are in operation.

As these examples suggest, identification is a complex and shifting process. Identification with an organisation can exist even in the absence of a comprehensive knowledge of its aims and activities. Citizens can rally to the flag of a social-movement organisation – or, for that matter, a state – even when unaware of its 'exact' agenda. And this, it seems to me, is a useful way of conceiving of the relationship between the general public and the civic groups: activists designed and planted the flag, its image was disseminated (by opposition supporters and the West German media), and large numbers came to identify with it. In the following pages, these processes are examined more closely.

As platforms claiming national scope, the civic groups assembled into a central force activists whose primary affiliation had hitherto been to local church-based groups, as well as wider layers with no political experience. From September onwards they became transformed from formal platforms into active forces in the form of members connected through structures. Existing oppositional circles regrouped around the civic organisations, and spread word of their activities through established networks. Large meetings in cities attracted individuals from surrounding towns, who would return home to organise similar events. Often at considerable risk, thousands of people set about gathering signatures and printing and distributing leaflets – 'whether with typewriter, with crude mimeographic technology or with photocopiers in workplaces and universities to which access was limited'. One New Forum organiser concealed lists of supporters in an envelope under his pillow – until it became so thick that he had to find somewhere else to hide it.[20] Uwe Rottluf, a printer in the postal service (who found himself 'in partial agreement with New Forum') printed out a bale of leaflets at work as a favour for a colleague.[21] Leaflets would then be passed on to friends, surreptitiously placed in prominent places or handed around at work. Donations were collected to support campaigns for detained demonstrators. Events were publicised via 'whisper propaganda', often with extraordinary success. One Stasi document from the Potsdam area – representative of many from late September and early October – warned that

20 Eigenfeld, 'Neues', p. 82; Grix, *Collapse*, p. 111.
21 Interview with the author. ('The state was not so omniscient!', he remarked wryly.)

Awakening '89, as well as calls for support for the 'Initiative New Forum', are being distributed by means of the misuse of cultural and other meetings, shop windows, wall newspapers, educational establishments and the Church, as well as by word of mouth and by the painting of enemy graffiti – all of which proceeds without the perpetrators meeting significant resistance.

These acts, the report continued, have led to 'large sections of the population developing an interest in New Forum's proposals'. Opposition activists, it concluded, 'feel strengthened and protected by this "positive" resonance amongst the population'.[22]

That the addresses of New Forum's founder members were published on their materials turned their homes into magnets which, despite the high perceived risk of arrest, drew thousands of sympathisers. On one day alone, Bärbel Bohley's flat in Berlin was visited by 190 people. And at her home, also in Berlin, New Forum's Tina Krone recalls, 'queues of people would be waiting on the stairs, every day! They continued into the evening, sometimes as late as 2:30 a.m. Some poured out their life stories to us; others would say "We want to do X, Y or Z: how did *you* do it?"' In Leipzig, a New Forum supporter has described how three members each gave their addresses as contact points. Upon 'discovering that we were no longer able to deal with the flood [of inquiries] – and people would be arriving even into the small hours' – they were obliged to expand the circle of organisers. Visitors at a Magdeburg contact address, in Hans-Joachim Tschiche's evocative description, 'engaged in inflamed discussion; often, forty people and more filled all the rooms; cigarette smoke hung in the air; the doors were still swinging long after midnight. It was euphoric.'[23]

Hives of organisation and debate also formed in churches and church halls. I recall one, at the Gethsemane church in Berlin. Without, a candlelit vigil demanding the release of those arrested at demonstrations. Within, several hundred people reading, or queuing to read, opposition propaganda. Whether in churches or in front rooms, these sites of organisation and discussion were known as contact centres. They were meeting places at which like-minded spirits would gather, helping to create a generalised and actualised awareness of common cause. They acted as transformers, raising the voltage of opposition.

Before long, letters were pouring in to the contact centres, conveying myriad hopes, concerns, demands, or simply greetings.[24] 'What should

22　Meinel and Wernicke, *Tschekistischem*, pp. 141–2.
23　Krone, *Briefe*, p. 12, and interview; Fehr, *Unabhängige*, p. 253; Tschiche, 'Herbst', p. 337.
24　Those that I viewed are located in the Robert Havemann Archive, Berlin. See also Krone, *Briefe*.

I do?' 'How can I get active?', were typical questions. One, from a rail worker in Frankfurt an der Oder, read as follows:

> As I walked past the main post office I noticed a group of people. A New Forum statement was pinned up there! At last I had found what I had been looking for for weeks: contact addresses. Please send me information, as my colleagues and neighbours have so many questions about New Forum.

Another correspondent wrote to New Forum's Dr Tietze of his 'elation' at hearing news of *Awakening '89*. 'Thank you for your courage!' was a common phrase. 'Warmest thanks for your leaflet', read another; 'It has filled me once again with a hope that had, I thought, gone for good'. Many correspondents proposed issues for the opposition to take up, some of which were general, others quite specific – in one case even down to the price that a loaf of bread should cost ('Three Marks and fifty Pfennig!'); in another, that citizens be allocated a fruit ration ('a kilogram of both oranges and bananas each month').[25]

By means of leafleting, petitioning, the contact centres and the amplification effect of these activities through West German media, the civic groups reached a wide audience. One East Berliner I interviewed was arrested at a demonstration; 'When a woman – in prison, of all places – gave me a New Forum leaflet it made me realise just how widely these critical leaflets were being spread.' This, she recalls, was one ingredient that contributed to feelings of 'solidarity and strength' amongst detainees. A more typical experience is that of Ollie, an interviewee who described himself as having been 'not very political' and mistrustful of organisations ('I'm the kind of guy who stays quiet most of the time but I turn stubborn when challenging something I don't like', he said). His memories are of

> New Forum leaflets that found their way, somehow, into our apprentices' hostel. Nobody knew where they had come from – but we read them and discussed them. It was all very interesting and so very new. 'Wow', I thought, 'What these say is actually so logical. Why did I never think of that myself?'

Ollie knew no oppositionists, did not contact New Forum nor attended any of its meetings. Yet he clearly did identify with its core aims and analysis and found encouragement in the process.

The circulation of *Awakening '89* in particular strengthened the impression amongst those who heard of and read it that a movement was crystallising, that demands for immediate and real change were now on the table. It acted as a focus for hopes in political reform and a stimulus

25 Krone, *Briefe*, p. 232.

to work towards alternative perspectives. It helped to fire tens of thousands with a sense of shared purpose, a belief that change was possible, and raised their confidence and commitment to movement building. As one young woman put it, *Awakening '89* 'really was a clarion call. I was electrified.'[26] Likewise, a young Berliner, Antje Neubauer, recalled: 'When I heard of New Forum it gave me a greater sense of confidence that things would work out (although I still couldn't imagine that it would ever be legalised).'

From the above, it seems that the more suggestive questions concern not whether or not the civic groups 'mobilised the populace' but the character of their activity. Here, a useful distinction can be made between agitation and propaganda – or, in Bert Klandermans' terminology, action mobilisation and consensus mobilisation. The former denotes 'the process by which an organization in a social movement calls up people to participate'; it includes the determination of times, places and themes of activities and the methods used to encourage attendance. The latter refers primarily to the dissemination of goals and of general arguments as to how these might be achieved; it 'is a process through which a social movement tries to obtain support for its viewpoints'.[27]

Although the civic groups occasionally engaged in agitation there is little doubt that their strongest suit was consensus mobilisation. In the vocabulary of David Snow and Robert Benford, they propagated a 'master frame' – a relatively coherent and comprehensible set of ideas that diagnosed a political problem and proposed demands and strategies, thus helping their audience to orient themselves to the unfolding political crisis.[28] *Awakening '89* in particular fulfilled several vital framing functions. It presented a clearly expressed interpretation of the political impasse and, in referring to the chasm between 'state and society', hinted that the chief culpability was the regime's. It proposed that 'something be done' to improve 'communication', to construct an open public sphere and pave the way towards a more democratic society. And it staked New Forum's claim, on behalf of the population, to be 'part owner' of the country's crisis, asserting its right to contribute to its resolution. *Awakening '89* 'resonated' widely. It keyed into widespread desires (or what sociologists call 'generalised beliefs') that political change take place, and that the regime should begin to listen to, and engage in dialogue with, the people.

26 Probst, *Kultur*, p. 46.
27 Klandermans, 'Mobilization', p. 586. See also Wielgohs and Johnson, 'Entstehungsgründe'.
28 Snow and Benford, 'Master', pp. 136–8.

In such ways consensus mobilisation by the civic groups contributed to collective action. Their forward-looking frames, especially the pitch that popular pressure could advance political reform, helped to ferment the belief amongst swathes of the population that something could at last be done, and that they themselves could play a part. Thousands felt connected through a shared political and oppositional identity, in a process that strengthened the norms of engagement and solidarity that were so important in the revolt's early, anxious stages. Opposition networks thus helped to boost confidence far beyond their own ranks. Their branches mobilised resources, in the form of people, venues, communications and propaganda materials, and coordinated activities and information exchange. They fed news to the western media, and helped to spark public political debate. They acted as seeds around which critical spirits from the wider population crystallised. Although not direct sponsors of the large Leipzig crowds of early October, they nonetheless played a significant part in generating a buoyant culture of protest. Their very emergence represented 'the signal for an attack on the SED's power monopoly, and with that, the signal for a general uprising'.[29] They played an important role in dispelling the clouds of resignation and fear that had held potential participants back from protest. Their rise to movement leadership was 'raisin like' but they also acted as 'yeast'.

Protest identity and the 'Third Way'

The relationship between social movement organisations and their constituents is, in mainstream frame theory, assumed to be transitive, with the former as agent, the latter as object, but recent contributions propose that it instead be conceived dialogically.[30] This seems sensible. And it is certainly appropriate in the East German case, in which groups such as New Forum evolved in interaction with their supporters and the public – the protest culture 'out there' had a significant bearing upon their character.

The initial conception of New Forum's founder members was that it would operate simply as a platform, but when protestors adopted it as a symbol of opposition this began to change. Of the letters that flooded in to the contact centres some referred to New Forum not as a mere 'platform' but as a 'movement'. On the streets, protestors appropriated the names and (selected) ideas of the civic groups as their own, as a 'banner' to wave against the regime. This process, in turn, cemented the civic groups' reputation. The critical moment came when Leipzig

29 Gehrke, 'Demokratiebewegung', p. 226; Stolle, *Aufstand*, p. 302.
30 Steinberg, 'Tilting', 'Talk'.

demonstrators, who had previously chanted 'We're staying here!' as a determined but ultimately vacuous counterslogan to the emigrants' 'We want out!', raised the concrete demand, 'Legalise New Forum!' This then became one of the most prevalent slogans on the streets, and helped to impart New Forum with a 'movement identity' linked to street protest.

New Forum, I am suggesting, became a 'flag' that signified a general oppositional stance. For example, Andrea, a secretary from Berlin, recalls that: 'My gut reaction to New Forum was positive – even though I knew very little about them. I just thought: "they're oppositionists, they're against the state, that's good." So when I went to a Monday demonstration in Leipzig I chanted "Legalise New Forum!"' Similarly, when a group of youths returning home from a disco in Prenzlau paused to tear down some GDR emblems they shouted 'Up with New Forum – Stasi out!'

With so many of East Germany's critical spirits adopting New Forum as a 'flag', it quickly became recognised as a central part of the wider movement. By the end of October some 100,000 had signed *Awakening '89*, and at the Leipzig demonstrations New Forum, 'although few in numbers' was 'thoroughly in charge. Whenever the words "Here Speaks New Forum" were uttered through the megaphone, the people cheered loudly and gathered round the speaker.'[31]

Before long, however, the civic groups were losing ground. Their popularity had derived in part from their function as a 'flag' of rebellion, and flags can relatively easily be dropped as others become available. A dissonance emerged between their culture, values and tactics, and those that prevailed on the streets. The following pages seek to understand that dissonance through an anatomy of the civic groups' origins, ideals and practices.

The German Question, to be discussed in chapter 9, formed one fault-line, but it was not the only one. Another, it is often argued, was the civic groups' socialist ideology, which set them apart from the masses and encouraged collusion with the regime. A strong version of this case has been put by Christian Joppke in his *East German Dissidents and the Revolution of 1989*. For him, the civic groups were composed not of 'genuine' oppositionists but leftist intellectuals who were fundamentally 'loyal to the communist regime'. In contrast to their counterparts elsewhere in Eastern Europe, their enthusiasm for the 1989 uprising 'was not about freedom from dictatorship but about the final arrival of utopia'. The utopia in question was to be a socialist form of participatory democracy: 'the utopian hope of a complete alternative, a thoroughly politicized

31 Langer, *Norden*, p. 120; Joppke, *Dissidents*, p. 156.

society of the virtuous citizen-activist.' Commonly tagged the 'Third Way', it tapped into German romantic traditions, with their antipathy toward 'western "civilization" and its "formal" democracy'.[32]

In treating the GDR opposition as the antithesis of its liberal nationalist counterparts in neighbouring countries, Joppke exaggerates its socialist character. Before I advance an alternative account, it is worth emphasising that 'socialism' was as elastic a concept in East Germany as it is elsewhere. The stance of oppositionists towards socialism was, inevitably, complex, and those who perceived the GDR as socialist would hedge the statement with qualifications. One New Forum activist even wrote that the SED preached socialism but practised 'an intensified form of capitalism', while Bohley caused a stir by pronouncing that 'The GDR hasn't experienced even five minutes of socialism.'[33]

Socialism was, of course, associated with the regime but also possessed more general connotations, including a communal ethic, a commitment to welfare and redistributive justice and some degree of collective (state or cooperative) ownership of major parts of the economy. Many oppositionists sought to reclaim the concept from the SED. Thus, Democracy Now declared for a socialism 'in which the labour movement ideals of a just, free and solidaristic society can flourish'. Such values and policies were far from unpopular: opinion polls reveal that a 'reformed socialism' was backed by a clear majority as late as February 1990, and that socialist ideas remain popular in eastern Germany today.[34]

Advocacy of 'reformed socialism' could also express the limits of oppositionists' horizons: they simply could not imagine any greater change than reform to the existing ('socialist') order. As Timmer has described, 'Long years of conflict with the SED had led to a fixation upon the SED and the socialist *status quo*'. Over years spent bravely and persistently chipping at the boundaries of permitted 'free space' it had seemed as if the game being played was a fixed one, and premised upon the SED's hold on power. Mainstream oppositionists in the 1980s adopted a 'system-immanent' approach: they took the SED's grip and the apathy of the masses as givens. Reform, they concluded, meant 'democratisation and the rule of law, achieved non-violently, in small steps, as an evolutionary change'; wherever possible, it would be legal, and involve cooperation with reformist factions of the SED and bloc parties. It is only a slight exaggeration to suggest that, by 1989, 'The civic groups' conception of socialism

32 Joppke, *Dissidents*, pp. 199, 161, 206–12.
33 Krone, *Briefe*, pp. 234, 250.
34 Poppe, 'Bürgerbewegung', p. 161; Förster and Roski, *DDR*, p. 56; Yoder, *From*.

was limited to attempts to assay new "models" and "programmes" together with discerning sections of the ruling Party.'[35]

In this sense, the term socialism sanctioned a strategy of 'self-limitation' geared to incremental reform within accepted political and systemic structures. As such, it bears a family resemblance to the concept of civil society elaborated by Polish intellectuals in the 1980s. In Poland, this term signified the public sphere independent from the state, which could be expanded without calling into question the parameters of the ruling imperial system ('self-limitation'). While accepting the existing state, it championed individual autonomy, in the tradition of eighteenth-century anti-absolutist struggles. As such, Krishan Kumar has argued, it belonged to the East European tradition of the 'Third Way'.[36]

In its simplest sense, the Third Way signified the quest for a *via media* between Communist dictatorship and liberal capitalism, with the best of both worlds combined (civil liberties and full employment, for example). Typically, its advocates would also espouse some form of direct or participatory democracy. In the 1980s, East European dissidents spoke increasingly in terms of civil society, which they posited as a realm of freedom against the coercive state. As such, it offered a more direct route to liberalism than had previous versions of the Third Way. In 1980s East Germany, opposition activists, with their emphasis upon tolerance, democracy, decentralisation, individual experience and opposition to state paternalism, were largely operating within the civil society branch of the Third Way tradition.

For Joppke, Third Way thinking is utopian, exemplifies the opposition's socialist leanings and has 'dubious precursors' in German romanticism, notably amongst the 'conservative revolutionaries' of the inter-war era.[37] Before further exploring the opposition's utopian and socialist inclinations, I should point out that the latter contention is a slur, and a ludicrous one at that. The conservative revolutionaries were ultra-nationalists, their guiding values were 'manliness' and violence; Mars was their god. East German dissidents, in contrast, worshipped Venus. Consider, to take a representative example, this vision from a founder member of Democracy Now:

> I wish for a Germany that stands neither above nor below other peoples, but beside them – a motherland. A Germany with no soldiers, neither its own nor those of others; whose economic power also benefits the poor

35 Timmer, *Aufbruch*, p. 73; Poppe, 'Weg', p. 260; Renken, 'Oppositionsgruppen'.
36 Kumar, *Civil*; Timmer, *Aufbruch*.
37 Joppke, *Dissidents*, p. 211.

peoples of the world; and which is able to share. A humane Germany. The motherland that I long for is colourful, friendly, and diverse.[38]

The same applies to the critique of representative democracy. The conservative revolutionaries opposed it because it contradicted their values of autocracy, hierarchy and the *Ständeprinzip*. By contrast, the civic groups' agenda represented 'an attempt to restore nineteenth-century liberal freedoms', as well as 'a new twentieth century form of grassroots participation, more responsive to popular wishes than parliamentary procedures or bureaucratic decisions'.[39] Their ideal responded to a 'deeply felt need for individual and group autonomy,' constituted 'an attractive counterimage to the centralized, ever-controlling, and initiative-suffocating East German party-state' and united dissenters, 'not with the capitalist West which they rejected, but with their critical counterparts in West Germany whom they respected'.[40] The emphasis was upon campaigning in one's immediate environs, and maximising popular participation. They were versed in standard left-wing criticisms of representative democracy: the domination of parties by their bureaucracies, the reduction of meaningful choice in the party system, the disproportionate political influence of the propertied classes, the manufacturing of consent, the seclusion of the workplace from democratic will-formation, the corrupting of the public sphere by market forces and the elevation of consumer over citizen.

In terms of intellectual heritage, oppositionists' ideas of grassroots democracy drew to a limited extent on anarchist thought as well as Marx's *Civil War in France* and Lenin's *State and Revolution* – texts that sat uncomfortably in the SED's canon. But, *pace* Joppke, much more central was the liberal republican tradition – a perspective that, while supportive of representative democracy, emphasises participation as a vital component of democratic life. In John Stuart Mill's original version, hands-on involvement in public service (such as jury duty or local government) fosters engaged, assertive, public-spirited citizens who are more likely to look to the common good and less likely to submit to their private partialities or to tyrants. In its East German update, the emphasis was upon movements and, later, the 'round tables', as schools of democracy. Accordingly, the civic groups distributed manuals with advice not only on campaigning and 'mobilising others', but also on how to 'assert one's interests without being overbearing', 'facilitate the

38 Weiß, 'Vierzig', p. 299.
39 Jarausch, *Rush*, p. 51.
40 Flam, *Mosaic*, p. 266; Degen, *Politikvorstellung*.

harmonisation of individual and collective interests', and 'assess whether to make decisions by consensus or majority vote'.[41]

Unlike Marx, for whom the maturity required for effective democratic participation is generated in the democratic struggle itself, opposition leaders tended to view the 'immature' masses with suspicion.[42] Some, like Mill before them, saw democratic participation as the proper preserve of those they deemed capable of educated deliberation. Thus, Bohley's critique of the decision to open the Wall was, in part, that it accelerated the political process such 'that free elections would be scheduled before the East German electorate was civically educated'.[43] When the electorate then voted in an 'uneducated' manner she felt her suspicions confirmed, as shall be seen in chapter 10.

Stage armies and think-tanks

In theory, opposition leaders espoused anti-elitist principles. They wished to break down the wall between political actors and passive majority. They did not envisage their organisations as 'representing' the movement but as 'networking' within it, as a forum for the interchange of ideas and experiences. Yet their practice fell far short of the ideals. Although thrilled to see public protests take off, they repeatedly warned of the 'incalculable risks' of 'spontaneous mass demonstrations', and advocated talks between the regime and themselves as an alternative. They were concerned primarily with gaining recognition from the state and 'therefore desisted from calling for demonstrations'. They viewed the masses as a stage army, a 'revocable force with which to pressurise the government'.[44] *Pace* Joppke, this was hardly 'socialist romantic' behaviour. Rather, it manifested reformist themes common to 'moderate' social-movement organisations; and in East Germany these adhered chiefly to social democratic and 'socialist liberal' ideas.

The character of the civic groups owed much to their forebears in the 1980s opposition. That decade had witnessed a proliferation of small but courageous social movements which the regime attempted to intimidate and police. One favoured method was the infiltration of informal Stasi agents into opposition circles, with instructions to foster divisions and

41 'Guidelines for *Basisdemokratie*', in 'Die ersten Texte des Neuen Forum'. Extracts are published in *Oktober 1989*.
42 Draper, *Revolution*, pp. 46–51.
43 As paraphrased in Maier, *Dissolution*, p. 198.
44 *Neues Forum Leipzig*, p. 105; Pollack, 'Bedingungen', p. 311; *die tageszeitung*, 17 January 1990.

encourage a preoccupation with internal issues. Another was to establish free spaces for dissidence within the Protestant Church in order to contain it there, in arenas policed by the clergy. The protection and resources offered by the church were a boon for activists, but – as one of the finest contributions to social-movement theory has shown – a reliance on established, powerful or rich institutions invariably dampens militancy.[45] Cloistered within the Church, opposition politics inevitably meshed with religion; moralism, and ethics of individual self-sacrifice and asceticism flourished. The strategy favoured 'system-immanent' strategies of value-based and lifestyle-oriented opposition, the proponents of which were freer to organise, and were thus in a position to set the agenda in 1989.

Although their isolation was largely imposed by a regime they despised and by clergy they mistrusted, many oppositionists came to feel at home in the 'ghetto', and developed ideas that made their seclusion seem natural. Unlike their fellow citizens – who, it was assumed, would never be drawn into oppositional activity – they were disproportionately church-goers, intellectuals and antipathetic to consumerism. Existing as if trapped between the apathetic masses and an intransigent state, their quest for social change appeared to rely upon their own beleaguered (and infiltrated) forces. An attitude of heroic altruism could result, a conception of political engagement in which an intrepid, risk-taking few acted on behalf of the indifferent many. As a result of the state's success in sequestering the opposition from ordinary folk, when the latter grew increasingly politicised in the late 1980s the ghetto dissidents were only dimly aware of the changes afoot. Coupled with their refusal to countenance the possibility of collective rebellion, they were ill-equipped to recognise signs of an incipient mass movement as these emerged in summer 1989.

The cleft between dissidents and masses followed political and ethical but also social lines. The former were often bound, for instance through marriage or tertiary education, into middle-class milieux. There was a preponderance of intellectuals (although a good many can be described as 'academic proletarians,' their careers cut short as a result of their seditious activities). It was these layers that provided the core activists of the civic groups in 1989. Such groups, Colin Barker has observed, typically rise to leadership in the early stages of uprisings, 'in part, because they are able to articulate the still cloudy and half-formed aspirations of newly awakened masses of people'. Whereas 'the everyday life of workers under "normal" conditions of class society does not promote

45 Piven and Cloward, *Poor.*

self-confidence in public speech', that capacity is more developed among 'intermediate layers' within society: 'sections of the intelligentsia, liberal clergymen, "professional" workers of various kinds – in short, the non-commissioned officers of class society'.[46]

The civic groups were not, of course, a single-class movement. New Forum in particular received much support from workers. Consider one published page of signatories to *Awakening '89*, from September. The occupations listed – six nurses, a plumber, a mechanic, a teacher, a fitter, a stoker, an engineer and a chartered engineer – are almost all working class, which may not be typical but was not unusual either. There were factories in which entire work teams joined New Forum or the SDP, and scores of New Forum factory groups were established, some of which involved themselves in workplace campaigns – to depose managers or establish enterprise councils, for example. Some workforces even used strike threats to force management to permit civic group activities on site.[47]

Yet workers tended to regard the civic groups with scepticism. Oppositionists were widely seen as aloof. 'Of course, hopes were invested in New Forum', Uwe Rottluf, a print worker, told me. But their activists were seen as 'people with nothing useful to say; as intellectuals they encountered a fair dose of mistrust too'. Research on New Forum conducted by Wilfried Wilkens-Friedrich has found that 'the accusation arose, mainly from amongst its working-class membership, that it was purely a discussion group rather than one aimed at effecting change in the wider society'. A married couple, describing themselves as 'ordinary poor GDR citizens', wrote to New Forum to gently explain that it was 'too intellectual – it isn't our world, when, mainly in the church, highly educated people are canvassing for New Forum. We are simple and – to put it crudely – secular workers, but honest of heart'. Another of New Forum's correspondents warned that in his locality it was becoming a 'game for intellectuals'.[48]

For their part, the civic groups placed little emphasis on workplace or working-class issues. According to Linda Fuller, activists would ignore, disparage, or rebuff workers, 'and in some instances purposely excluded them from their efforts'. It would be unfair to charge the civic groups with discrimination in their approach to workers; if any-thing, the opposite was the case. Yet, as this wry recollection by Gerd

46 Torpey, *Intellectuals*, p. 141; Barker, 'Perspectives', p. 235.
47 Eigenfeld, *Bürgerrechtsbewegungen*; Klenke, *Rationalisierung*.
48 Uwe Rottluf interview; Wilkens-Friedrich, 'Beziehungen', p. 44; Krone, *Briefe*, p. 165.

Sczepansky indicates, a positive attitude was not necessarily much more than tokenism:

> At the end of September I was a founding member of New Forum in the Karl-Marx-Stadt district, belonged to its leadership and was, yes, the only worker. It was quite hilarious, because the doctors and professors and intellectuals who were in the committee would always say: 'You're a worker, you must take a seat on the podium, you'll be in the front row.' To which I'd reply: that's not what I want; that's how the SED always behaved too.

And, he continued, it was those very same committee members – 'the artists, paediatricians, intellectuals' – who insisted that 'politics must stay out of the workplace'.[49] In some districts, such as Görlitz, workplace New Forum groups survived into 1990 but elsewhere, it was argued, resources should be concentrated upon local and 'theme' groups instead. 'We were originally involved in groups based on locality, theme and workplace', Uwe Rottluf recalls,

> But in mid-November a resolution was passed to pull out of the work-places – although I now know that was a mistake; it led to conflicts in our local groups too. Yet the dissenters were outvoted. The argument was that we should focus on one thing: *political* goals. The intellectuals [in the leadership] fought shy of any association with 'union' activity. They wanted politics alone. I saw this as unrealistic, because the power to really change things lies where value is created, in the workplace, and because workers were primarily interested in shop-floor issues.

Perhaps in reflection of their class composition there was a distinctly cerebral slant to the civic groups' activities. At the outset of the uprising, they were generally conceived as think tanks. Hans-Jürgen Fischbeck (DJ) proposed that 'the task of our civic movement is to reflect together about the means and ends of democratic change'. DJ groups were 'above all forums for information and discussion rather than activity'; accordingly, it advised its new members to devote their energies to selecting 'themes' and drafting discussion papers. New Forum advertised itself as 'a place for new thinking'; its founder members conceived its task as establishing workgroups to develop oppositional theory. Innumerable theme groups were set up, on issues ranging from housing policy to preservation of historical monuments, from ethics to accommodation for the elderly, from literature to the problems suffered by victims of accidents and bereavement. Already by the first week of October, Halle New Forum had established groups on farming, art, and landscape design, as

49 Fuller, *Working*, p. 78; Gehrke and Hürtgen, *Aufbruch*, pp. 42, 122.

well as women and family, economy, education and the environment. Sometimes sub-divisions were deemed necessary; the ecology theme group in Karl-Marx-Stadt, for example, partitioned further into 'urban ecology, water, soil, air, transport, social ecology and nature conservation' sub-groups. As for the VL, theme groups were not a prominent feature of its organisational structure but it did share the general 'think-tank' orientation. Thus, two of its Berlin activists told a reporter: 'We don't exist as a formal organization but as a group initiative which works out perspectives in different areas, like political democracy, economics and art.' At its meetings, and even at its conference in November, the balance between analysis of 'the next step' and of 'the future society' tended to lean towards the latter (with Stasi agents eagerly pulling that way).[50]

Of course, there was a necessary aspect to the thematic orientation. Activists lacked political experience and were keen to develop their ideas. As old certainties crumbled and opportunities for change widened, myriad questions were thrown up. What reforms are needed in education and health? How can pollution be reduced without jobs being lost? What kind of democracy is required? The theme groups were one arena in which such issues could be aired and substantive proposals elaborated. 'People would come and get involved', Tina Krone, a prominent activist, told me; 'people who wanted to engage in different areas – education, for example – and thought they had something to offer. They'd say "I can contribute something here" '.

But this came at a price. The thematic focus detracted from movement building in the here-and-now, thereby reducing the opposition's broader appeal. New Forum wanted to proceed 'step by step', as one of its founders put it, 'but the people, who were now coming in their thousands, didn't want to work out theoretical models of socialism, they wanted to do something, and right away'.[51] Similarly, Bernd Lindner notes that the specialisation on themes was accompanied by 'a critical lack of a tight, organised net of territorial structures', and this helps explain, no less, why 'the civic groups steadily lost their influence over the transformation process over the course of the autumn'.

50 Fischbeck, 'Marktwirtschaft', p. 200; Poppe, 'Bürgerbewegung', p. 162; Wielgohs and Müller-Enbergs, 'Bürgerbewegung', p. 117; Stolle, *Aufstand*, p. 128; Eigenfeld, 'Neues', pp. 84–5; Krone, *Briefe* p. 128; *Socialist Worker*, 18 November 1989.
51 Paraphrased by Uta Stolle, *Aufstand*, p. 129. New Forum's thematic orientation, Stolle concludes (p. 302) 'suited the dynamics of mass activity as the proverbial fish to the bicycle'.

Some opposition activists expressed concern at the thematic focus. One New Forum correspondent worried that the organisation was 'fragmenting into single work groups, separated from one another'. Another advised Bohley that

> The people do not wish to see New Forum degenerate into a debating club . . . but want strategic and tactical goals to be stated more clearly. The creation of 'territorial structures', from the local right up to the national level, must be greatly accelerated. The people need functioning associations into which they can bring their enormous commitment. Important though theoretical workgroups are, it is nonetheless . . . much more decisive that the many, many people in the movement are able to organise themselves in solid and binding ways.[52]

To a degree, responses to the thematic orientation reflected class differentiation. 'Our theme groups', Tina Krone of New Forum maintains, 'were more representative than those of Democracy Now. They didn't only include intellectuals.' However, Marianne Schulz's research has shown, even New Forum's structures were tailor-made for, and dominated by, intellectuals. 'The priority accorded the theme groups', she maintains, 'is essentially a manifestation of modes of professional behaviour that are specific to the intelligentsia'. According to activists, she reports, 'the predominance of this form of organisation impeded the engagement of individuals from other social groups, especially workers, who were more interested in activity-oriented campaigning'. The theme-oriented structure, she concludes, formed an obstacle to the extension of local branches and thereby 'functioned to seclude New Forum, *to impede communication with the population*' and to reduce its capacity to recruit potential sympathisers for practical activity.[53]

Tina Krone herself was later to become disenchanted with theme-centrism. In a speech to a New Forum gathering in early 1990 she warned that

> New Forum has lost its claim to represent citizens. If the experts from the various theme groups continue to waffle away in their ivory towers, that will never assist the rest of us . . . in achieving the ability to make competent decisions . . . Take the example of the Berlin economics theme group: it cultivates connections to other economics groups, but did it ever initiate discussions with, for example, [New Forum's workplace] group from the nearby television factory? They are the people who will have to suffer the consequences of [the economics group's] clever insights, should these ever win a majority in society.

52 Lindner, *Revolution*, p. 60; Krone, *Briefe*, pp. 156, 90.
53 Schulz, 'Neues', pp. 21–2, emphasis added.

Others vented similar frustrations. According to Wolfgang Schmidt, an elderly engineer who helped establish New Forum workplace groups in the Görlitz district, the theme groups were not overly attractive to workers:

> They addressed issues such as education, ecology, the health service, social services, urban development, youth, law, and so on . . . there were themes, like culture for example . . . yes, culture; I mean, I ask you, did that interest us at that moment in time? Everything was at stake! Ultimately, our workplace and jobs too! Culture has to take a back seat!

Workers, he adds, 'didn't feel comfortable at New Forum meetings; when they began to speak of their concerns, they were not really understood'.[54]

Demos and clerisy

The democratic agenda of the civic groups, this chapter is arguing, contained both participatory and elitist impulses. The latter did not arrive as add-ons but were present from the outset. Already in April 1989 Rolf Henrich, soon to become New Forum's leading theoretician, published what with only slight exaggeration can be described a clerisocratic manifesto. Although his book, *The Tutelary State*, extols democratic values such as 'civic courage' and 'what has, since the Enlightenment, been called self-determination', it also sketches a vision of a reformed GDR in which power would be vested in councils in which 'the representatives of free cultural life' are guaranteed key positions.[55]

In the 1989 uprising, a preoccupation with 'competence' in the elaboration and implementation of reform programmes drew Henrich and his colleagues to seek support from established pools of expertise. Spokespeople from New Forum and DA repeatedly affirmed their respect for the 'huge potential of expertise and achievement' that existed in the SED. United Left spokespeople believed their organisation possessed great potential 'because at the base of the SED, in academic circles and even among top functionaries there is considerable sympathy for our project'.[56]

The tension between participatory and elitist modes was even visible in the discourse of 'dialogue' that was such a core concept for the 1980s opposition. From statements and speeches of oppositionists, one can distil three separate senses of the term. The first was dialogue as *immediate goal*. Here, it signified 'freedom of speech', opening the public sphere to a plurality of voices, the accountability of powerholders and

54 Krone, 'Keine', p. 60; Gehrke and Hürtgen, *Aufbruch*, pp. 273, 283.
55 Henrich, *Vormundschaftliche*, pp. 260, 290–2; Hürtgen, 'Henrichs'.
56 Schorlemmer, *Träume*, p. 103; *die tageszeitung*, 4 September 1989.

recognition of opposition. It expressed that demand for and celebration of 'voice' which characterise the early stages of most mass movements ('citizens, raise your voices, clamour for change!'). It also implied that leaders should *listen*, and if they was unwilling to do so that they should yield to others who were prepared to, as had occurred in the Soviet Union. For some, dialogue also referred to communication with the masses; 'it was always applied', one New Forum leader told me, 'deliberately, in order to bring us an ever-broader mass base'.[57]

Second, dialogue represented a *regulative ideal for political action*. Together with the cognate term 'communication' it had been a keyword of the 1980s opposition. It could be used in a rather vague and utopian sense, as in Friedrich Schorlemmer's call for 'a survival pact of humanity with the Earth', the achievement of which depended upon the development of a 'dialogue of survival reason'. More commonly it signified a preparedness to talk to all parties, regardless of ideology or position. The conception of politics involved was, Detlef Pollack suggests, 'harmonistic': it posited 'politics as primarily a form of discussion aimed at the achievement of a broad consensus'.[58] It is an outlook that may be described as Habermasian, in that it posits politics as a field of discourse rather than as interest articulation within an agonistic arena. In Habermas' vision, generalised dialogue (communicative action) undergirds a political strategy geared towards the creation of 'communicatively-created power' and entailing a 'communicatively-dissolved sovereignty' that is constituted by 'free-floating public communication'. Such communicative action, Habermas argues, becomes transformed into policy via 'the decisions of democratically constituted institutions' that express a consensus achieved through rational debate. In Habermas' schema, the part played by activists is to stimulate a ferment of consensus-oriented, 'domination-free' dialogue which acts as a solvent upon social contradictions and invests institutions with democratic life – precisely how GDR oppositionists envisaged their mission in 1989.[59]

'Dialogue' also referred, thirdly, to the desire for *negotiations between state and society*. 'For me', one activist told me, 'it meant the need for ordinary people to talk with representatives of the state'.[60] Unlike the others, this meaning directly addresses the question of which parties should be engaged. With the civic groups proposed as representatives of

57 Poppe, 'Weg', p. 253; Schorlemmer, *Träume*; Wolfram, interview.
58 Pollack, drawing on John Torpey, in Findeis, *Entzauberung*, p. 278.
59 Habermas, *Revolution*, pp. 199–203, see also *Legitimationsprobleme*, pp. 140–52. On Habermasian influences in 1989 Czechoslovakia, see Jirí Suk, in Auer, 'Paradoxes'.
60 Steffen Geißler.

the people and the SED representing the state, dialogue in this sense acted as a complement and potential alternative to mass protest. It did not indicate a disavowal of demonstrations, or indeed of conflict. ('Dialogue', Reich insisted, is conflictual: 'it is not the main course but the hors d'oeuvre; and it is prepared not with candy floss but with pepper and paprika.')[61] Yet it did signal that the opposition's strategy was moderate, that it preferred a mediating role within a negotiated transition and not a confrontational role in a revolutionary rupture.

In the autumn's early phase, the accent was upon the first of these meanings, but as freedom of expression was gained and a framework for negotiations evolved it was increasingly displaced by the third. Influenced by Polish events, activists had floated the notion of a round table already in the summer, and in October, at the 'contact group' at which the civic groups coordinated activities, IFM, DJ and SDP representatives had begun to push it more vigorously. Dialogue in this 'round table' sense meant talks between themselves and regime representatives. (One suggested that talks include 'New Forum, parties, and experts – for example, economists').[62] It would entail the civic groups substituting themselves for 'the people' and, at least formally, recognising the constitution and government as legitimate. On the latter point, Sebastian Pflugbeil recalls, a 'mutual basis' for dialogue had to be fashioned:

> We had demanded fundamental reforms for a long time. But we had always tried to phrase such demands in a way that would make it clear that we stood behind the principles of the existing constitution. We thought it was necessary to create some kind of mutual basis for conversations and controversial debates. And we felt that the constitution could very well be used for such an endeavor.[63]

From dialogue *qua* negotiation it was a short step to acceptance of the constitution. Yet this step encountered a signal difficulty. As Pflugbeil recognises, 'the "leading role of the party" was just as much part of the constitution' as were civic rights. The hope was that this difficulty would resolve itself in time, that the 'fight for a full guarantee of basic human and democratic rights . . . would eventually lead to an inevitable self-

---

61 Poppe, 'Weg', p. 253.
62 Meinel and Wernicke, *Tschekistischem*, p. 135; Krone, *Briefe*, p. 64.
63 'Our initial goal had *not* been to bring down this state', he adds; 'In fact, at first that had not been our intention at all'. After all, basic democratic rights, including freedom of speech and association, 'were all guaranteed by the constitution . . . We did not want to break any laws, but, on the contrary, wanted those laws abolished which were in clear conflict with our constitution.' Philipsen, *People*, p. 311, emphasis in original.

dissolution of the phrase "leading role of the party" '. In line with this perspective, Pflugbeil and other New Forum leaders, including Bohley and Henrich, as well as Ibrahim Böhme of the SDP, publicly endorsed the existing constitution. Other supporters of New Forum and the other groups were not prepared to go quite so far, but consensus did exist on the broader point that reform, as Schorlemmer put it, 'must be tackled in cooperation with the SED'.[64]

Conclusion

This chapter has suggested that the civic groups, particularly New Forum, gained a 'protest identity' that reflected recognition by the crowds of their important role in the revolution's early stages but which partially contradicted their inner nature. That, in turn, had been shaped by the previous history of political opposition and protest, some key points of which are summarised in the following paragraphs.

Before 1989, East Germany's most turbulent period was its first decade. The 1940s witnessed powerful labour movements, culminating in a mass uprising in 1953. After that date, public protest lay dormant, but low-level industrial action was endemic, as were forms of 'refusal' – refusing promotion at work because of the compromises entailed; refusing to join the FDJ or FDGB, to perform certain duties in the army, to call 'the Wall' by its official title and the like. A state-sanctioned grievance procedure existed in the shape of the 'Eingabe', by which individuals or groups could petition the authorities (typically over terms and conditions of work, housing, trips to the West, and access to higher education).[65] By engaging in industrial action, submitting Eingaben and learning to utilise the 'mass organisations' for their own purposes, citizens generated what Joyce Mushaben has called a 'rudimentary civil society'.[66] Their 'infrapolitical' activities were sometimes successful in pressuring company managers and state leaders to withdraw unpopular measures – whether pay restraint or restrictions on rock music – and to make concessions – such as permitting naturist beaches, and 'Construction Soldier' units (as an alternative to weapons-toting military service).

---

64 Neubert, *Opposition*, p. 859. See also Wolle, *Diktatur*, p. 313; Gutzeit, 'Opposition', pp. 98, 108; *die tageszeitung*, 6 September 1989.
65 Over the decades, millions of petitions were submitted. For many citizens, Hans-Jochen Vogel told me, it was 'the most active way of combating partial aspects of the system. For many, it was, frankly, a hobby. It corresponded to the mental outlook of the majority: exercising opposition, but in legal ways.'
66 Mushaben, 'Lehrjahre', p. 99.

Opposition also came in the form of intellectual dissidence which, from the 1950s to the 1970s, was generally of a 'revisionist' disposition. Dissidents accepted the 'socialist' (state-owned) character of the GDR's economy while criticising the 'Stalinist distortions' of the political super-structure – the archetypal revisionist desire was 'that socialism in the GDR frees itself from its bureaucratic sclerosis'. Invariably they appealed to the Marxist classics for vindication of their heresy. 'Because I had read the classics thoroughly', one poet recalls, 'I knew how radically they of all people had opposed every tendency towards any ossification of party and state organisation. This knowledge gave me great encouragement.' Their chief goals were to establish the rule of law and civil liberties, along with some form of participatory and/or parliamentary democracy. They placed their hopes in SED-led reform and repudiated collective rebellion. Their numbers included philosophers and poets (notably Brecht), and numerous middle-level functionaries. Fritz Schenk has summarised the biographical trajectory of the typical dissident: 'Rebels emerge, again and again, from amongst those on whose desks reports of policy failures pile up.' These

> shift at first into 'Practicism', i.e. they try to address the visible abuses with a multitude of administrative measures . . . As soon as they realise the futil-ity of their efforts they slide into 'Revisionism', i.e. they are wracked by doubts about the system, come into conflict with the ideology and the Party apparatus and search for fundamental change.[67]

In the 1980s, small social movements arose, geared to issues such as peace, ecology and human rights, and the character of dissidence altered. The new generation placed greater emphasis on individual lifestyle change, were more likely to be churchgoers and less likely to advocate work within the SED. But in several other respects they resembled their predecessors. First, they identified with the GDR. Bohley, for example, was driven by a desire to enable East Germans to identify more closely with their state. Her associates concurred; one stated that: 'Our reformism was a search for a Third Way, tied to GDR sovereignty.'[68] Second, they tended to advocate respect for the constitution, and would, in Bohley's formulation, 'always appeal for the law to be respected'.[69] Third, they placed their hopes in gradual, non-conflictual change, via dialogue with the regime. (One activist in the mid-1980s grumbled that

67 Fuchs, *Gedächtnisprotokolle*, pp. 26, 36; Jänicke, *Dritte*, p. 92.
68 Hilsberg, 'Interview', p. 140; Degen, 'Forum', p. 107; Findeis, *Entzauberung* p. 74.
69 'It took a while', she adds, 'before we began to see that some situations demand that laws be transgressed'. Findeis, *Entzauberung*, p. 52.

it was 'as if we could, or would wish to, engage Erich Honecker in some kind of Geneva negotiations!') Finally, like earlier generations of dissidents, their approach to the working classes was fraught and ambivalent. Predominantly intellectuals, they viewed workers with some suspicion (and the feeling was reciprocated). In the words of one Karl-Marx-Stadt activist, 'we didn't manage to engage "the people" in communication, even though some attempts were made. And that was most frustrating: we failed to reach the masses, they weren't interested in us.' As a result, in the late 1980s 'We weren't so aware of how much things were bubbling' amongst the population at large.[70]

In October 1989, as illustrated earlier in this chapter, the oppositionists and the 'people' did begin to find one another and this 'confrontation', as a study by Leipzig sociologists concludes, 'forced the grassroots groups to recognise that the population could act politically'. The groups contributed significantly to the development of protest norms, and came to mediate between the emerging movement and the public sphere (including the western media). Their activists were motivated by the desire 'to encourage *self-activity*', as Tina Krone put it.[71] The autumn mobilisation boosted their confidence in the effectiveness of collective action and strengthened participatory-democratic norms. Thus, one Leipziger has described how her experience staffing a New Forum 'contact centre' revealed that 'the capacity to think together, act together, plan together and govern together is present to an amazing degree'.[72] Oppositionists played a significant mobilising role, particularly in the early stages, and the civic groups' association with the demonstrations was hugely strengthened by protestors appropriating them, notably New Forum, as a 'flag'. Yet although this embrace was welcome in many ways, a bold, streets-centred identity was partially at odds with New Forum leaders' conceptions. The narrow limits to action and thought that had prevailed during previous decades, in which 'system-immanent' pragmatism had seemed the only viable strategy, had become internalised. Accordingly, the civic groups tended to attract those whose hopes lay in effecting change within the bounds of the existing system, in reconciliation with the SED, and in 'dialogue'.

It is not uncommon to find an over-representation of the educated middle classes in social-movement organisations, particularly their cadre

70 Büscher and Wensierski, *Null*, p. 159; Stefan Geißler, interview; Hans-Jochen Vogel, interview.
71 Pollack *et al.*, *Gruppen*, p. 50; Krone, interview.
72 Petra Lux, from a New Forum leaflet distributed in Leipzig, 22 October 1989.

and leadership. Such individuals tend to possess greater supplies of resources that facilitate organisation: leisure time, experience in analysing information, articulating ideas and influencing opinion and confidence in one's ability to intervene effectively in the public realm. This was abundantly so in East Germany. The SDP leadership, for example, consisted largely of clergymen plus one other who was able to quit his job thanks to assistance from wealthy relatives. The class structure of the surrounding society works its way into the social-movement organisation. For example, as Tina Krone complained at its January conference, New Forum's spokespeople consisted of

> those who are able to take the time off that's required for all the journeying around the country and participating in the day and night discussions to create organisational networks. But in the meantime all those who are not priests, self-employed or the like, so cannot so easily leave work or stay away for days, remain relatively helpless in the face of political events.

Perhaps a concentration of 'intellectuals' in the civic groups was inevitable. However, this chapter has shown, it was also directly encouraged by the groups' self-conceptions as 'think-tanks', their organisational structures that privileged thematic discussion and their reluctance to relate to workplace–political issues.[73]

New Forum and the bulk of the other civic groups decried bureaucratic politics and, as an antidote, advocated 'grassroots democracy'. They feared that their organisations would 'substitute' for activity at society's grassroots and would ossify into hierarchical political parties. But this calculation was based upon a mistaken (and Michelsian) assumption – that the roots of bureaucratisation lie in organisation *per se* – particularly centralisation and the leadership principle. Even as they strove to maintain their organisational fluidity and decentralism, the civic groups were unwittingly marching down what is in fact the royal road to bureaucratisation. As subsequent chapters will show, the tighter their relationship with existing institutions and the closer they clung to the coat-tails of the ruling class, the more their behaviour began to reflect established hierarchies.

73 Herzberg and von zur Mühlen, *Anfang*, p. 143; Krone, 'Keine', p. 60.

7

'Last night in Munich for a beer, then back again for the demo here'

> In amazement, we watch these contortionists, whom the people dub
> Wendehälse – which, the dictionary tells us, 'are able to adapt quickly and
> easily to a situation, handle it skillfully and exploit new opportunities'.
> (Christa Wolf) [1]

> Those who cried 'Stalin hooray!' now shout 'Reform, today!'; Away with
> the Wendehälsen![2]

The media-spectacular images of East Germany's revolution were of the
summer exodus, the October 9 demonstration and the fall of the Wall.
But what happened thereafter? Did protest tail off, as the country cruised
towards German unification? Many historians of East Germany assume
precisely this. 'Once the Berlin Wall had been breached', says one, the
movement's demands were met and 'the theme binding many participants
and compelling them to undertake public action no longer existed, clearly
shown by the huge drop in the numbers at demonstrations at the end of
1989 and beginning of 1990'.[3] Yet in this chapter and chapters 8 and 10
I show this to be a misleading statement. Indeed, by some measures the
very opposite was true. Protest numbers (of both participants and events)
in January 1990 far exceeded those of October 1989. And, while the
movement did indeed peak in early November, it revived only a fortnight
later, surged in early December, and crested yet again in mid-January.[4]

A regime sheds its skin

As daily life slowly returned to normal following the fall of the Wall it
was clear that a new phase in the revolution was in the offing. In their

1 From a speech at Alexanderplatz, 4 November 1989.
2 Banners at Leipzig demonstrations.
3 Grix, 'Recasting', p. 272.
4 Johnson, 'Massenmobilisierung', p. 93.

general outlines, certain developments – such as closer relations with West Germany – became inevitable, but which precise directions would be taken, and what roles would be played by the SED, occupying powers, civic groups and the masses was less clear. What reforms would be instituted, whether the regime would collapse or restructure and whether the movement would radicalise or dwindle, all these questions remained to be answered.

In the month that followed the fall of the Wall, the regime experienced intense and unremitting stress, and began to disintegrate. Numerous functionaries resigned and hundreds more took leave of absence, typically on grounds of illness ('sleeping disorders, sickness, stomach problems and vomiting', were complaints cited in one report). In the SED, the upper echelons were in turmoil, with long-standing authority figures resigning in disgrace and new appointees struggling to find their feet, while the lower ranks continued to buckle and fray. Having already lost 300,000 members, around half a million more followed in December. Critics of the incumbent leadership pressed for root-and-branch change, and further personnel turnover at the top; they called for a special party congress to be convened, the delegates to which would be empowered to elect an entirely new Central Committee. 'The stream of bad tidings from the Party branches swelled', Schabowski remembers of this period; 'Mass resignations, mistrust of the leadership, helplessness.' Krenz's memoirs reveal similar, if more self-critical, thoughts:

> The Party is in a desolate condition. We're paying the price for having many passengers, but too few committed members. Comrades, in their thousands, are resigning. They say they've been let down by the corrupt leadership . . . Each new day makes it clearer that I cannot retrieve the lost trust. In October I still believed that I could succeed in halting the crisis. But, for many, my long period of cooperation with Erich Honecker means that I'm incapable of engaging in reform.[5]

In the security forces, the picture was likewise one of disarray. Police officers, some wearing butterfly badges in their lapels, joined the demonstrations. The factory battalions were disarmed, and calls mounted for their complete dissolution. In the army, reformist officers, under pressure from the ranks, issued calls for policy and personnel changes in the military leadership. Divisions opened up within the officer corps, as the reform movement within the army provoked a countermovement among hard-liners determined to resist change. Even the Stasi was not immune

---

5 Richter, 'Revolution', p. 932; Hertle and Stephan, *Ende*, p. 84; Schabowski, *Absturz*, p. 181; Krenz, *Herbst*, pp. 305, 331.

to the virus of disintegration. Already before the fall of the Wall, officers had been alarmed by mounting disobedience on the part of the Stasi's officers and informal agents, including 'the disappearance of "our best forces", the informal agents' and, worse, that 'The [Stasi's] ability to function is in question'. After the fall, signs of indiscipline multiplied. With the organisation coming into ever-sharper focus as a target of popular wrath, with the first moves towards a reduction in its size and remit, and with the 'fog of revolution' rendering its guiding precept, 'who is who?', ever more difficult to operationalise, morale plummeted. It was not helped either by the Stasi's hapless rebranding as the Office of National Security, a name that abbreviated to 'Nasi'. From mid-November, numerous officers and informal agents emigrated to West Germany. Disgruntled officers sent petitions to SED leaders complaining of deception on the part of the Stasi leadership. One, for example, wrote to Modrow to urge that the 'incapable, arrogant, alcoholic and privileged cadre in our organisation be discharged and called to account'. As regards informal agents, although a majority (perhaps 80 per cent) continued to cooperate with their guiding officers, others were deemed unreliable. Some renounced their role or even crossed sides to become genuine supporters of the opposition groups upon which they had been spying.[6]

The general sense of disintegration was sharpened further when all the old-regime institutions – SED, police, bloc parties, Commercial Coordination (KoKo, see p. 143), the ministries and mass organisations and especially the Stasi – began the systematic destruction of files. Stores of painstakingly assembled information went up, literally, in smoke. In the case of the Stasi, this began in earnest in early November under its new leader General Schwanitz and was accelerated later that month. The shredding process, some officers believed, was nothing but a spineless surrender to public opinion. The SED leadership, in their view, had no aim other than to remain in office long enough to give the file-shredders time to bury the incriminating past, so as to reduce the likelihood of further scandals arising that might damage their image during the impending transition.[7]

The gathering pace of file-shredding might appear to indicate that prospective defeat was envisaged – and, in retrospect, the period following

6 Menge, *Ohne*, p. 236; *die tageszeitung*, 9 December 1994, p. 12; Richter, *Staatssicherheit*, p. 47; *Telegraph*, 10; Mitter and Wolle, *Befehle*, p. 230; Mitter and Wolle, *Untergang*, p. 533.
7 That a significant minority of Stasi officers held this view was communicated to me, off the record, by the wife of a senior Stasi officer in early December 1989.

the Wall's fall can appear as one in which the regime surrendered. Indeed, some scholars go further than this. One study limns it as a moment in which power *dissolved*. East Germany in 1989, it suggests, experienced a revolution in which '[t]here were no buildings to seize, no palace to attack, no capitalists to dispose of, no Red Army to fight'. Power, it avers, in Foucauldian idiom, 'was everywhere and nowhere. The crowds just stayed in the streets until the Other fell away.'[8]

The crowds themselves, however, were not so naïve. They expressed scepticism towards claims that the old elites were 'falling away' in banners such as 'SED – still has a secure grip on: media, economy, organisations, sport, judiciary, administration, schools, police, culture, etc.!' and, an old Russian proverb, 'A snake may shed its skin, yet it remains a snake!' A similar, if more nuanced, metaphor was invoked by an opposition activist: 'The administration's head has been chopped off, but the body lives on.'[9]

It is indisputable that the storming of the Wall dealt SED leaders a greater blow than any had expected, and in retrospect it can be seen as the beginning of the end of the GDR. But it did not occasion a scuttling of the ship of state. 'On the contrary', Schabowski recalls, 'we expected a process of stabilisation'. The regime's commitment to retaining control of the transition process remained intact, and parts of the power apparatus, including some Stasi sections and company managers, even attempted to combat tendencies of disintegration with a hard-line stance. Although increasingly frayed, the reins of power remained with the SED leadership, passing from Honecker's ageing Politburo via Krenz to Modrow. As the most reviled officeholders resigned, people with new ideas and greater flexibility came to the fore. But they were not new faces. Modrow's original appointment as a functionary occurred during the purges that followed the June 1953 uprising, while the Stasi's new chief, General Schwanitz, had long been Mielke's right-hand man. Nor were their records lily-white. Schwanitz's elevation provoked discontent among Stasi officers, who alleged that in early October he had ordered that they should open fire even on fellow SED members if the situation demanded.[10] Modrow had many admirers,[11] but was implicated in the

---

8 Eyerman and Jamison, *Movements*, p. 158.
9 Krone, *Briefe*, p. 257.
10 Schabowski, *Politbüro*, p. 139; Klemm, *Korruption*, p. 41.
11 One biography (or hagiography) portrays him thus: 'Modrow has about him something of the monk, with a pure heart, and something of the knight, who can fight like a demon . . . This man is, and can only be, thoroughly honest.' Arnold *Modrow*, p. 105.

May 1989 election fraud and in recent police and army brutality in Dresden. Krenz supported his promotion because, while reform-inclined, he was essentially 'on message'. Justifying his move to a sceptical colleague, Krenz pointed out that 'Modrow has been in the Central Committee since 1958. In all this time he has unswervingly toed the Party line.'[12]

The new leaders did, nonetheless, belong to that section of the *nomenklatura* that had become convinced, even before the fall of the Wall, that some form of democratisation along lines charted by Poland and Hungary was inescapable. Perhaps even a transition to parliamentary democracy was the only realistic means of avoiding what Christa Luft, a rising star in the regime, called the 'gathering chaos'.[13] No longer were democratic reforms seen as piecemeal concessions to the mass protests; a shift to some form of democratic polity was regarded as inevitable, and yet, existing powerholders and their supporters in the SED and bloc parties believed, *they* would be the architects of transition. Although democratisation would undermine their position, they would nonetheless succeed in maintaining a pivotal role in a future parliamentary democracy, thanks to their control of the economy, state bureaucracy and scientific establishment and to the influence of informal Stasi agents within the civic groups. In election campaigns these contacts, as well as funds, and decades of political experience, would be put to advantage. Already in early December, the SED and bloc parties began to gear up to campaign in (as yet unannounced) parliamentary elections. In a telling contribution at the 3 December Central Committee plenum, Politburo member Gerhard Beil warned that 'whether we like it or not, we are already in an election campaign' – even if, he added, 'others have forced this upon us'. (Rival parties, he went on, were bound to use underhand methods, and the SED should adopt such tactics from the outset.)[14]

The incoming government of 17 November attested in its very form to the fundamental character of the reforms underway. With Modrow's election the apex of power shifted from SED General Secretary to prime minister, and the Council of Ministers was freed from its subordination to the Politburo. It was a coalition government, with eleven of twenty-eight ministries in the hands of the (increasingly independent) bloc parties, and with CDU leader Lothar de Maizière as deputy prime

12 Krenz, *Herbst*, p. 215.
13 Luft, *Wende*, p. 11. See also von Plato, *Vereinigung*, p. 110, and Modrow's speech to the Central Committee on 9 November, in Hertle and Stephan, *Ende*, p. 285.
14 Hertle and Stephan, *Ende*, p. 475.

minister. In his inaugural speech, Modrow indicated that his government would endeavour to regain popular trust and to ensure that 'the democratic renewal of public life in all its aspects, which has just begun, will be profound and lasting'. In the weeks that followed, steps were taken towards more transparent and democratic governance. For example, a reinvigorated *Volkskammer* appointed a commission to investigate functionaries' privileges and corruption, and the Attorney General initiated proceedings against members of the security forces accused of abuses against demonstrators.

The Modrow administration also followed Poland and Hungary in economic reform. An early target was the subsidising of basic consumer goods and rents. For Honecker, this had been a shibboleth. 'The 17 June 1953 began with a rise in the price of jam', he would remind colleagues; and 'the people need cheap bread, a dry flat and a job. If these three things are in order, socialism is secure.' Now, such subsidies were progressively reduced. Next, private property rights were expanded. In a ruling that appeared merely semantic, so-called 'people's property', it was decreed, had all along been nothing but state property. The very real consequence was that paramount control of businesses could be devolved from the central planning apparatus to company directors without constitutional ado. Furthermore, companies were encouraged to look west, in particular to form joint ventures. The combination of cheap East German labour with western technology, expertise and markets would, it was hoped, prove a winning formula. In this regard, a representative example of the ideas circulating in East Berlin was that which Soviet ambassador Valentin Falin pitched to Krenz towards the end of November. The GDR, he proposed, should seek to establish an economic relationship with West Berlin akin to that of China with Taiwan. He had already broached this with West Berlin's mayor, Walter Momper, who 'had found the idea interesting'. Cooperation of this sort, Falin suggested, would prove highly profitable. For example, Berlin's Schönefeld airport could be expanded to become a 'second Frankfurt'. Joint ventures in the automobile and electronics industries, with Soviet involvement, were potentially promising, too. In the Soviet Union,

> for example, a small car, 'OKA', has been developed. If this car were produced, at a volume of one million per year, by a joint GDR–FRG consortium and with Soviet participation, the price would be two-thirds or half that of today's cheapest FRG model.[15]

15 Steiner, *Plan*, p. 190; Stark, 'Wirtschaftspolitische'; Krenz, *Herbst*, pp. 277, 315–18.

Contemporaneously with the restructuring of domestic polity and economic policy, the SED underwent an internal transformation. Under pressure from the membership, Krenz reluctantly agreed to call a special party congress which, unlike a party conference, was empowered to replace the entire leadership (thus upping the prospect of an internal split). For the leadership, the event offered the opportunity of adapting their organisation to the uncharted terrain of the impending pluralist system through repackaging as a left-reformist parliamentary party. At the top, Krenz was replaced by a bright and youthful lawyer, Gregor Gysi. In demeanour, and in his approach to politics, the media-savvy Gysi brought an air of freshness to the SED leadership; the contrast to the arrogant and wilfully deaf Honecker or to the insincere Krenz could hardly have been greater.

A fundamental transformation of the SED, it seemed, was underway. Yet in other respects the old ways continued. In the run-up to the congress the leadership pulled strings to prevent the election of radical delegates, and the resolutions from the more radical platforms that had sprouted in previous weeks were bureaucratically suppressed. One such, which was established at a Berlin television factory and then spread to the Humboldt University and other local branches, called for the complete dissolution of the Party, including dispersal of its funds and property, to be followed by refoundation as a left-reformist parliamentary party. Had this cause succeeded – and there is evidence that it was a popular one – the SED would probably have split, and something akin to 'regime collapse' might have ensued. When the congress convened in mid-December, the new leadership fought against the proposition. An acknowledged reformist, Gysi was especially well placed to appeal to the middle ground. He invited delegates to consider the fate of the thousands of functionaries whose livelihoods depended upon the Party, and to bear in mind the disputes about legal entitlement to its vast property holdings that would arise if a number of successor parties were founded. Appealing to delegates' fears of 'anarchy', he warned that if the proposal were accepted, 'a political vacuum would arise that nobody would be able to fill, and that would exacerbate the crisis, with unforeseeable consequences'. Finally, he urged that all those 'who have committed themselves to reforming the Party' would see their hard work come to fruition only if the SED held together and retained its resources.[16]

In the event, a majority of delegates voted for continuity, and refused to sanction the dispersal of the Party's funds. Thanks in part to his

16 Glaessner, *Demokratie*, p. 75; Falkner, 'SED', p. 35; Liebold, 'Machtwechsel'; Barker, 'SED', p. 2.

dynamic image, Gysi had played a crucial role in preventing a radical renewal. The congress succeeded in slowing the disintegration of the SED: enough was conserved that it could remain secure in its position at the heart of the regime, enough was reformed to present a semblance of democratic credibility – and this latter was reflected in an upward turn in the party's poll ratings. Symbolising the balance between continuity and change, the Party's name was retained, but with the words Party of Democratic Socialism appended, to form SED–PDS.

A further area that witnessed major restructuring was the Party's relationship to the opposition. Three changes arrived in short order: the civic groups were legalised, they were granted resources for campaigning (such as offices, vehicles and telephones) and their cooperation was actively sought by the SED–PDS. Indubitably, this was a remarkable turnaround. Yet here too, change occurred within an overall framework of continuity. If Modrow's game plan *vis-à-vis* the opposition was a bold one, it was not an entirely new departure but rather a deepening and institutionalisation of Krenz's earlier 'dialogue' tactic. In the context of renewed protests and heightened instability, the attempt to persuade opposition leaders to cooperate in the restitution of social order had become a matter of urgency. Enlisting their help seemed the only way of restoring order and helping the regime to regain a modicum of credibility. In addition, it was a strategy that was becoming ever-more viable, given the refraction of what the SED liked to call 'the critical potential' into moderates and radicals. That a prominent New Forum member had given Modrow 'a vote of confidence' regarding his selection of government ministers (with two exceptions, Gerhards Schürer and Beil), was one of many indicators of oppositionists' inclination to cooperate.[17]

Modrow's calculation was, as *die tageszeitung* put it, that 'a weak opposition is likely to accept co-optation'.[18] The tactic was transparent at the time, but since then more has been revealed of the detailed thinking that underlay his overtures. The most revealing insight is contained in the transcripts of a meeting, attended by Modrow and Wolfgang Schwanitz, in mid-November. Prime Minister and Stasi chief agreed that instability was rising and could worsen considerably, but neither considered that the time had arrived to raise the white flag. The authority of the state, Modrow insisted, must be preserved at all costs. Calls for 'the constitution to be sliced up' should be resisted. We must win back public trust and go on the 'political offensive' again, he argued, but we must also 'engage in serious rethinking. There is no way around that.' In

17 Neues Forum, *Wirtschaftsreform*, p. 10.
18 *die tageszeitung* Journal 1, p. 152.

particular, the assumption that 'everyone on the streets is the enemy, against whom we must do battle' should be jettisoned. Instead, 'the game that we should play' with the 'friendlier' sections of the movement – the civic groups – is to involve them in the petty paraphernalia of work within state structures. Offer them a morsel of power, he proposed, and then, when their leaders begin to shoulder political responsibility and carry the can for unpopular decisions, their allegiance to the state will strengthen, even while the key levers of power will have remained untouched. Schwanitz agreed, adding that 'New Forum etc. are, like us, for democratic socialism, so we should be able to achieve consensus'.[19]

The planned cooptation of the civic groups did not negate the use of traditional police methods. Rather, they offered new scope, in particular for the Stasi's network of agents. Those planted in the opposition leadership, such as Ibrahim Böhme and Wolfgang Schnur, were invaluable in the eyes of state leaders. 'In their fantasies', the historians Armin Mitter and Stefan Wolle speculate, senior functionaries 'envisaged themselves as partners in a . . . coalition government alongside Böhme's SDP'. Hence, as Schwanitz pointed out in the same meeting, the new commitment to cooperation with oppositionists necessitated a 're-activation of the activities of our informal agents, with the maintenance, of course, of the highest levels of secrecy and conspiracy'.[20]

If the Modrow–Schwanitz plan was clear in its outlines, it was not immediately apparent how the civic groups would respond. But answers to this question soon emerged. On the same day as the aforementioned meeting, Democracy Now issued a call for 'round table' negotiations to begin a process of constitutional reform. Dialogue with the regime, oppositionists hoped, could begin to 'transform policy making into a discursive process of communication about the normative legitimacy of political claims to power'.[21] Put more simply, round tables seemed to offer them the prospect of influence over the incipient process of democratisation while evading the uncertainties inherent in a confrontational course of mobilising against the regime.

The round table's precise shape would emerge through negotiation. One proposal, by Wolfgang Ullmann (DJ), may be dubbed 'democratic corporatist'. Designed to ensure that representatives of the old order would be outnumbered, it was envisaged with five sides, drawn from parliament and government, workplaces, the churches, the opposition

19 The document is archived in BStU, ZA (ZAIG 4886). Modrow's speech is reprinted in Stephan, '*Vorwärts*'.
20 Mitter and Wolle, *Untergang*, p. 532; Kowalczuk, 'Artikulationsformen'.
21 Elster, 'Introduction', p. 109.

and the 'technical, scientific and artistic intelligentsia' (the latter on condition that its representatives had contributed to the 'democratic transformation of the GDR'). In Ullmann's vision, the round table would be the site of historic negotiations over the transition to democracy; to it would devolve the task of drafting a new constitution in which the SED's monopoly of power would finally be annulled. But it also offered a new model of political mediation, a means of achieving consensus through communicative interaction as contrasted to agonistic parliamentary politics.[22]

Hardly had the suggestion of round table talks been formally announced – by the Church – than it was taken up by old regime parties, first the LDPD then the SED. The eagerness with which they seized upon the offer put opposition groups in a quandary. With the Party signalling willingness to accept them as negotiating partners, the round table could perhaps provide a forum for genuinely democratic discussion. Yet why was the SED so keen? Did it envisage round table talks as a side-show, with negligible influence on policy and involving no more than a supervisory function for the opposition? The latter judgement, as it happened, was closer to the mark. As outlined above, round table negotiations suited Modrow's strategy of cooptation. He was aware that round tables at the local level, which had arisen upon the ruins of the old structures of local government, were proving as committed to the maintenance of order as they were to political reform. For the old forces, as Ullmann feared, the round table was conceived not as 'a representative committee, a kind of emergency parliament, but as a sort of extraordinary senate that would serve to bind all existing authorities behind the shared aim of recreating effective institutions of government'.[23]

As early as 23 November, Schabowski delivered a speech that left no room for uncertainty on this point. East Germany, he said, was in danger of entering a 'dual power' situation, and the round table would not be permitted to replace parliament and government, as had occurred in Poland. 'Parliament is the country's highest organ of power, above or beside which no other decision-making body can be placed', he concluded – as if that was self-evidently the case and had been so for time immemorial.[24]

---

22 Ullmann, *Demokratie*, p. 148. Others, notably Ullmann's DJ colleague Konrad Weiß, had still grander visions. For him, the round table was, potentially, the embodiment of 'the ancient ideal of the teutonic assembly'.
23 Schlegelmilch, 'Politische'; Schulz, 'Neues', p. 26.
24 Fehr, *Unabhängige*, pp. 326–7.

'Where has all the hard currency gone?'

Despite the announcement of far-reaching reforms and the commence-
ment of round table negotiations, mass protests did not disappear. For
a time, to be sure, the monumental concession to popular demands in
the shape of the liberalised border regime did take the wind from the
sails of protest and this gave an initial breathing space to Modrow's
incoming government. With the attention of millions deflected from the
domestic scene towards newly opened vistas to the West, the upward
trajectory of protest was halted; in Leipzig 'only' 210,000 demonstrated on 13 November. However, although the turnout in Leipzig on
this and the following week was relatively low, and the streets of Berlin
remained quiet, it soon became apparent that travel and protest were
quite compatible. As one banner put it: 'Last night in Munich for a beer,
then back again for the demo here.' Indeed, with Munich beer priced
in Deutschmarks, the demand for hard currency only added to the
motives for protest. Before long, the crowds in the streets and squares
of some towns and cities, such as Dresden, were surpassing previous
records.

Following the fall of the Wall, protestors paid greater attention to
socio-economic issues, particularly as these connected to the East–West
chasm in living standards, and the related question of German unification. Among ordinary East Germans there was no shortage of grievances over income and consumption issues. One gripe concerned access
to Deutschmarks. In the 1980s, those who lacked them had become
increasingly irritated by the growing income and status gap separating
them from Deutschmark recipients – citizens with an 'aunt in the West'
and the elite. Another grievance concerned senior functionaries, who
were widely perceived as avaricious and corrupt. In its reports on the
'mood' of the population, the Stasi noted the ubiquity of workers' complaints that they bear the brunt of economic problems, of the wish that
elite groups should sacrifice their privileges and of criticisms of the
abuse of power by officials. A common grumble was that export
receipts flowed directly 'into the hands and pockets of privileged functionaries'. Rumours and mutterings of this sort circulated widely. A
typical story that I recall was of a neighbour's cousin who worked in a
carpet factory; a visit by Harry Tisch, although intended to boost
morale, had precisely the opposite effect when the FDGB leader
departed, taking with him one of the factory's finest products.
Similarly, a Berlin shop steward tells of 'a construction supervisor who
told me that they were sometimes asked, for an extra 1,000 Marks a
weekend [about the average worker's monthly income], to leave their

real jobs and build houses for functionaries, mostly with Western materials'.[25]

Tales of *nomenklatura* greed were legion and discussion of distributive injustice was endemic, but in the autumn of 1989 these grew ever more heated. Stasi reports from early October warned that

> progressive forces in the workplaces are being confronted, on a large scale, with arguments concerning the existence of a so-called privileged class in the GDR (including functionaries of Party, state and economy) and of a massive increase in profiteering and speculation. The thrust of the argument, which is conducted very aggressively, is that these groups have been the true beneficiaries of socialism.

Questions of privilege and class had begun to arise on demonstrations in October. One march, in Jena, made its way to the headquarters of the largest local firm, Carl Zeiss, where chants of 'Biermann, get yer Volvo out!' were intoned and the building was almost stormed. In the middle of the same month, a worker in a Karl-Marx-Stadt vehicles plant reported to the New Forum leadership that, as things stood, his colleagues saw no future with either their firm or the state. 'Them at the top drive big western company cars that are paid for with urgently needed hard currency', was one grievance outlined in his letter, which added, 'We passed a resolution stating that this state of affairs should be abolished, with supervision by ourselves'.[26]

In mid-November, demonstrators in Leipzig were heard singing 'Where has all the hard currency gone?' (to the tune of 'Where have all the flowers gone?'). Within days, their question began to be answered, in the form of a spate of revelations of corruption and high living by functionaries. An announcement that the reservation of hunting grounds as *de facto* private playgrounds for functionaries was to be ended only drew attention to this particular privilege. It was also revealed that the homes of Politburo members' children, constructed from Canadian timber, Italian floor tiling and West German ceramics, had swallowed large sums in hard currency. Journalists had long held leads on stories of this sort, which they had hitherto been unable to follow up; now this backlog began to reach the public sphere. Further opportunities for investigations proliferated; the pressure on the government had intensified to such an

25 Klenke, *Rationalisierung*; Mitter and Wolle, *Befehle*; Meinel and Wernicke, *Tschekistischem*, p. 134; Philipsen, *People*, pp. 124–5.

26 Mitter and Wolle, *Befehle*, p. 205; Klenke, *Rationalisierung*; Krone, *Briefe*, p. 84.

extent that it was increasingly difficult to deny access even to sensitive information.[27]

In order to demonstrate a commitment to transparency and, presumably, in the hope that only a few 'bad apples' would be uncovered, the *Volkskammer* had earlier established a commission to investigate abuses of power. Although its head, Heinrich Toeplitz, was a compromised figure – as president of the Supreme Court he had gone so far as to sentence a man to life imprisonment for assisting citizens to flee the country – his commission took its task seriously, and was assisted in this by thousands of letters that poured in, alleging all manner of injustices from the docking of wages and the confiscation of property to major miscarriages of justice that had led to wrongful imprisonment. Thousands rang a phoneline set up for the purpose with reports of corruption; in some instances, groups of workers supported their claims with strike threats.[28]

Thanks to the efforts of whistleblowers and investigative journalists, people discovered that their rulers were more rapacious than they had dared to suspect. The Toeplitz commission's remit included recent cases of police brutality, the prevalence of which, and the similarities displayed in the methods used across a range of towns and cities, pointed to the existence of a central strategy. Victims of repression began to speak out, too. Political prisoners told of the use of torture. Villagers in Wolletz (near Berlin) reported that Stasi officers had thrown them out of their homes, wanting them for themselves. Women workers from a village in Saxony alleged that Stasi officers had locked them in their factory when they had attempted to organise a strike, and subjected them to abuse.[29]

Reports of brutality by the security forces were supplemented by stories of high-handed behaviour by state leaders. The revelation that Honecker used a servant as his gun-rest on hunting expeditions, eventually causing him to go deaf in one ear, was very widely discussed, as was the rumour that Honecker and Mittag were given to shooting wild animals while these were feeding at the trough. Such tales resonated with people's resentments against the multitude of local 'Honeckers' – arrogant officials, bullying managers and the like. As so often, a Leipzig demonstration banner expressed the matter with wit and concision: 'We were the animals in the hunting grounds!'

In addition to functionaries' privileges and police/Stasi abuses, a third set of scandals concerned the transmutation of state funds into the private property of *nomenklatura* members. To give one example that stands for

27 Ash, *People*, p. 70; Links and Bahrmann, *Volk*, p. 147.
28 Klemm, *Korruption*, pp. 23–4.
29 Hawkes, 'Tearing', p. 77.

many, bureaucratic control of prices enabled a villa that cost 400,000 Marks to build to be sold to a Politburo member's son for under a third of that sum. A trickle of allegations of this sort quickly became a flood. Wandlitz, the secluded and normally tranquil exurb that had, since the 1953 uprising, accommodated Central Committee members and their families, became a centre of journalistic attention and a symbol of *nomenklatura* privilege and hypocrisy. Each year, it was revealed, tens of millions of Marks were diverted from the hard-pressed economy to its 280 residents for the purchase of western commodities. A special shop sold western goods at knock-down prices for the fortunate inhabitants and, as the GDR began to collapse in late 1989, they made intensive use of it. In one trip the Krenz family spent over 10,000 Marks – equivalent to an unskilled worker's annual income. In a few days just before the fall of the Wall the Sindermanns spent over 23,000 Marks, a third of which on gold jewellery, while the Schabowskis spent over 10,000 Marks on clothes alone.[30]

A series of further reports in media outlets confirmed that these revelations were but the tip of an iceberg. The SED regime had tirelessly preached equality and austerity to its subjects. Now, it seemed, its leaders themselves lived in luxury, squandering 'the people's' resources on hunting lodges, tennis courts and yachts. Honecker and his wife owned a fleet of fourteen cars, including a Mercedes, while presiding over a system that obliged those who required even a single Trabant to queue for fourteen years for the privilege. SED leaders used a state-owned flight of jets for private purposes and held exclusive rights to the Baltic Sea island of Vilm. Functionaries' private hunting grounds occupied 20 per cent of the entire region of Neubrandenburg, and the maintenance of these alone took 6 million Marks from the state budget each year – much of it in hard currency. At several of his estates Honecker retained a full complement of staff on a permanent basis, despite hunting at them no more than once a year. Mielke had at his personal disposal the Stasi's hunting lodge near the Polish border, where 3,000 hectares were set aside for himself and his family. The grounds were stocked with game, some of it imported and, on Mielke's orders, the animals received the best nourishment money could buy. This reportedly included hundreds of tons of assorted fruits, rice, and turnips, 65 tons of soy beans and 10 tons of chestnuts. When these figures were revealed, 'East Germans grumbled aloud that some of these products were not readily available for human consumption in food stores'.[31]

30 Klemm, *Korruption*, pp. 72–3; Schabowski, *Absturz*, p. 33. These figures did not represent a major drain on the public finances, but relative to ordinary citizens' consumption they were astronomical.
31 Keithly, *Collapse*, p. 198.

A fourth string of revelations began to unfold from 2 December. Just a day after the Toeplitz commission presented its first report to parliament, activists near Rostock uncovered a cache of weapons. These, it emerged, belonged to a company that sold arms clandestinely to Third World governments and transferred the earnings to an organisation known as Commercial Coordination ('KoKo'), headed by a Central Committee member and minister in Modrow's government, Alexander Schalck-Golodkowski ('Schalck' for short). Although Modrow had pleaded successfully with the Toeplitz commission to keep Schalck from its line of fire, and had decreed that KoKo's files be kept secret, the furore that followed the apprehension of Schalck when he attempted to flee the country, with DM500,000 and stacks of East-Marks in his suitcase, left the premier no option but to allow public investigation into KoKo's affairs.[32] KoKo's arms exports, it emerged, had been motivated by profit yet had been dressed in ideological clothing, as support for national liberation movements.[33] It profited from deals with western and Japanese pharmaceutical firms in which unknowing citizens were offered as guinea pigs for medical experimentation. KoKo companies supervised the collection of blood from East German citizens, who donated on the assumption that its recipients were to be selected on humanitarian criteria of 'international solidarity', and sold it to West Germany in order to further its core aims of lessening the GDR's balance of payments deficit and providing an annual sum of DM6–8 million for senior functionaries' hard-currency consumption.

These insights into the insulation of state leaders and functionaries from the lives of ordinary people, their cavalier use of scarce hard currency, the extent to which the regime engaged in what it forbade the rest of society – making money in the West – and the depths to which it was prepared to sink in pursuit of this end, all focused popular attention on the GDR's hard-currency revenues and on questions of the justice (or otherwise) of distribution. Workers had long demanded of managers and officials: 'Why is so much of what we need for ourselves being exported to capitalist countries?' to which the stock response had been: 'Because we urgently require hard currency in order to successfully implement our economic strategy.'[34] These earnest assurances now appeared faintly ridiculous, not to say disingenuous, in the light of the news that Schalck and his deputies had been taking a hefty cut for themselves and their friends in Wandlitz, and of the rumours that they had spirited hundreds of millions of Deutschmarks out

32 Koch, *Schalck-Imperium*, p. 90; Klemm, *Korruption*, p. 40.
33 Przybylski, *Tatort 1*, p. 133.
34 Eckelmann, *FDGB*.

of the country into Swiss bank accounts and networks of conspiratorial cover firms. It is telling that, of all the exposés, it was those concerning the activities of Schalck and KoKo that were given particular exposure on noticeboards in East Germany's workplaces.

In their attempts to rebut charges of corruption and avarice, SED leaders only deepened the hole they were in. When the issue of *nomenklatura* privileges had first arisen in October, Schalck appeared on television to defend his class, but was unconvincing – 'bumbling', viewers said. For his part, Krenz attempted to present a 'regular guy' image by declaring that 'I had no hunting estate, neither then nor now. Nor did I have a hunting lodge or a hunting house', but the feebleness of this pitch for popular sympathy earned only ridicule. If Krenz's efforts brought smiles, Schabowski's were met with hilarity. On one occasion he tried to explain to foreign reporters that, although a top functionary, he was also an ordinary bloke. Like many GDR citizens, he told his audience, he would come home from work, relax in his easy chair, turn on the television and open a can of beer. These remarks, according to Raymond Stokes,

> may or may not have had the intended impact on foreign audiences. But they certainly had the effect domestically of further undermining the credibility of the GDR regime. For everybody knew that beer was not generally available in cans in the GDR, but only in bottles. The ability to purchase beer in cans meant privileged access to foreign currency and to the special shops in which to spend it.[35]

The raftloads of revelations cut in two directions, at once deepening the alienation of the public at large from the regime and further undermining the moral self-assurance of its members and supporters. They fuelled a resurgence of protest. In the first weeks of December, in every town where public protests occurred with only two major exceptions (Berlin and Leipzig), attendance either equalled or surpassed those of previous months. On the streets, the issue of wealth distribution came to the fore. Although economic issues, including the failure of the regime to provide hard currency for travel purposes, had been thematised before, these were now plugged into the ascendant frame of social justice, and gained an added charge in the process. Chants and banners now targeted the privileges of functionaries and called for resource distribution:

- 'We make the money that you spend!'
- 'You in the Central Committee have preached water and drunk wine – now pay the bill!'

35 *Neues Deutschland*, 1 December 1989; Stokes, *Constructing*, p. 160.

- 'No to functionaries' privileges!'
- 'The "people's servants" should drive the people's cars!'
- 'The isle of Vilm for the people!'
- 'The bosses lived like on *Dallas*, in luxury – what they had should go to the elderly!'[36]

The change in mood was unmistakable. Demands for reforms were rivalled by calls for a clean sweep – that *all* bosses and functionaries, and not just those guilty of corruption, should have their privileges removed, and that the savings made be put to good use. In early November, Krenz noted in his diary:

> For a while, [media reports] have been hitting the Party and state leaderships on a sensitive spot: corruption and the abuse of power. These revelations are falling on fertile soil amongst GDR citizens, including SED members. They suggest: the rulers are preaching water but drinking wine. Not only leading functionaries are under suspicion. The rage at the grassroots is also directed at functionaries in workplaces, localities and districts. *Distinctions between parasites and the many functionaries who engage themselves for the GDR without privileges are no longer made.* All are thrown in the same pot.

At the end of the month he was more exasperated still: 'No political lull has set in over recent days either. News items about corruption and the abuse of power are decimating the remaining trust that we possess. Many more comrades are resigning from the Party.'[37] The question was no longer whether the bad apples could be removed but what was to be done with the rotten barrel. The demand for complete, systemic change was in the air; slogans expressing this mood, such as 'socialism – never again!', grew louder.

Privilege as a social relation

The last week of November and first of December marked a major climax of the revolution, and it is puzzling that so many accounts skip over it.[38] In Charles Maier's otherwise comprehensive treatise, for example, the episode is telescoped into a few terse lines that present the exposés as drawing attention to a few 'taints':

> During the winter, anger surged at the representatives of the old order, symbolized above all by the Stasi and the nomenklatura's suburb of official

36 'Bonzen lebten wie in Denver und Dallas – gebt den Rentnern nun alles!'
37 Krenz, *Herbst*, pp. 221, 331, emphasis added.
38 An exception to the rule is Jarausch, *Rush*, p. 81.

residences at Wandlitz. By most standards the privileges were modest: well-stocked food stores, well-tended lawns, a comfortable enclave of houses – but hardly great luxury. Corruption there certainly was in the system – pervasive even. Later it would be charged, for example, that officials got health care [at a special hospital] while elsewhere modern medicine was scarce and rationed. The party was not to overcome these taints, and bitterness would grow.[39]

What is misleading about this précis is not so much its assessment of the degree of luxury enjoyed by the residents of Wandlitz and their colleagues – although, as even the few examples presented in this chapter indicate, it does understate its scale, especially in respect of the sensitive question of access to western imports. Rather, it is its disregard for the relational nature of privilege and corruption and the moral and political interpretations thereof. Anger was directed not at the comfortable lifestyles *in themselves* but, as one analyst has put it, at the fact that 'the bosses have enriched themselves *at the cost of the general public*'.[40] The vehemence which the revelations elicited spoke of offended values of distributive justice and of the disparity between the regime's avowed commitment to egalitarian ideals and the evidence of systematic flouting of those values. As a Berlin shop steward related to Dirk Philipsen, although the simple desire for higher living standards played a part in the late autumn uprising, this

> was not the key issue. You see, we also had people in the GDR who had everything. In fact, as we later found out, some of the party hacks had far higher living standards than anything we had ever suspected . . . There was an incredible degree of injustice everywhere.

It was not that *nomenklatura* members' refusal to live by their ostensible creed was a discovery. In pre-1989 'hidden transcripts', cynicism regarding the integrity of powerholders, not to mention their personal commitment to their own regime's values was ubiquitous. East Germans were aware of the resemblance between their country and Orwell's *Animal Farm*. What changed at the end of 1989 was that the transcripts were no longer hidden, nor reliant upon limited, anecdotal sources. Now the evidence was there for all to see, and it exceeded the worst suspicions. Even cynics were shocked to learn of the scale of corruption and privilege and realised that, far from being exaggerated, previous allegations had in fact been comparatively tame. And all this, let us not forget, took place within a few weeks, concentrated in the first week of December. One could almost hear a sharp intake of breath across the land.

39 Maier, *Dissolution*, p. 164.
40 Hall, *Fernseh-Kritik*, p. 114, emphasis added.

To East Germans it appeared that their leaders had not only shown ineptness in the management of the economy, brutality in the repression of dissent and unfairness in the distribution of resources, but had been thoroughly hypocritical to boot. Regime supporters felt betrayed. They had devoted their energies to defending a system that, it now appeared, had been channelling wealth to a corrupt clique. Some had collected donations for charities to alleviate suffering in the Third World only for the funds to be secretly diverted to the FDJ. Revelations of this sort severely dented the regime's legitimacy, based as it had been on the claim that its 'socialism' was ethically superior to the alternatives. As to those who did not support the regime, many had long held that they had been badly led and exploited. The scandals amplified these sentiments, and compounded citizens' sense that they had been systematically lied to. *Dignity* was at issue here: people felt *insulted* by their rulers' behaviour.

The analysis here is not unlike that of Francis Fukuyama, in *The End of History and the Last Man*. For Fukuyama, the ferocity of emotions displayed in the December days is best understood with reference to *thymos*, Plato's term for a well-spring of human motivation that complements reason and desire and which can be translated as 'spiritedness' (albeit with strong connotations of 'self-esteem'). 'What swept the Socialist Unity Party out of power completely and discredited its new leaders Krenz and Modrow', he writes, were the exposés of the opulence of life at Wandlitz. Is there not something odd about this, he asks. For,

> strictly speaking, the enormous anger that these revelations provoked was somewhat irrational. There were many causes for complaint against communist East Germany, above all relating to the country's lack of political freedom and its low standard of living when compared to West Germany. Honecker for his part did not live in a modern version of the Palace of Versailles: his home was that of a well-to-do burgher in Hamburg or Bremen. But the well-known and long-standing charges against communism in East Germany did not raise nearly the degree of thymotic anger on the part of average East Germans as viewing the Honecker residence on their television screens.[41]

This 'thymotic anger' was fuelled by the perception, discussed above, that the public had been systematically deceived and mistreated by their leaders and by their subordinates in positions of company management and the state apparatus; that these had profited from the exercise of power and enjoyed the material fruits thereof and yet had, all the while, arrantly professed a belief in the justice of their cause. 'The tremendous

41 Fukuyama, *History*, pp. 178–9.

hypocrisy those images revealed, on the part of a regime that was explicitly devoted to equality', Fukuyama concludes, 'deeply offended people's sense of justice and was sufficient to get them into the streets to demand a total end to the Communist party's power'.

A final aspect of the December anger, which Fukuyama discusses only in the abstract, is that the issue of distributive justice was entwined with that of *democracy*. The amassing of wealth in the hands of a few was not simply a matter of inequity but entailed an implicit and practical rejection of *community* and, consequently, prevented state leaders from attending to, let alone representing, the interests of ordinary citizens. This notion – that class division imposes a limit upon, or even contradicts, democracy – is a well-worn theme in the canons of radical political theory, but rather than citing Rousseau, Marx or Jefferson, for present purposes the point is better illustrated by the words of an East Berlin shop steward, interviewed by Dirk Philipsen. When asked for his views on *nomenklatura* privileges, his response begins, predictably enough, with a condemnation of the 'quite unbelievable' degree of distributive injustice. But he then moves at once to the implications for political representation: 'Some people had everything *and hence did not give a damn about what common folks at the bottom of society had.*'[42] One cannot say for certain whether his views were shared by the mass of the population, but it is plausible that they were. Numerous Stasi documents on working-class opinion, both before and during the revolution, report that the privileged elite were widely viewed as living comfortably, aloof from the masses, and that they had 'lost sight of the needs of ordinary citizens'. To these people, the notion that material inequality is an impediment to democracy made eminent sense.

From this discussion of the scandals of the late autumn and the popular response, I would draw attention to three key points. One is that the revelations simultaneously weakened the morale of the SED and its supporters and strengthened the view that the regime was thoroughly bankrupt and should be swept from power altogether. They served to shift the popular agenda towards demands for thoroughgoing regime change. Just as Imelda Marcos' shoe collection doomed her husband, the hunting lodges were the nails in the coffin of the SED, observed a US historian residing in Berlin at the time.[43] Second, the 'distorted communication between state and society', of which New Forum spoke with such urgency and eloquence, was not simply the mark of a dictatorship but was also – and on this point New Forum was largely silent – a product

42 Philipsen, *People*, p. 125, emphasis added.
43 Darnton, *Berlin*, p. 94.

of the chasm in material privilege between rulers and ruled, and was viewed by many citizens in just these terms. Related to this, third, the December rage testified to a radicalism that focused on issues of material justice and demands for the redistribution of wealth and power. It may be described as a social democratic consciousness, in the nineteenth-century sense of the term. If the East German revolution is approached with the preconception that it was simply liberal and nationalist, in contrast to revolutions with radical and social agendas, this aspect will be (and indeed often is) overlooked.

Workers and prisoners

The protest movement shifted gear in December, in a way that is familiar to students of revolution: periods when old regimes suffer a rapid withdrawal of support and when protest activity spreads to previously 'unmobilised' sectors tend also to be characterised by the emergence of radical currents of opinion and the diversification of sites and techniques of contention. On the streets, issues of distributive justice came to the fore, and in workplaces, discussion moved beyond general political themes to concrete demands and possible action. In late November and early December a major wave of industrial action occurred, involving tens of thousands of workers in over a hundred workplaces. The motivating issues were various, but in most cases were connected to political events on the national and international stages. One source of inspiration was a two-hour general strike in neighbouring Czechoslovakia. A widespread demand was that old-regime institutions be driven from the workplace. Strike threats in factories from Frankfurt an der Oder to Karl-Marx-Stadt and all points in between won concessions on issues that included the abolition of factory battalions and the closure of the SED's workplace offices as well as those concerning enterprise management, such as the sacking of unpopular managers or the establishment of workers' codetermination. In the Hennigsdorf steelworks a demonstration was even called to force the closure of the FDJ office.[44]

An additional spur came from the corruption scandals. Although these focused on senior functionaries, their appointees in factories and offices for the most part remained at their posts, and the investigations underway at the national level encouraged employees to follow suit in their workplaces. At Carl Zeiss Jena, workers threatened to strike unless its influential general director, Wolfgang Biermann, stood down which, on December 8, he did. At Bergmann-Borsig in Berlin, a workplace council

44 *Der Spiegel*, 11 December 1989, p. 28.

was elected, and charged with investigating management corruption and the abuse of office. Hundreds of workers from the same firm marched on parliament to demand that Schalck be dismissed. 'With each new revelation of corruption', recorded *Der Spiegel*, 'the workers' bitterness grows'; indeed, there is little doubt that the scandals incensed the working classes in particular – with consequences for the protests. As Jens Reich describes,

> The rage over the relative luxury and corruption of the *nomenklatura* was one of the strongest motives behind the uprising at the beginning of December which led to the overthrow of Krenz. According to my observations it was much broader, 'closer to the people' and much more energetic and ready for action than were the peaceful demonstrations of September and October.[45]

This same period also saw strikes and hunger strikes in prisons, including those in Berlin, Magdeburg, Brandenburg, Halle and Zeithain. The GDR's *per capita* prison population was among the highest in the world. Because their labour contributed over ten *billion* Marks each year to state coffers, prisoners possessed not only the power of disruption within their institutions but could affect the national economy, too.[46] At the epicentre of the movement was the infamous prison at Bautzen, which had attracted considerable publicity in preceding weeks over reported abuse of political prisoners held there, notably those arrested at the battle of Dresden Station. The reports elicited a flood of petitions and protest letters from individuals and workplace 'collectives' to prison and state authorities. Even family members of prison officers added their voices, and an investigation into abuses was duly announced.

Within prison walls, the political opportunity structure was undergoing a similar transformation to that of the state and workplaces: incumbents in positions of power suffered a weakening of morale, a loss of strategic perspective and an erosion of support. In mid-November, to cite one well-publicised case of what was a widespread phenomenon, the government department with responsibility for prisons expressed concern that the enormous 'psychological pressure' upon Party members among prison staff at Bautzen had resulted in such intense insecurity and discontent that mutiny was a real danger. Among the prison population, critics could see the possibility of replicating the transformation of national politics within their institutions. It takes little imag-

45 Klenke, *Rationalisierung*; *Der Spiegel*, 11 December 1989, p. 104; Reich, *Abschied*, p. 17.
46 Bahrmann and Links, *Chronik 1*, p. 169.

ination to see that news of the breaching of the Berlin Wall or indeed of the core demands of the protest movement – the freedom to travel, democracy and justice – could gain a peculiar charge within the walls of prisons, these manifestly undemocratic institutions the purpose of which is the dispensation of 'justice' through the denial of the freedom of movement.

Democracy and justice were indeed the terms in which inmates' demands were framed when the strikes began on the first day of December. Most centred on calls for improved conditions, the establishment of accountability and democracy – that inmates be given opportunities to influence decisions affecting the prison regime – as well as a general amnesty. The latter is a common feature of prisoners' movements; in East Germany it gained added weight from the fact that the system under which guilty verdicts had been passed had been presided over by what many considered to be a 'bunch of crooks', some of whom were themselves under arrest and facing charges far graver than ordinary prisoners had known. In some cases the accusations against senior functionaries connected very directly to prisoners' own experiences. Inmates at Bautzen, for example, had been forced to build holiday homes for functionaries, and many had suffered at the hands of prison officers who were now being publicly criticised by the Toeplitz commission. Some prisoners, notably the politicals but also many of those accused of property crime, rightly perceived themselves to be victims of systematic and politically directed injustice, but their criminal neighbours also possessed strong arguments in favour of amnesty. One of them insisted that the call for a general amnesty was not issued with the aim of trivialising their crimes; nonetheless, 'in comparison with the crimes of the Party and state leaderships against the entire people that are now being exposed', those still in prison see themselves as 'small-fry'; they are asking, rhetorically, 'Who are the real crooks?'[47]

The prison strikes were for the most part well supported and successful. On 1 December, almost 2,000 inmates at Bautzen began a hunger strike, while the few who eschewed this form of action showed solidarity by refusing labour duties. A strike committee of some thirty inmates was formed, and issued a list of demands, including an immediate general amnesty (with the exception of Nazis and war criminals), reform of the criminal code and improvements to the prison regime. The government, fearing that another front was about to be opened, quickly showed willing to compromise, and declared an amnesty for 15,000 prisoners. The Bautzen strikers, suspicious of the government and confident of the

47 *Ibid.*, p. 165.

efficacy of protest, refused to accept the government's promise until it was televised, a demand that was promptly granted.[48]

Citizens' committees

If workplaces and prisons represented two new sites of contention that emerged during the movement upswing of late autumn, Stasi premises formed a third. Only now was the Stasi's monstrous size being revealed, and in early December it came sharply into the sights of protestors. Dozens of demonstrations and strikes demanded its dissolution, or sought to prevent company managers from hiring former Stasi officers. The issue was commonly linked to that of resource distribution – exemplified in the banner that read: 'Stasi, you get the resources that should go on us nurses!' Other typical slogans of the time included:

- 'Work down the pits, Stasi gits!'
- 'Lock the Stasies in their prisons!'
- 'Put the Stasies to work in the factories; only then should they get their salaries'.[49]

In view of the impending danger that its offices would be stormed, the Stasi accelerated file destruction from 29 November. Such was the intensity of this programme that a shredder shortage ensued, and agents had to cross over to West Berlin to purchase additional machines. At one site alone within the gigantic Stasi headquarters in Berlin, members of the civic groups were later to find over 100 burnt-out shredders. Little by little, news of these activities emerged. One Stasi officer admitted that 'huge amounts of [material] are being incinerated'. For Justus Werdin, and others living close to Stasi buildings in Frankfurt an der Oder, this seemed only too plausible. On the evening of 4 December 'my wife, Inken, and I were looking out towards the Stasi building', he recalls, and saw 'thick clouds of smoke billowing from its chimney'. The Werdins proceeded to inform acquaintances; people then gathered together to demand entrance into the Stasi building – with success.[50]

Elsewhere, similar events were unfolding on the very same day. In Suhl, a New Forum meeting was informed that files were being destroyed. In

---

48 For prisoners elsewhere, a partial amnesty was not enough. They continued to strike in support of total amnesty. See Israel, *Freiheit*, pp. 264–6.
49 'Stasi in die Produktion – Nur für Arbeit gibt es Lohn!'
50 Süß, 'Bilanz', p. 602; Richter, *Staatssicherheit*, pp. 36, 61; Funder, *Stasiland*, p. 67; *die tageszeitung* Journal 1, p. 162; Werdin, *Unter*, p. 9.

defiance of New Forum organisers' appeals for calm, a majority of the 4,000-strong meeting marched – accompanied by shouts of 'arrest them all!' – upon Suhl's Stasi headquarters, where they overcame resistance (including tear gas), and forced entry. Later, in order to prevent Stasi employees absconding with files, municipal bus drivers blocked the entrances with their vehicles. In nearby Erfurt, also on 4 December, a member of 'Women for Change' noticed containers being loaded and driven away from the local Stasi headquarters, and smoke rising from its chimneys. She urged acquaintances to action and before long several dozen people were blocking the road; all lorries were prevented entry or exit; cars were allowed through only after being searched. A delegation of blockaders was permitted entry to the Stasi building to put their demands – access to every room, and to the computer. Negotiations on these appeared to be stalling, when someone entered the room to report that a crowd several hundred strong was storming the building, having brushed its way past three or four officers with machine guns. One contingent made straight for the furnace to pull documents out of the fire, before seizing machine guns and pistols and locking the Stasi guards in a cupboard. Others fanned around the town to build support for the occupation, asking bus drivers to announce it over their tannoys and inviting shoppers to lend support. One group approached a construction site and appealed to workers there: 'Come on, drop your hammers! You're needed. Remember 1953!'[51] A 'citizens' guard' was organised to seal the building and ensure that files remained in place. Over subsequent days and weeks, the 'citizens' guard' and 'citizens' committee' gained further support, not least from members of political parties (except the SED). All told, some 3,000 participated in the Erfurt occupation.

The news from Erfurt, Suhl and Frankfurt spread, and encouraged similar activities elsewhere. Stasi premises in over two dozen towns were occupied. In some places underground bunkers were discovered and searched. Activists in Berlin, upon hearing that files had been transported from Friedrichshain town hall, successfully demanded its archives be sealed. Dresden oppositionists, after hearing rumours of file destruction, appealed on local radio for citizens to demonstrate at the local Stasi headquarters. Around 5,000 were able to gain entry and, in a dramatic reversal in power relations, they interrogated Stasi employees within.[52] All officers were ordered to leave, and control of the building was assumed by police and oppositionists, while others went on to occupy a

51 Dietrich and Jander, 'Revolution', pp. 330, 319; Mosler, 'Klassenkämpfe', p. 16; Dornheim, *Politischer*, pp. 72–6.
52 Richter and Sobeslavsky, *Gruppe*, p. 181.

Stasi-run radio station. In the case of Dresden, the Stasi had already determined that the doors would be opened – after all, the most critical files, particularly those implicating officers, had already been destroyed. Nonetheless, one chronicler of the event concludes, 'the "occupation" of the Stasi building was an important symbol of the assertion of popular control over a major instrument of power'.[53]

From out of these occupations, and spurred by the breaking news of Schalck's attempted flight, citizens' committees mushroomed across the land, upping the pressure on the government to dismantle the Stasi. Practically, their task was to monitor Stasi activities and prevent further file destruction. As organs not merely of protest but of control, they marked a milestone for the movement – and, one standard work on the Stasi remarks, 'citizens occupying a still-intact secret service in order to oversee its work is historically unprecedented'. And they hinted at the real power the movement could exert if it chose to. For example, when the Dresden Stasi chief reneged on his promise to stop officers spying on New Forum, the citizens' committee placed him under house arrest.[54]

Yet these hints of the movement's ability to take charge remained only hints. To see why the anti-Stasi rising was contained, consider, first, the perspective of Stasi officers. Their organisation was rudderless, its leadership could do little more than react to events. They were confronted by the seething hatred of a mobilised population. Their strength had always depended upon a weak and fearful citizenry; now, as fears were dispelled, their power was evaporating. The only apparent choice – armed resistance to the uprising or an orderly retreat – was not really one at all. Armed resistance would involve internal division, mutiny and resounding defeat; it would set back the cause of reform (which many officers had come to see as inevitable), and had negligible support. Orderly retreat spelt defeat, but with minimal losses; it would allow precious time in which to wipe away traces of malfeasance, secure resources and attempt to establish a good footing from which to step securely into whatever new society awaited. In this context, it is not difficult to imagine the thought processes of Stasi officers in Leipzig when a delegation from New Forum and DA came to the door. It was 4 December, and news of file burning and forcible occupations was trickling out. 'You've doubtless heard of Erfurt', the oppositionists began, 'and if you would rather not have 100,000 do it, we can do it in a manner that you may prefer'. The Leipzig officers grabbed the opportunity, and even provided

53 Dyke, *Dresden*, p 233.
54 Gill and Schröter, *Ministerium*, p. 184; Weber, *Alltag*, p. 49.

megaphones to the oppositionists in order that they could ward off the crowds when they arrived.[55]

On the national scale, the Stasi pushed this tactic as far as it would go. Guntolf Herzberg has described it well: 'At this critical conjuncture the Stasi had a remarkably astute thought: it contacted its former enemy – the civic movement – and pushed for a security partnership.'[56] Although, during the furore that followed the apprehension of Schalck, civic groups had helped to instigate the occupations, with calls for citizens to form committees to prevent malpractice by functionaries and the Stasi, and although their leaders (notably Jochen Lässig and Konrad Weiß) gave vocal support to the occupations, when the oppositionists placed their faith in 'security partnerships' with the police, the committees turned rapidly from organs of popular control over, into 'security partnerships' with, the Stasi. Now, when citizens broke into Stasi buildings, they commonly found them already in the hands of the police or interior ministry forces, with oppositionists' assent. The process of dissolving the Stasi remained in the hands of the security services, including the Stasi itself.

After the initial successes of the occupations the same refrain was heard from countless committees: their activities were being blocked. The government gave verbal support to the committees and ruled that their members should be given paid leave by employers, but behind the scenes file destruction continued, in some cases on Modrow's direct orders.[57] The committees aimed at politely requesting control over the Stasi's effects but were generally denied it. They were refused entry into many Stasi properties, and – thanks in part to infiltration by informal agents – were tricked into thinking that they were in control even as business went ahead as usual. And although the police were supposedly in 'partnership' with the committees, they protected Stasi properties less from file-burning officers than from protestors. Occasionally police did intervene on the side of the committees, but much more frequently they collaborated with the Stasi – as they had been doing officially and efficiently for decades.

When confronted by mass action, Stasi officers had been forced to relinquish keys and secrets, but when politely asked by committees of concerned citizens their attitude was, at best, prevarication. Thanks to their moderation and gullibility the Stasi was, in the words of one disappointed committee member and clergyman, never 'properly

55 Knauer, 'Opposition'; Timmer, *Aufbruch*, pp. 329–30.
56 Herzberg, 'Zusammenbruch', p. 13.
57 Werdin, *Unter*, p. 25; Worst, *Geheimdienstes*.

dissolved'.[58] With hindsight, he argues, the committees should have immediately locked out all Stasi employees. In so far as they tapped the immense popular antipathy towards the Stasi and channelled it into occupying Stasi premises, the committees were powerful, and posed a real threat to the regime. To the extent that they accepted 'partnership' with the security forces, they were harmless.

58 Königsdorf, *Adieu*, p. 111.

8

'Power lies on the streets': December rebellion and the Great anti-chaos coalition

Fists/clutching candles/for the overthrow!
Careful/that no wax/drips onto the cobblestones
None of them should fall. (Reiner Kunze)[1]

The workplace-based protest and occupations of Stasi buildings in early December posed a direct challenge to the power of the *nomenklatura* and signalled the potential for a further upswing in the protest cycle. The term 'protest cycle' refers to a series of phases commonly observed in mass social-movements. They commence when 'early risers' make claims that resonate with others. During upswings, wider numbers are mobilised and protest branches out, geographically and sociologically. At the peak, one usually sees a proliferation of forms of collective action, as well as bargaining between social-movement organisations and the authorities, and it is to these groups that initiative shifts as the cycle then winds down.[2] The notion of a cycle, while identifying a frequently observed series of phases, does not imply an automatic progression from one to the next, let alone predictability in the timing. Here, the strategies of the authorities and of movement organisations are crucial.

In early December, the East German movement faced in contradictory directions. On the one hand, it appeared to be moving towards confrontation with the regime, involving a deepening and widening of protest. It also foreshadowed more direct forms of interest articulation, in the form of citizens' committees and workplace councils.[3] On the

1 Owen, 'Wenn', p. 153.
2 Tarrow, *Power*, p. 168.
3 These began to address a problem that the playwright Volker Braun identified at the time: 'The will of the streets . . . is diffuse, dark and fickle, and it has no representative organ in which conflicts of interest can be argued out amongst the workforce and in the neighbourhoods, and then conveyed upwards.' Braun, 'Kommt', p. 19.

other, tendencies towards demobilisation and institutionalisation were strengthening. Whether the cycle would ratchet upwards again or begin its descent was far from clear.

Civic groups at the crossroads

'Modrow's shakiest moment', Jens Reich accurately observes, 'was at the beginning of December, when the SED collapsed and the people's anger at the revelations of privileges grew'.[4] Despite major restructuring, including even the abandonment, on 1 December, of its claim to a monopoly of power, the SED's popularity among the public was at rock bottom, and the mood internally was even worse.[5] The Party, complained Modrow, had 'fallen into a coma', while the Politburo was behaving 'like a goldfish tossed from its bowl into a stormy ocean'. Former leaders Willi Stoph and Horst Sindermann were expelled from the SED, Tisch, Mielke and Mittag were arrested, and juridical proceedings commenced against Honecker, yet Krenz, too, faced mounting pressure to resign, including from functionaries as senior as Modrow. On 2 December, he faced the ignominy of booing and chants of 'resign!' at a demonstration of Party members. On the next day he drew the conclusions and resigned. The Central Committee and Politburo dissolved themselves; in so doing they referred explicitly to the uproar within the SED at the findings of the Toeplitz commission.[6] For almost a week, the Party was headless.

The apparatuses of state were in no better condition. Singling out the border to West Germany and the condition of sections of the army, a senior Stasi officer cautioned that national security was 'in certain areas limited, or no longer guaranteed'. The 400,000-strong factory battalions were dissolved in early December. The Stasi was in turmoil: some sections demanded the 'cleansing' of the SED at all levels; district offices, including Leipzig and Plauen, submitted hard-hitting criticisms against the national leadership; 500 members of the elite 'Dzierzynski' regiment blockaded the national headquarters to prevent the removal of files, and there were similar demonstrations at provincial premises. The Stasi leadership resigned on 4 December, but protests by local sections continued. In the same week, Deputy Soviet ambassador Maximytschew noted with consternation

---

4 Reich, 'Revolution', pp. 356.
5 According to Maximytschew, 'Mauerfall', p. 32.
6 Modrow, *Deutschland*, pp. 357, 379; Bahrmann and Links, *Chronik 1*, p. 159.

that: 'The government is still weak, it has no levers of power at its command.'[7]

As governmental authority declined, questions of strategy came into sharper focus for the civic groups. Although their popularity curve had begun to decline, they remained influential. Opinion polls suggested that, were an election to be held, they would reap a third of votes, and that New Forum was the country's most popular political organisation. On the streets, chants of 'Power to New Forum!' had gained widespread popularity – including among supporters of German unification. One of these, a Leipzig worker, Manfred Bär, addressed a rally in November at which he called for free elections and for a New Forum or SDP vote, 'so we can truly win democracy and freedom!' And while these two organisations possessed the greatest name recognition, other civic groups were gaining in stature too. Democracy Now, for example, launched a petition calling for an end to the SED's monopoly of power which gathered over 175,000 signatures.[8]

In their demand that the SED relax its grip on power, the civic groups spoke with one voice, but when and how this could be achieved was less clear. Prominent New Forum members, notably Jochen Lässig, advocated the immediate convocation of a constitutional assembly, pending free elections. Yet, to realise that purpose would require a commitment to consolidating the processes of radicalisation on the streets and mobilisation in the workplaces. New Forum was inundated with letters calling for it to take decisive political initiative. Even a declaration of intent would galvanise support – for the very 'consciousness that power is at stake' functions as a mobilising force in a revolutionary situation.[9]

On 1 December, the choice facing the civic groups was illuminated in stark relief. With Modrow's offer of negotiations still on the table, Karl-Marx-Stadt New Forum proposed a two-hour general strike for later that week. The idea was inspired by the recent strike in Czechoslovakia, and was winged by workers' frustrations at the slow pace of reform. The strike demands were for drastic reductions in the SED and Stasi apparatuses and the separation of Party and state, for the (gradual) introduction of a social market economy, for the property of political parties to

7　Hertle and Stephan, *Ende*, p. 98; Knauer, 'Opposition', p. 723; *die tageszeitung*, 9 December 1994, p. 12; Maximytschew, 'Mauerfall', p. 33.
8　Wielgohs and Johnson, Entstehungsgründe', p. 352; Bahrmann and Links, *Chronik 1*, p. 120; Fehr, *Unabhängige*, pp. 251; Timmer, Aufbruch, p. 295.
9　Timmer, *Aufbruch*, p. 360; Hartung, *Neunzehnhundertneunundachtzig*, p. 58.

be returned to the people and for the prosecution of functionaries suspected of corruption and misuse of power.[10]

The strike call did not receive unanimous support within the civic groups. 'We were opposed', one Karl-Marx-Stadt VL activist told me, 'in part because we believed – wrongly, it now appears – that the strike call had not come from workers, but also because we thought it would lead to German unification'. However, she adds, 'we knew that New Forum would be able to pull it off anyway – they had the numbers behind them'.[11] Certainly, the appeal gained a widespread resonance. On the next day, a demonstration in nearby Plauen showed clear support, prompting the local New Forum group to throw its weight behind it.[12]

It was not only in the South that this issue was a live one. 'In November, the political situation and the mood became much more tense and feverish', Klaus Wolfram recalls;

> In many large factories there was a genuine readiness for strike action – the workers wanted to get involved but weren't quite sure what the demands should be. One of [our members], a worker in [a large factory in Berlin], regularly reported that his colleagues were extremely curious and would repeatedly say: 'OK, what's going on?: if we're going to strike, then tell us what for, and we'll do it!'

When asked if that was not an exceptional scenario, Wolfram replied: 'No, we didn't have that impression. I would say that the question was not *whether* such a situation existed in many workplaces, there was not the slightest doubt about that. Rather, for us [the New Forum leadership] the question was whether and for what demands strikes were appropriate.'

Against this background, word of the Karl-Marx-Stadt appeal

> spread like wildfire through the land; everyone was talking about it, there was a widespread readiness to strike, and strikes already began to break out in many places. And we were initially surprised – for who on earth was doing it? These were people that we [New Forum leaders] scarcely knew.

10 Reum and Geißler, *Auferstanden*, p. 114. For details, see Gehrke, ' "Wende" Streiks', pp. 256–60.
11 Interview, Gabi Engelhardt.
12 For Plauen New Forum, the strike demands included, in addition to those mentioned above, the opening of SED finances to public scrutiny, and uncensored media access for non-state organisations. See Küttler and Röder, *Volk*, p. 68. Many strikers, however, saw its main demand as a referendum on German unification. Certainly, this was central for workers at one of the larger factories involved (MLK), who delegated their union (BGL) chair to write to parliament threatening strike action unless a referendum on the issue was granted.

On 3 December, New Forum leaders, then in emergency session, heard word of a further strike call. 'Representatives from all parts of the country were at the meeting', Wolfram reports,

> and then Jochen Tschiche arrived from Magdeburg and said: the town square was overflowing, 100,000 people wanted him to tell them what should now happen in the GDR, and the workers from SKET – a heavy engineering factory of 12,000 workers, an enormous thing – had told him that they were determined to take strike action, on the 8th, or at the latest the 15th, and that he should suggest the demands. So Tschiche came to the meeting and asked: 'So what should I tell them, what demands should be proposed?' And that was the Magdeburg strike scenario: it fitted the psychological situation exactly; everyone knew at once that the story was true – Tschiche wasn't exaggerating.

For Modrow, this was, in his words, a 'very worrying' scenario but, one would imagine, a happy one for New Forum.[13] A mobilised public had taken the streets but not the institutions. The latter had begun to occur with the occupations of Stasi premises and now, it appeared, the regime could be toppled, *tout à fait*. That was the significance of the strike issue: it would galvanise, mobilising wider layers and testing the movement's capacity to dictate terms to government. A widespread readiness for industrial action was reported by activists – in Saxony it was 'overwhelming'.[14] Following the Napoleonic maxim '*on s'engage, puis on voit*', the call to action would reveal the extent of support. As Wolfram has argued:

> That would have been the opportunity to force the government to resign, by saying: we oppositionists want to form a government and if not, we'll call upon the country to strike. And that could have begun in Magdeburg – that particular offer [from SKET] could have played a decisive role. And the political situation was such that – I don't think this can possibly be denied – Modrow's government would have been forced to yield, and would have been prepared to do so. Shots wouldn't have been fired. The readiness to strike of the largest factories (in Berlin similar enquiries had been coming in since October) would have left the government no choice.

It was a moment of 'alternativity', a potential turning point. The issue was not German unification but state power. Frank Renken has put this succinctly: 'The German Question that the Wall's fall had thrown up hid the real heart of the matter. New Forum found itself at a crossroads:

---

13 Modrow, *Deutschland*, p. 381.
14 According to Jens Reich, in Joppke, *Dissidents*, p. 163. More recently, Reich has changed his mind. See Reich, 'Ich habe'.

Would it help the mass movement to power or would it act as bailiff for the old regime?'[15]

'Let's carry on talking'

With the government in disarray, Stasi premises under occupation and general strike a real possibility, the question of power was immediate. By this point, one SDP leader told me, 'we knew that the SED had effectively lost power'. Similarly, Wolfgang Berghofer remarked that 'Power lies on the streets'. But, he added, 'nobody is picking it up!'[16] In the opposition leadership 'many of my colleagues', Wolfram recounts (listing Reich, Eppelmann, Bohley and Reinhart Schult) 'were aware of the opportunities at an early stage, yet these did not appeal. "Yes yes, power lies on the streets", they would say, "And so? Well, let's carry on talking. We'll sound out the membership – for everything is decided at the grassroots".' When Karl-Marx-Stadt New Forum then issued its general strike call, they 'took fright, and the New Forum leadership met and we hurriedly denied the call and said "it won't happen!" and "we're all opposed" and "impossible!" and "what on earth are they up to?" and "why general strike?" That was the stance of most of those in leadership positions.'

Karl-Marx-Stadt New Forum's spokesperson was promptly suspended, and the national leadership condemned the strike proposal, and that from Magdeburg for good measure. In justifying their negative response, New Forum spokespeople argued that strike is a 'last resort' in political conflicts and should be exercised 'with great caution'. In the current situation, they said, 'political' (by which they meant 'institutional') means must be fully utilised, to wit, the impending round table talks; and their success required the rescinding of the strike call.[17] Moreover, a badly organised strike could fail, while a successful one might, 'in the current economic situation, bring about economic and political collapse, as well as the danger of an uncontrolled and accelerating strike dynamic'.[18] Similarly, an SDP spokesperson declared: 'We are opposed to a general strike, because it would drive our economy even further towards collapse.'[19]

15 Wolfram, interview; see also Wolfram, 'Machtfrage'; Reich, 'Revolution', p. 44; Renken, 'Oppositionsgruppen'.
16 Martin Gutzeit, interview; Müller-Mertens, *Politische*, p. 32.
17 The question could arise again, it was conceded, but 'only if the Round Table were to collapse'. Schulz, 'Neues', p. 28.
18 From New Forum leadership discussion papers, Robert Havemann Archiv. See also Schulz, 'Neues', p. 28.
19 Bahrmann and Links, *Chronik 1*, p. 175.

Members of Plauen New Forum were likewise pressured to steer against industrial action there – but they did not budge. The decision, they maintained, was democratic, and local demonstrations had repeatedly shown clear support for political strike action.[20] On 6 December, the Plauen strike went ahead, involving tens of thousands of workers in forty-four factories, as did industrial action involving upwards of 10,000 workers in Markneukirchen, Crimitschau, and elsewhere in Saxony and Thuringia.

If opposition leaders were loath to see the government toppled 'from below', they equally mistrusted offers to assist them to power 'from above'. On 4 December, West Berlin's SPD mayor, Walter Momper, proposed to New Forum leaders that they, together with their counterparts in DA and SDP, take steps towards assuming governmental power. Bohley and Schult, representing New Forum, 'politely rejected the suggestion', but in private their reaction verged on outrage: ' "well, what is all that about?", "what crazy idea is that?", and "he wants to persuade us to take power but we won't comply!"[21] In this instance, Wolfram explains, their indignation was entirely predictable. For,

> Momper was proposing a government with himself as father, so to speak, with Eppelmann – and he was already playing footsie with the CDU – and with a few other oppositionists, as mascots. And that really is a good reason to say 'no', because neither the founders of the SDP, who wanted to throttle the civic movement, nor Eppelmann with his close ties to Kohl and the CDU, were appropriate partners. And the whole thing would be proclaimed in West Berlin, in an antechamber of the Schöneberg city hall! I mean, what a cheek!

But 'what was correct', he adds, 'and in this Momper was not wrong, was that this was the moment when such things were possible, when the horizon was suddenly wide open'.

'The children must have their milk!'

If the argument in this chapter is correct, and the 'horizon was wide open', it would be as well to consider in greater detail what led opposition leaders to close down the new openings in favour of inter-elite negotiations. At a superficial level, one can point to their political rawness and the turbulent nature of the period. In the New Forum leadership the atmosphere was marked by considerable confusion, with the sense that

20 Küttler and Röder, *Volk*, p. 68.
21 Wolfram, interview, and 'Machtfrage', p. 3.

'events are piling up ever faster, the questions raised are ever larger, and we are no longer even sure of what we actually want'. Their lack of experience, combined with 'movementist' organisational forms, meant that the opposition lacked a stable platform from which to launch a bid to topple the SED. New Forum, in particular, was a very broad coalition, and members' views as to its purpose diverged sharply. Pastor Tschiche noted four distinct positions: 'Some say, take political office. Others would prefer us to remain some sort of extra-parliamentary opposition. Still others opt for a party structure. I believe we should follow the Solidarność model: a platform with a political arm.'[22]

Tschiche's reference to Solidarność notwithstanding, familiarity with labour-movement traditions was scarce in the opposition milieu, and had long been so. The trajectory of workplace-based resistance in East Germany had, from 1953, sloped downwards. From the early 1960s until late 1989 strikes had been rare; in the 1980s only a smattering occurred, and most of these were small in scale and defensive in nature. Therefore, lacking experience of workplace politics, opposition leaders were wary of industrial action, and their scepticism was heightened when the news media ran an extravagant anti-strike campaign in early December. The FDGB daily, *Tribüne*, transformed itself into an anti-strike propaganda organ, while other newspapers condemned what they dubbed 'adventurism' which is 'against everybody's interests', and appealed to 'all the forces of reason' to publicly condemn the strike call.[23]

'Because we ourselves had little to do with everyday economic life', Wolfram explains, 'they [the government and media] were able to scare us'. Opposition leaders were being told, in effect:

> 'so then, if economic organisation falls apart, then it's your lot's job to make sure that the potatoes and bread arrive at the supermarkets on time!' The government repeatedly warned: 'Milk distribution will collapse, the children will get no milk because the farmers no longer deliver it, the truck drivers are no longer working', and the like. And we would think: 'Doh! We can't manage all that! *You* must do it, you from the Party!' That's the line of argument they were taking.

This had indeed been anticipated back in November, when industrial action affected a dairy business.[24] Upon New Forum's higher councils the experience

22 Wolfram, interview; Timmer, *Aufbruch*, p. 309.
23 Renken, 'Oppositionsgruppen'.
24 Cf. Arnold, *Modrow*, p. 102.

made a resounding impression. Although the strike lasted only four hours, all these TV teams arrived here and implied that 'now there'll be no milk for Berlin's children, chaos is breaking out'. So everyone felt 'God, this poor country; if a general strike breaks out too, what will become of us? The economy is ruined anyway, and it'd decline even further!'

If these premonitions were footed in a paranoid calculation that a token strike could bring a city to its knees, they also betrayed an assumption that the existing regime acted as guarantor of social order. In Wolfram's words, the antipathy towards strike action,

> is really about order, in other words the functioning distribution of goods, that goods are on sale in the shops, and so on. And that people can draw money from the bank when they need to. That was the feeling, and the government knew how to manipulate it. As if everything would suddenly stop if the Modrow government was not maintaining order! That was the great dread – of being unable to cope with disorder. It was felt by people in New Forum but also in the other opposition circles.

The opposition leaders' aversion to political strike action did not simply reflect their existing ambivalence attitude towards mass self-activity and their belief in the social-order creating properties of the incumbent administration. It was also that such tactics bore the prospect of propelling them into the offices of state. They hailed from an 'anti-political' culture that perceived power to be related directly to violence and inversely to legality, that emphasised 'individual, ideal, and hence evolutionary change' and hewed to 'a strategy of political self-limitation'. 'We never wanted power', said Reich, for it 'would have conflicted with our commitment to legality'. He and his colleagues were also fearful 'of losing that moral integrity' that had accompanied their actions hitherto. Elsewhere, the New Forum leader put the point graphically: 'It would be an illusion to imagine Gandhi with a machine-gun under his arm.'[25]

Over the course of the autumn, the principle of non-violence evolved. At first it announced demonstrators' pacific intentions, in order to lessen the chance of provoking a 'Chinese reaction'. Increasingly, thereafter, it came to encompass the rejection of any radical demand or any action that could lead to the need to exercise power, even as an interim measure. To illustrate the reasoning involved, consider the refusal of the Erfurt citizens' committee to call upon the (unelected) town council to stand down. Such a confrontational approach, it announced, would oblige it to assume municipal power itself, and if that then led to 'panic buying

---

25 Knabe, 'Politische'; Maier, *Dissolution*, p. 169; Reich, *Abschied*, p. 17; *Rückkehr*, p. 183.

and looting, the citizens' committee would have to issue orders to shoot looters'.[26]

At the national level, Rolf Henrich did raise the question of power. 'If you want to achieve anything then you must take over the state prosecutor's office and the interior ministry', he said; 'Everything else is just chatter'. Yet his was a minority position. In Reich's recollection, 'non-violence prevented us from even thinking about taking power. Henrich said "we would have to make arrests!", and it is precisely from this that we recoiled.' Others, such as Ingrid Köppe, held that the politicians 'who got us into this mess should also now be responsible for getting us out of it'.[27] But, on the whole, the entire issue was evaded. 'The worst aspect of the discussion', Klaus Wolfram maintains,

> is that it was never conducted with adequate clarity and purpose. This issue was never given room at a formal meeting, but would be debated amongst ourselves in informal chats while going about other business. Jens Reich? He generally evaded the question, preferring not to speak about it. For Pflugbeil, too, it was too hot. Bohley . . . I can't recall a clear opinion.[28]

Swinging from sour apple trees

Opportunities were missed, this chapter has argued, due to the opposition's political philosophy, lukewarm attitude to mass mobilisation, wariness towards industrial action, as well as the metamorphosis of the non-violent tactic into a justification for negotiation and against confrontation. It was as if the Sorelian maxim that progressive social change is fuelled by *'violence enlightened by the idea of the general strike'* had been inverted.[29] (The 'myth of non-violence', it could be called.) In this regard, it is pertinent that New Forum leaders opposed strike calls in part because they 'could contribute to a pogrom atmosphere'.[30] This argument is also mentioned, even privileged, in the only English-language account that treats the 'December rising' in detail. In his *Rush to German Unity*, Konrad Jarausch contends that it was 'the rising threat of violence' that compelled cooperation between opposition and regime, which 'kept the revolution from spiralling out of control'. If this were so, it

---

26 Timmer, *Aufbruch*, p. 361.
27 Reich, *Rückkehr*, pp. 182, 117; Philipsen, *People*, p. 325.
28 And when Wolfram himself suggested that power was there for the taking, his colleagues would scoff: 'Taking power? There you are with your theories again! Do you want a new councils' republic or something?'
29 Sorel, *Reflections*, p. 249, emphasis in original.
30 From New Forum leadership discussion papers, Robert Havemann Archiv.

would suggest that a major element is missing from the above analysis; a digression on this issue is therefore required.

There is no doubt that, in December, the spectre of violence was in the air, and the growing anger on the streets certainly brought anxious moments to East German Communists. From my diary, an entry from the time notes this colloquy between my line manager and a colleague:

> 'It's worrying. The demands that are being voiced now – almost fascist.'
> 'Yes, exactly. Blood, that's all they want.'
> 'I know. It's become mob-like. These people are always the same, especially in times of crisis.'

For Stasi officers, the spectre loomed with a peculiar intensity. 'If we lose, they'll string us all up', Mielke told his men. One officer was warned by a colleague, with reference to the fate of their Hungarian counterparts in 1956, ' "If someone identifies you, five minutes later you'll be swinging" '. Nor was concern at the potential for pogroms restricted to Communists and Stasi officers. Western liberals were perturbed, too. The West German social scientist Thomas Schmid described this period as one in which the movement polarised between 'bourgeois' and 'vengeful proletarian' sections. 'The mood turned sour', was how *Observer* journalists summed up the shift:

> Until the border was opened, most East Germans had thought of East Berlin as seventh heaven. Having seen the splendour that was West Berlin, they suddenly [!] wanted to hang their district secretary from the nearest sour [!] apple tree. There were attacks on Stasi offices. Ugly-sounding 'citizens' councils' and 'vigilance groups' were formed across the country. In East Berlin, more than one Western diplomat found his Mercedes brought to a halt by angry young men smelling privilege. In the countryside, state guest houses were put under lock and seal, Honecker's country estate was raided and hunting lodges stormed.[31]

This is, of course, a crude depiction, drawing its strength not from sober analysis but from its appeal to clichéd images of social movements as reflex reactions of mobs driven by envy or greed. But more sophisticated explanations of the turn to 'self- justice' are available. An article in *Der Spiegel*, for example, rather than bracketing the 'ugly-sounding' citizens' committees together with vigilante groups, describes how the committees were ridiculed for having agreed to 'security partnerships' with police and Stasi, even though it was common knowledge that the latter deliberately obstructed their work, through tricks such as 'losing' keys.

---

31 Funder, *Stasiland*, p. 240; Schmid, *Staatsbegräbnis*, p. 59; Hawkes, 'Tearing', pp. 78–9.

'With the committees being made a laughing stock in this way', the article concludes, 'the call for self justice is growing ever louder.'[32]

Not finding expression in the politics of the organised opposition, the escalating anger directed against SED and the security forces manifested itself instead in calls for popular justice. And there is no doubt that this anger was at times expressed in an inflammatory manner, not least against the Stasi. During the occupation of Stasi premises in Suhl, cries of 'Get the rope out!' were heard. In Plauen, Stasi officers attempting to make an arrest were beaten up by demonstrators, and one young woman spat in a soldier's face. In Dresden, New Forum members stepped in to rescue a group of Stasi officers from a crowd that was, allegedly, seeking to administer hands-on justice. Personnel managers in several workplaces were confronted by 'threatening behaviour' when they appointed former Stasi officers, and one officer's holiday home was burnt down. The police, too, faced shouts of 'pigs!' at several demonstrations. A few police officers alleged that they were denied service at petrol stations, another, that his child was refused admission to kindergarten. There were death threats against functionaries and, according to one Politburo member, the call came for Wandlitz to be stormed.[33]

One can scarcely read an account of the revolution without encountering mention of the threat of 'self-justice' – notably of pogroms against functionaries – or of its twin, 'chaos'. But having trawled through innumerable histories, chronicles, memoirs and documents I have only found the few examples listed above. Of pogroms against functionaries, not a word. Mostly it was phantasmagoric. Indeed, Karsten Timmer has perceptively compared December 1989 to the *Grande Peur* in France two centuries earlier. In both, rumour played a key part in catalysing collective action; in both, the fears were largely invented.

What was going on? That the loudest warnings of lynch justice came from SED representatives was not without irony. Only two months earlier, prominent opposition activists, such as pastor Christian Führer, were on the receiving end of countless death threats, in all likelihood from Stasi officers and other SED members, and yet neither organisation showed any concern for their adversaries' nervous health. Also ironic was the timing of the spectre of pogroms against functionaries, for it came precisely in the period when, as Wolfgang Templin put it, 'former top functionaries were feathering their own nests with astonishing

32 *Der Spiegel*, 18 December 1989.
33 Küttler, 'Wende', pp. 119–20; Weber, *Alltag*, pp. 55–6; Hager, *Erinnerungen*, p. 444.

brazenness'.[34] Given the cooperation between opposition circles and the *nomenklatura*, the December days were in certain respects the very antithesis of the *Grande Peur*. In the French episode, peasants' fears of attacks by brigands prompted them to arm themselves and to organise collectively, a process that fed into the destruction of feudalism 'from below'. In East Germany, elements of militant collective action could be glimpsed (in the citizens' committees), but the centre of the political process was shifting to institutional actors: delegations at the round table, parliamentary parties and representatives from Bonn, Moscow and Washington as unification approached. The spectre led to mobilisation in the French case but to demobilisation in East Germany.

Where the 'ugly' cry for justice was heard, moreover, it was for the *lawful* punishment of SED leaders. And it did not come only from 'the mob'. Bernhard Quandt, one of the SED's oldest and longest-serving functionaries (a KPD member since 1922 who had served time in Sachsenhausen and Dachau), addressing a Central Committee plenum on 3 December, declared 'I am in favour of reintroducing [capital punishment] and that we summarily execute all those who have brought such disgrace upon our Party', and proceeded to heckle other delegates with 'You'll get your punishment!'[35] In factories, too, calls for top functionaries to face the death penalty were heard, particularly after the execution of Romanian tyrant Nicolae Ceausescu.[36] But more commonly the demand was simply that judicial procedure begin. 'Put the bosses on trial!' rang the chants on the streets, while banner slogans included 'Cats don't let their mice flee – every boss before a jury!', and 'Former political prisoners demand: Stasi before the courts!' as well as the more common 'Management onto the factory floor' and 'Lowest pension for sacked functionaries'.[37] Where notes of collective 'self-justice' *were* sounded – as in 'Harry [Tisch] stay in your forest, we're soon coming hunting; the people' – the meaning was, surely, metaphorical.

This was no mob driven by a frenzied desire for revenge. These demands, rather, formed part of a wider movement calling for a wholesale *Abrechnung* (settling of accounts) with an elite suspected of corruption and the abuse of power. Its well-spring was not envy but a sense that injustices had been perpetrated, and this, in turn, connected to the class

34 *die tageszeitung*, 7 January 1990.
35 Lest anybody target their guns on him, he insisted 'I am honest. There's no doubt that my shirt is white . . . I have nothing in common with criminals!' Hertle and Stephan, *Ende*, pp. 469–72.
36 *Tribüne*, 19 December 1989.
37 Lang, *Wendehals*.

consciousness discussed in chapter 7 – the pervasive feeling that 'them up there' had been lining their pockets at the expense of 'us down here'. Its political character was based upon an expansion of democratic participation, in the streets, workplaces, educational establishments and neighbourhoods, where ordinary people discussed social and political affairs, formulated demands and planned action. The agenda was fundamentally democratic: it centred on sweeping aside the (undemocratic) Stasi and the (unelected) SED regime, and calling corrupt powerholders to account. The break desired was a clean one, not a half-hearted affair – the bridge of compromises across which tens of thousands of Stasi officers and functionaries hoped to reach comfortable positions on the other side.

In this light, the problem was not an overabundance of promoters of *self-justice*, but a lack of organisations standing for the popular conception of *justice*. 'There's much wild talk about witch-hunts and lynch justice', said one of the opposition's wiser voices, 'but it's nothing but diversionary tactics. There is no instance of such things happening.' Markus Wolf had been the first to invoke the spectre, in the face of a chorus of booing, on the 4 November demonstration in Berlin. Two weeks later, the CDU's *Neue Zeit* denounced a rival newspaper for reporting corruption scandals: exposés of this sort would, it cautioned, only encourage 'self-justice'. By December, such scaremongering had become a media staple, and West German politicians joined in too, appealing for faith to be placed in the 'Rechtsstaat' as opposed to self-justice. But the greatest play with the spectre was made by the SED. In his debut speech as leader, Gregor Gysi appealed to citizens to respect the law and warned of the threat of self-justice. Although, being a lawyer, Gysi's accession to the SED leadership was seen as a blow for the principle of legality against arbitrary rule, the same principle, he recognised, could be deployed against the demands for justice (*qua* '*Abrechnung*') that were echoing on the streets. In the process, the civic groups could be pressed to accept the false dichotomy of legality and self-justice. Just as *Observer* journalists wrote of 'ugly-sounding "citizens' councils" *and* "vigilance groups" ', so did SED spokespeople speak, in the same breath, of vigilante activity *and* 'forced entry into public buildings' – i.e. the Stasi occupations.[38]

Thus did the SED present the civic groups with a choice. They could denounce the scaremongering as a moral panic, insist that calls for *Abrechnung* were legitimate and argue that, for the course of justice to be followed, the SED should be deprived of its law-making powers. Or they could accept the SED's message that violence loomed, that strikes,

38 Editors, *Keine*, p. 28; *Neues Deutschland*, 5 December 1989.

occupations of Stasi buildings and vigilante activity were leading to 'chaos' and conclude that the alternative to violence was cooperation with the regime.

The 'Grand Coalition of Political Reason'

The decision to accept the dichotomy of 'negotiation versus violence', coupled with their rejection of political industrial action, entailed a hardening of the opposition leaders' position. Already in mid-November they had voiced concern at the prospect of rapid regime change. 'It wouldn't help us', said Jochen Lässig, 'if the SED swiftly perished and pulled us down into the depths as it sank . . . For the time being we are only interested in coalition government, participation in power, and supervision.' In early December they charted a clear course towards cooperation; in Ulrich Preuss' words, they felt 'forced to pursue an almost unconditional strategy of consensus building'. The three parties that formed this consensus – the civic groups, regime and Protestant Church – appealed in unison for citizens to 'remain calm and sensible' in the face of 'chaos' (as represented by strikes and occupations).[39] Proclaimed the 'Grand Coalition of Political Reason' by Rainer Eppelmann, the consensus had been presaged by the 'security partnerships' between civic groups and the Interior Ministry, was institutionalised at the round table and was then sealed in mid-December with the appointment of a New Forum member as Deputy Minister of Education.

In the space of a week, opposition leaders rethought their position towards the round table. Caution yielded to absolute commitment, even as the round table itself was becoming, explicitly, a tool in the regime's crisis-management strategy. Whereas they had previously viewed the round table as a means to commence a negotiated process of democratisation, when it first convened on 7 December it defined its own role as seeking ways 'to overcome the crisis', while New Forum's delegates declared its aim to be 'preventing anarchy and chaos'. The few voices that suggested that the opening of talks be used as an opportunity to demand that the government step down – and thus 'to mediate the processes of crisis and articulate them before the whole country' – were sidelined. 'By this stage the motives for calling a Round Table', Karsten Timmer has stated, 'were almost exclusively the fear of anarchy and chaos'.[40]

39 Timmer, *Aufbruch*, p. 357; Preuss, 'Roundtable', p. 111; *Der Spiegel*, 11 December 1989, p. 23.
40 Wolfram, interview; Timmer, *Aufbruch*, pp. 352–3.

The long-term goals of the round table were undoubtedly admirable. They included supervising the dissolution of the Stasi, setting a date for parliamentary elections, drafting a constitution, drawing up a charter of economic and social rights and furthering the democratisation of industrial relations and economic stabilisation. Clearly, the round table was a grand project, and some lofty claims have been made on its behalf. For Dieter Rucht it was 'a direct expression of an emerging civil society'; in Jon Elster's view it embodied a form of 'bargaining between the government and society'; while Charles Maier rates it 'as a unique moment of renewing a social contract'.[41]

The grain of truth in these asseverations is that the round table and its local offshoots did indeed function, at an elementary level, as 'schools of democracy'. Citizens were able to switch on their televisions to witness quite novel forms of institutional politics, enlivened by extempore contributions and agonistic debate. Questionable, however, is the supposition that the round table represented a democratic expression of 'society' *vis-à-vis* the regime. The negotiations were modelled on the Polish precedent, which has been described as 'a classic corporatist scenario' in which negotiators from government, Solidarność and the official trade unions, 'none of which had been elected for the purpose, met in a series of closed-door sessions to work out a social contract binding upon all'.[42] The East German version was similarly corporatist, but distinct in two respects. Whereas Lech Wałesa and his colleagues had gained respect through practical leadership of struggles down the years and, formally, through election within Solidarność, their Berlin counterparts 'possessed nothing but self-assumed authorizations . . . They had never been democratically elected in any way. At no point had they thus been democratically entitled to speak for New Forum in negotiations with the government or with anyone else.'[43]

A second – and not unrelated – difference was that in Berlin the round table was treated with scant respect by government. In Warsaw, opposition delegates dealt with high-ranking functionaries; in East Berlin they generally faced lesser officials drawn from sundry old-regime institutions. Modrow seldom 'sent responsible Ministers along, [and these]

41 Rucht, 'Unification', p. 44; Elster, 'Introduction', p. 3; Maier, *Dissolution*, p. 187. That these are all western social scientists may be more than a coincidence. As Ehrhart Neubert avers (*Opposition*, p. 901), East Germans were less likely to buy into the 'myth of the Round Table'.
42 Ost, 'Solidarity', p. 83.
43 Harald Wagner, a prominent member of Democratic Awakening, in Philipsen, *People*, p. 234.

answered questions even more rarely', while he himself did not even attend until mid-January. And when opposition delegates asserted themselves, proposing the right of the round table to veto government policy, and their own participation in Modrow's forthcoming talks in Bonn and at meetings of the Council of Ministers, their demands were casually dismissed by de Maizière. Such an 'interdiction of the government', the deputy prime minister insisted, was simply unacceptable.[44]

As historians of the round table have detailed, the floor it was pitched on was anything but level.[45] Representatives of old-order institutions were familiar with the terrain, and possessed in-built advantages in terms of access to information and experience in dealing with procedural issues. The state bureaucracies were on their side and consistently sabotaged proposals by opposition representatives – for example through withholding essential information. Furthermore, the opposition delegations contained numerous informal agents, who ably assisted the 'other' side, for example by playing upon fears that the Stasi would mount armed resistance if its powers were trimmed too quickly. One may assume that they joined in the general mirth when a proposal was submitted to the round table that delegates be checked for Stasi membership. The proposal was quashed.

Because the old forces were masters at the arts of blocking and evasion, and because it was dedicated to alchemising conflicting positions into consensus, the round table's work proceeded sluggishly. That it remained stuck in the thick mud of filibusters and procedural side tracks was, of course, especially detrimental to the side that sought more rapid change – the opposition delegations. Yet they could see no easy alternative. 'Most of us movement spokespeople', Klaus Wolfram recalls,

> were aware of the danger that the Round Table would only create a smoke-screen. This was a very very strong feeling, and it was also articulated at our [leadership] meetings. People would say: 'how can we combat that danger?' and, 'hopefully an idea will come up', and, 'be wary', and . . . but nobody thought of a way of avoiding it.

At local round tables similar hazards were seen. The SED and its allies would make concessions where unavoidable but evade and block wherever possible. Oppositionists, grumbled Christoph Kleemann, a New Forum spokesperson in Rostock, were gradually becoming aware

44 Renken, 'Oppositionsgruppen'; Klein, 'Modrow-Regierung'; Süß, 'Unwillen', p. 472; Müller-Mertens, *Politische*, p. 56.
45 Lohmar, *Entwicklung*; Thaysen, *Runde*.

that not only were negotiated agreements being blocked, but 'the real political and economic decisions are not being made at the round table' at all. Opposition delegates, he added, 'increasingly had the feeling that the town council was misusing them in pseudo-democratic ways'. If the round tables were the centrepiece of an 'elite settlement' road to democracy, it was clear which elite was at the wheel and which was the back-seat driver. The overall process has been summarised concisely by Opp and Voß: 'The central round table debated endlessly over procedural questions while the regime got on with the task of securing its inheritance.'[46]

A modification to the above picture did emerge in mid-January. The government appeared more forthcoming at the round table, and, some analysts have suggested, the opposition groups negotiated major victories – a date for parliamentary elections and agreement to dismantle the Stasi. Yet it would be fallacious to see these developments as resulting from the round table talks – this view reminds one of the flea on the lion's back that marvels at its formidable power as the savannah herds part before it. The date for elections was forced by the mass protests – indeed, these raged near to the building in which delegates met and clearly influenced their belief that, for further radicalisation to be avoided, 'credible signals' must be given. The election date was later brought forward due to pressure not from the round table but from 'events'. As to the dismantling of the Stasi, this could be deemed a success only from the organisation's own standpoint. Indeed, according to one high-ranking Stasi officer, 'the Stasi was dissolved by the Stasi', and in enabling this, the civic groups and round table played no small part.[47] When, in early January, the round table established a sub-committee that was intended to oversee the dismantling process it was chaired by an SED–PDS member together with a Stasi 'informal agent'. Not until February was a commission to dismantle the Stasi actually set up, and it was composed not of members of the citizens' committees but largely of Stasi employees, with key advisory roles entrusted to Generals Engelhardt and Braun – who had until then headed the organisation – and 337 other officers. The government refused even to inform the round table of the whereabouts of the Stasi's central computer and insisted that no member of a citizens' committee be permitted entry into the Berlin headquarters of the HVA, a core Stasi section – to which the round table agreed. The HVA was permitted to hold on to a key

46 Probst, *Ostdeutsche*, pp. 98–9; Glaessner, *Unification*, p. 55 ; Opp *et al.*, *volkseigene*, p. 204.
47 Richter, 'Exiting'; Thaysen, *Runde*, p. 52; *Der Spiegel*, 4/1995, p. 114.

database, enabling its members to access files, even while round table delegates acquiesced to the destruction of other databases.[48]

Prevarication in the dismantling process was continued by the conservative-led government that entered office following elections in March 1990. The new regime took over the authority set up under Modrow to administer dismantling, even though it was packed with old-regime functionaries and former Stasi officers. Indeed, those citizens' committee members who remained members were driven out by the new Minister of the Interior, Peter-Michael Diestel. The entire process was placed in the hands of western and eastern bureaucrats, and the round table subcommittee charged with supervising the dismantling was not permitted to interfere. Stasi officers, meanwhile, were able to continue destroying and laundering files, including those of informal agents. Later, Diestel would boast that 'around 100 per cent of the really explosive documents have been destroyed, along with around a third of the total collection'. Although a democratically elected conservative, 'Diestel, more than anyone else, hindered the proper public investigation of the Stasi's activities', Stasi-researcher Anna Worst has concluded.[49]

As regards the round table's other goals, they were equally noble, but were for the most part 'overtaken by revolutionary actuality'[50] or were rejected out of hand by government – as with its proposal for the establishment of supervisory councils in firms, with worker and trade union representation and also a resolution calling for all existing managers to step down and for replacements to be elected by the workforce. Its most time-consuming activity was the drafting of a constitution, but this issue found only weak resonance in the wider public; the plan did not get beyond the drawing board.[51] Perhaps its most impressive achievement was the elaboration of a social charter that guaranteed rights to work and housing, free education and health care, social welfare and a definite share of state property for every citizen. Here too, sadly, its visions were published only to be binned by the incoming CDU-led government that was as determined to marginalise radical ideas as it was to rescue the old elite.

The round table was, in sum, the child of the marriage between a beleaguered regime and an opposition which was searching for ways of

---

48 This particular decision was laden with irony, given that opposition negotiators had, in early December, pledged their opposition to industrial action in part as a quid pro quo for the government's agreement to protect files and databases. Modrow, *Aufbruch*, p. 68.
49 *Der Spiegel*, no. 4, 1995, p. 115; Worst, *Geheimdienstes*, p. 43.
50 Renken, 'Oppositionsgruppen'.
51 Rucht, 'Unification', p. 42.

evading the looming question of state power. The former was seeking ways to brake the protest upswing and offered negotiations as a means of binding the opposition into its strategy of crisis management. The latter accepted the offer as, in Marianne Schulz's words, the best possible 'alternative to their taking power'. In its effects, the round table operated less to accelerate the demise of the old regime than to further divide the popular movement by coopting its 'moderate' section. Until mid-January it possessed, at most, weak supervisory powers, yet as a much-publicised experiment in 'democracy' it burnished the image of the regime. Klaus Hartung has summarised its purpose as the attempt to 'contain the radicalisation of the masses through a programme of democratisation. A great anti-chaos coalition . . . standing against the mass movement itself'. Rather than an 'organ of civil society' it is more accurately described as an 'institution of reconciliation between the new and old political forces, and only partially about institutionalising a democratic public sphere'.[52]

Among the population, the round table received a mixed reception. In popular parlance it received the moniker 'talking shop' (Palaver Club), while on the Monday demonstrations it was 'regarded as an irrelevance'.[53] Ambivalence characterised the responses of my interviewees. Typical was that of Ollie, from Dresden: 'I welcomed the Round Table and followed it intensively on television. Everyone was talking together, and there was a voice for the opposition. Hey, that looks like democracy!, I thought. But, then again, no solutions seemed to come from it.' In retrospect, even prominent oppositionists voice scepticism. When asked if the round table was an attempt by the regime 'to create a playground for oppositionists in order to quiet them down', a New Forum negotiator, Ingrid Köppe, replied in the affirmative.[54] Jens Reich – who did not participate at the round table, claiming to have seen through the 'lullaby function of that talking shop' – has written its epitaph:

> In early December a popular uprising and general strike were very real threats, and the Round Table was set up as a tranquilliser. The intelligentsia, its old cadre as well as the new forces, united in an unspoken alliance to ensure that the self-dismantling of the system proceeded in the form of palaver. They succeeded.[55]

52 Schulz, 'Neues', p. 28; Hartung, *Neunzehnhundertneunundachtzig*, p. 55.
53 Herles and Rose, *Parlament*, p. 5; Schmid, *Staatsbegräbnis*, p. 34.
54 Although, she added, 'we did achieve more than they would have liked us to'. Philipsen, *People*, p. 325.
55 Reich, *Abschied*, p. 17.

Conclusion: 'the wrong side of the tracks'

A common narrative of the 1989 uprising tells of unity in the early autumn, symbolised by the slogan 'We are the people!', after which point divisions began to emerge between the original protestors (the 'civic movement'), representing an 'authentic' politics of radical democracy, and a nationalistic movement for unification, seen as 'inauthentic', conservative and mesmerised by the gleam of Western commodities. This and previous chapters suggest that such interpretations are flawed. A fault-line did exist, but it is better described in different terms. Its origins lay in the 1980s, it first became a talking point following the Wall's fall, but it then deepened drastically in December, as the opposition groups, hitherto a movement to be 'crisis-managed', became crisis managers themselves. Locked in their embrace with the regime, oppositionists exhorted reconciliation even as swathes of the population were moving into radical opposition to the state, particularly in early December when exposés of the lavish lifestyles of the *nomenklatura* emerged.

There were exceptions to this general rule. Some oppositionists, such as Jochen Läßig, called for miscreant functionaries to be brought to account for their deeds, and for the SED's ill-gotten funds to be redistributed – but many others preached forgiveness.[56] The Stasi formed another exception. On this issue, the civic groups were more militant. Their supporters were active in the occupation of Stasi premises and in the formation of citizens' committees to supervise the dissolution process. Yet the oppositionists' hostility to the Stasi, although understandable given its central role in administering political repression, was inconsistent, for it was merely one pillar of a regime with which they were, increasingly, cooperating. (One rueful Stasi officer compared the oppositionists' logic to that of a snake which, after being hit by a stick, bites the stick instead of the hand that holds it.[57] In this case, I would add, the 'snake' was positively entreating the 'hand' for friendship.) And here too, cooperation won the day: the citizens' committees were integrated into a wider 'security partnership' strategy in which they were marginalised, enabling the Stasi to oversee its own demise.

In veering from a strategy of mobilisation to one of negotiation,

---

56 Take, for instance, Thomas Küttler's appeal to the citizens of Plauen: 'Many people are demanding reprisals and the punishment of miscreants . . . But we shouldn't let an atmosphere of hate arise . . . We'll have to live with the Wendehälsen. Indeed, in a sense we need them. Everyone is needed.' Küttler and Röder, *Volk*.

57 Richter, *Staatssicherheit*, p. 72.

opposition leaders found themselves in Catch-22 territory: the power they brought to the negotiating table depended on their popular support, but this was diminishing due to their embrace of a regime that was itself haemorrhaging popularity with each new day. The gap between the movement on the streets and the civic groups was far from absolute, but was widening. Even as the number of protest participants was escalating in most of East Germany (outside Berlin and Leipzig),[58] the opposition-ists turned their backs on collective action – with exceptions only in cases of 'symbolic' protest that were designed as an alternatives to concen-trated mass gatherings, as with the 'human chain for democracy and non-violence' that looped around the country on 3 December.

As autumn passed into winter, the political culture of the civic groups seemed increasingly out of synch. Berliners who attended Democracy Now meetings grumbled 'that they were still expected to sing'. And when former dissident Wolf Biermann, appearing in concert in Leipzig, sang 'against revenge and for pensions [for Stasi officers and functionaries]', the applause evaporated. 'On the streets', meanwhile, 'ever fewer slogans expressed support for the opposition'. The civic groups now found them-selves, one journalist remarked, 'on the wrong side of the tracks, urging restraint where the crowd wanted resolve, and caution where the crowd wanted action'. New Forum's failure to support the general strike call was widely seen, both by the general public and by its own membership, as an indication of impotence and, according to a survey of Leipzig demonstrators, it saw its support tumble from 70 to 54 per cent in the month following the fall of the Wall. 'The people stopped listening to New Forum', one Leipzig demonstrator recalls, 'because the reformers hadn't recognised that the whole system had to go'.[59] Similar sentiments were expressed in letters to New Forum. One seventeen-year-old wrote, in early December, 'Now people are waiting for strike action. But *you* rejected it. The newspaper's line was: "Will our country sink into chaos?" Why don't you admit that chaos is here already?'[60]

In short, a remarkable reversal had occurred. In the 1980s, dissidents

---

58 Calculated from Johnson, 'Massenmobilisierung', p. 93, with the 'working month' of December assumed to last three–four weeks.

59 Jakob Moneta, *Sozialistische Zeitung*, 7 June 1990; Neubert, *Opposition*, pp. 869, 883; Hawkes, *Tearing*, p. 79; Haufe and Bruckmeier *Bürgerbewegungen*, p. 46; Mühler and Wilsdorf, 'Montagsdemonstration', p. 40; McFalls, *Communism's*, p. 50.

60 The organisation, the teenager concluded, should desist from 'sucking up to the old state apparatus, and instead push for our demands, in united fashion, through strike action'. Krone, *Briefe*.

had courageously engaged in protest activities, and were frequently scornful of 'the masses', seen as compliant with the system. Now, with hundreds of thousands of people entering into active opposition to the regime, many of those same dissidents were preaching rapprochement.

In retrospect, opposition intellectuals have recognised this as a problem. They did nothing, Ludwig Mehlhorn of Democracy Now regrets, to stop the widening rift between themselves 'and the people in the streets'. To allow such a gap to develop, he adds, 'is always very dangerous, because you lose all control of events'.[61] And here one may note a further irony. The organised opposition had 'lost control of events' as a result of policies that were tailored precisely to prevent the revolution from 'spiralling out of control'. Negotiations, they hoped, would offer a clear way forward. Instead, the scissors that opened between civic groups and crowd, combined with the latter's escalating hostility to the regime, generated a deepening political crisis. Disappointed by the alternatives at home, growing sections of the population looked elsewhere for inspiration, as chapter 9 will show.

61 Philipsen, *People*, p. 370.

9

The German Question

And you just sit there talking about deals and timetables. Or the terrors of fast food and Coca-Cola. (Victoria Brodskaya)[1]

The alternatives are not 'two states' or 'annexation', but an unconditional orientation to the aim of radical democratisation, in which decisions are ceded to those who will bear the consequences. (Jürgen Habermas)[2]

When the streets of Leipzig and Dresden began to fill with the black–red–gold flags of the Federal Republic, most people, East Germans and outside observers alike, were taken by surprise. The issue had not figured prominently hitherto. Although attitudes to unification in pre-revolutionary East Germany are difficult to assess, the polling evidence that does exist suggests that, while Honecker's policy of *Abgrenzung* ('demarcation' from the FRG) did not reflect majority opinion, neither was unification a popular vision. It was simply not conceivable as a realistic option. In addition, East German analyst Heinz Niemann has suggested, a critical disposition towards market capitalism and West German imperialism played a significant part among a considerable section of the public.[3]

Before the fall of the Wall, calls for unification were seldom heard. Of innumerable letters to New Forum that I have read, only one even broached the issue in this period, while a survey of Leipzig demonstrators in early November indicated that as few as 1 per cent considered it a motive to participate.[4] On the first Monday after the Wall's fall, the issue raised its head in Leipzig, and on the following week pro-unification speeches met with applause. Yet it was not until late November that it was raised as a priority issue on a demonstration. That was in Plauen, while

1 David Edgar's, 'The Shape of the Table'.
2 *Revolution*, p. 160.
3 Niemann, *Hinterm*.
4 Krone, *Briefe*, p. 18; Mühler and Wilsdorf, 'Montagsdemonstration', p. 161.

elsewhere other themes – *nomenklatura* corruption, free elections, social justice, economic reform, the environment – remained the primary foci. Opinion polls taken at the time indicated at least 16 per cent support for unification; in mid-December, the figure was in the region of 27 per cent and climbing. By early February it had risen to at least 40 per cent, and probably considerably higher.[5] Whatever the truth of these figures, it is apparent that the swing to unification was no tsunami, no rapid, automatic response to the fall of the Wall, but a gradual, tidal change.

Why, exactly, did this turnaround occur? There are those, such as *Schutzstaffel* officer-turned-journalist Wolfgang Venohr, who perceive in the desire for unification deep pools of yearning for an authentic German nation, which required only the right conditions to well up at the surface. But this is far-fetched. It may well be the case that, pre-1989, positive attitudes towards the Federal Republic were more widespread than the aforementioned polls suggest. And supporters of unification undoubtedly held their tongues until late autumn because, had the demand been raised earlier, it would have shortened the odds on a 'Chinese solution'. (One Leipzig demonstrator recalls that, 'From the very start we all wanted unification, but it would have been a tactical blunder to demand it right away'.) Yet the turn to unification is ill-described as the expression of a fervent patriotic urge. This was 'not the nationalism of an emotionalised *Volk*', Claus Offe has argued, but was pragmatically grounded and 'instrumental' in nature.[6] The comparatively 'emotionalised' slogan 'We are *one* people', popularised by stickers supplied by the West German CDU, was not an especially common chant on demonstrations, even when these had become a sea of black–red–gold flags. Unification was seen as a routemap towards political and social advance; and when, in the 1990s, disappointments with the route taken burgeoned, many Germans (of east and west) rapidly reversed their position, arguing 'We're *not* one people'.[7]

Unification from above

In terms of its driving forces, unification can be viewed from two angles, as the project of elites, and as that of public opinion and the streets. Beginning with the first of these, the main player was Bonn, ably backed by Washington. In late November, Chancellor Helmut Kohl and

5 *Der Spiegel*, 18 December 1989; Förster and Roski, *DDR*, p. 53.
6 Venohr, in *Zurück zu Deutschland*; McFalls, *Communism's*, p. 50; Offe, 'Wohlstand', p. 286.
7 In 1990, 74 per cent of easterners polled were proud to be German, in 1995 the figure was 16 per cent. Dennis, *Perceptions*, p. 93.

his advisors, concerned that Modrow was attempting to shape the agenda with his proposal that the two Germanies establish a federation, and thrilled by indications that Moscow was willing to entertain the possibility of unification,[8] launched a 'Ten Point Plan' that shrewdly adopted Modrow's federation idea, not as a goal but as a stepping stone to unification. Announced on the very day that the SED Politburo was elaborating its concept of federation, Kohl's intervention wrested the initiative from East Berlin.

The second elite, the GDR *nomenklatura*, was opposed to unification. Indeed, its members regarded the black–red–gold flags filling the winter streets with horror.[9] The GDR regime slammed the front door, so to speak, on Kohl's proposal. However, other doors were left ajar. First, as described in chapter 7, *nomenklatura* members were mutating into enthusiasts for market capitalism, parliamentary democracy and rapprochement with Bonn. As a liberal capitalist state with friendly (not to say mortgaged) relations to West Germany, the GDR would possess no *raison d'être*. This conundrum was widely discussed at the time, most famously in the formula, 'Poland minus Communism is Poland, East Germany minus Communism is . . . West Germany'.

A second 'open door' was the Kremlin's strategy (or lack thereof) on the German Question. Months, if not years, before the GDR uprising, Soviet policymakers had begun to face up to the inevitability of unification, even as they sharply criticised Bonn for forcing its pace. In autumn 1989, Moscow's official stance was to oppose unification, yet highly placed sources were conceding that the GDR was on its last legs. 'Doesn't the left hand know what the right hand is doing?', grumbled Krenz, in view of Moscow's equivocation.[10]

When Krenz's successor, Modrow, announced his government's conversion to German unification he alluded to a third 'open door': the SED's own traditions. Adopting a line, 'Germany united fatherland', from the GDR's original national anthem, he drew attention to the Party's original advocacy of German unification and, in the idiom of the early SED, he proclaimed that his vision drew upon 'patriotic, progressive ideas and movements for the unity of the German nation'.

As regards the civic groups, on issues of foreign policy, including unification, and market reform their positions generally resembled those of the SED. At a conference on economic reform organised by New Forum

8 Diplomatic misunderstandings were involved in this critical issue. See von Plato, *Vereinigung*, pp. 113–19.
9 Maximytschew, 'Mauerfall', p. 32.
10 MccGwire, *Perestroika*; Krenz, *Herbst*, p. 318.

in late November, for example, most of the proposals made were akin to those under discussion in government. There was plentiful talk of market reform, enterprise autonomy and joint ventures; of Western aid, East-Mark convertibility and integration into the international division of labour; and of cuts in consumer goods subsidies. Some voices spoke in favour of 'sharper differentiation among employees' in wages and conditions, and one New Forum delegate, a company director, proposed that capitalist relations be introduced (but only in the 'economic sphere'). The Green Party, meanwhile, called for 'proprietorial consciousness to be strengthened'. There was also support for social cushioning and industrial democratisation, in the form of trade union rights and the right of work: 'As much market as necessary and as much social security as possible' was later to become a New Forum election slogan. New Forum also advanced the idea of a corporatist ownership structure, in which industries would be managed jointly by representatives of the workforce and the state in addition to company managements.[11]

Albeit unintentionally, tracks towards unification were being laid, by the regime and with support from the civic groups, through the 'back door' of market reform, even as Bonn, and the crowds on the streets, pushed at the 'front door'.

Unification from below

What motivated the black–red–gold flag-wavers on East Germany's streets? The irresistible attractive power of Western commodities, goes one answer. The Wall's fall revealed to them, in the words of sociologist Zygmunt Bauman, the 'enticing and alluring spectacle of lavish consumption enjoyed under capitalist auspices'.[12] In addition, they regarded West Germany, with extraordinary naïveté, as a utopia. For example, when an FRG television crew asked a group of Leipzig demonstrators why, given that 6 million West Germans lived in poverty, they nonetheless supported unification, the reply came: 'That's not true. Everyone who wants work there can get it.'[13]

So, at any rate, run two common assumptions regarding the movement for unification. In my view they are wide of the mark. Consider, first, the supposedly insatiable desire for Western commodities. In fact, on their

---

11 *Neues Deutschland*, 8 December 1989; *Märkische Volksstimme*, 2 February 1990; Stark, 'Wirtschaftspolitische', p. 1191.
12 Bauman, *Intimations*, p. 171.
13 Schomers, *Deutschland*, p. 138. One wonders if they would defend those words today.

first shopping trips to the West after the fall of the Wall, Easterners generally 'bought one or two small items, perhaps some fresh fruit, a Western newspaper and toys for the children', while West Berlin book shops sold out of GDR dissident literature. Similarly, after currency union, instead of 'buying in a frenzy, cautious customers preferred to window shop. Before they parted with their hard money, most wanted to compare cost and quality . . . Unsure about their own future, four-fifths of East Germans wanted to save their "new money".' These are journalistic impressions, but are supported by the relevant statistics. When in possession of Deutschmark incomes, Easterners were not driven to spending frenzies; rather, the savings-rate *climbed*, from 12.7 per cent – already a high level – in 1989 to 14 per cent in 1991, before stabilising at 11 per cent.[14]

As regards visions of a 'utopian' FRG, while starry-eyed East Germans did exist in numbers, many others had a realistic outlook. For example, when *Spiegel* interviewed a group of Rostock dockers, most of whom supported unification, there was considerable scepticism towards Western capitalism. 'We workers always get shat on, whether in East or West', and 'I don't care whether I live in socialism or capitalism – living well and in security, that's the main thing' were prevailing views. And although the 'enticing and alluring spectacle' of West German capitalism exceeded the expectations of many, others were less impressed. One school student who crossed into a poor part of West Berlin following the fall of the Wall recalls: 'We were, obviously, expecting fantastic shop-windows and so on. Instead we saw shabby housing, which wasn't so very different from that in East Germany.'[15]

The unification movement was far more complex in its causation than the 'seduction thesis' allows, with its reduction of political behaviour to consumption cravings, but what were the salient factors? As a first cut, one may concede that it did represent a sublimated expression of the desire for West German consumption levels. Its supporters wished for the Deutschmark – and not, primarily, for identity-related reasons but as notes and coins in their wallets. The Deutschmark had long functioned as a parallel currency in East Germany. Those who possessed it could access all manner of goods and services – a new car, spare parts, a prompt visit from the plumber – that those who lacked it were denied. Its distribution thus divided the populace in two, and for the excluded section, unification offered the prospect of overcoming their second-class status through the generalisation of Deutschmark ownership.

14 Ash, *People*, p. 62; Sinn and Sinn, *Jumpstart*, p. 79; Akerlof, 'East', p. 33.
15 *Der Spiegel* 18 December 1989, p. 55; Olaf Klenke, interview.

Unification would bring the Deutschmark, and with it, access to mate-rial goods. As such, the movement is sometimes seen as 'materialist' in nature. However, it also promised greater fulfilment of what some, fol-lowing Ronald Inglehart, have dubbed 'postmaterialist' needs – those that enable 'self-actualisation', such as foreign travel. Especially for young people, it offered a means of cultural escape from the parochial and stultifying GDR. The menu of music, films and books available across the border was markedly greater, as was the range of college courses and careers. The desire for Western-style consumer choice, in short, was no mere 'stampede for glittering kitsch'. It 'embodies wishes for things', in the words of GDR author Lutz Rathenow, 'which project into democratic structures. One has to differentiate: The desire for travel is not the same as the desire for thirty different types of yoghurt.'[16]

For East German workers, unification promised Deutschmark wages, but also a more productive use of labour time. When asked why they favoured a Deutschmark economy, workers would say: 'with western technology higher quality production can be achieved at a lower price', 'wasteful stoppages would be minimised thanks to the replacement of worn-out machinery' and 'spare parts could be speedily procured instead of created in makeshift fashion with scissors and glue'. Unification would bring western capital and, as one docker put it: 'There's no other way of getting out of the muck.'[17] The same sentiment adorned banners at demonstrations, such as: 'Mercedes, buy the Sachsenring factory; the German market economy is "in".'[18]

A more productive use of labour time, GDR workers believed, would fuel growth and benefit them, too. Not only was average annual labour time around 10 per cent higher in East than in West Germany, but they had to work longer than their counterparts across the border to earn the price of equivalent goods: 215 against 30 hours for a fridge, 20 against 10 minutes for a basic lunch of bread and cheese and a beer.[19] In East Germany the working week was long and holidays short, yet many of the goods received in return for one's 'aluminium chips' were shoddy. Deutschmark wages seemed to promise proper recompense for the lengthy hours; 'For hard work, hard currency!' read a banner at a Leipzig demonstration. In addition, the efficient use of leisure time was at issue; West German supermarkets were coveted not simply for the commodi-ties on display, but also for the relative lack of queues.

16 Interviewed in Jäger and Villinger, *Intellektuellen*.
17 *Der Spiegel*, 18 December 1989, p. 46.
18 Ash, *People*, p. 72.
19 Merkel and Wahl, *Deutschland*, p. 76; Mögenburg, *Revolution*, p. 70.

Support for unification, in short, was bound up with the 'postmaterial' desire for a less stressful life. It was as much about 'wasted life-time', Klaus Hartung has argued, as about commodities. It 'contained a democratic radicalism: D-Mark, that meant recognition, taking stock, drawing a line [under the past]. No more campaigns to construct a new society, not even in the name of a new democracy, but immediate recognition.'[20] This 'democratic radicalism' tapped into perceptions of justice and exploitation. GDR workers, as Michael Hoffman and Dieter Rink have perceptively observed, experienced a twin shock in late autumn 1989. They discovered the high quality of life across the border and, domestically, the extent of economic crisis and ruling class corruption. 'Taken together these generated a feeling, especially among older workers, that for decades they had been betrayed of the fruits of their labour.'[21] As an interim conclusion, it appears that issues of labour time and exploitation provided vital fuel for the unification movement. An implicit corollary is that the assertion – by economic historian Jeffrey Kopstein – that the movements of 1989 should be understood as the 'actions of dissatisfied consumers, not, as Marxian social theory would have us expect, of dissatisfied producers', cannot withstand scrutiny.[22]

The turn to unification, I am arguing, needs to be understood in the context of the wider protest movement. As previous chapters have detailed, the latter underwent a process of radicalisation in late autumn, fuelled by revelations of the extent of Stasi power and *nomenklatura* privilege and corruption. The belief that the whole ruling class should be swept aside gained ground, and frustration grew as the 'old forces' maintained their grip. The following excerpts from letters sent to New Forum indicate the range of popular concerns that prevailed in December and early January – precisely the period in which support for unification

20 Hartung, *Neunzehnhundertneunundachtzig*, p. 120; Hartung, 'Radwechsel', p. 76.
21 Hoffman and Rink, 'Leipziger', p. 120.
22 Kopstein, *Politics*, p. 192. The 'revolution of consumers' thesis has been convincingly critiqued by Mathieu Denis ('Labour'). 'Did the workers shouting "Wir sind das Volk" distinguish between shortages in production, that threatened their pay, and shortages in consumer goods? Would they have had any reason to make such a distinction?' Producers and consumers, he points out, are in most cases the same persons and, for them, wages and consumption are inextricably linked. It is, moreover, nonsense to suggest that Marxian approaches assume social movements to be based exclusively upon production-related issues. A cursory glance at any Marxist-authored history reveals studies of social movements breaking out over 'bread' and 'peace' as well as 'land'.

soared: 'The SED still controls the media'; 'The Stasi isn't giving up its power'; In workplaces,

> the SED-Directors are deciding, completely on their own, the firm's future, how many employees will be dismissed, and they're establishing joint projects with western countries . . . They can now take decisions autocratically, which will be decisive for the economy, environment, and thus for the future of our country as a whole.

Summing up these frustrations, one correspondent concluded that 'The revolution has got stuck half way'.[23]

For its supporters, German unification offered a means of completing the revolution. It represented a sure-fire means of achieving a better quality of life, with institutionalised political freedoms (such as parliament and independent trade unions), a more rational organisation of production and, to boot, the deracination of the 'SED–Stasi state'. Unification was a nationalist formulation of the goal of regime change; its proponents, as Ulrich Beck suggests, were 'acting, *within the horizons of the GDR*, in a revolutionary way; for they helped to power the rival system'.[24] Equally, however, the turn to unification also *short-circuited* the radicalisation process; it expressed at one and the same time a radicalisation and a halt to the upward curve in the movement's self-confidence. It was accelerated by ordinary people's simultaneous experience of Western society and their own poverty, as well as by revelations of corruption and the abuse of power. 'The collapse in trust' that these occasioned, Peter Przybylski has described, 'was not limited to individuals but challenged the whole'.[25]

Until mid-November, the progress of demands from the limited ('please let us demonstrate!') to the radical ('freedom to travel!, Stasi out!') developed in tandem with a waxing sense of collective empowerment – best expressed in the slogan 'The people are not supplicants!' But that connection then broke down. A tone of sober powerlessness infiltrated the crowds. Typical is this excerpt from a flyer that called upon Dresdeners to welcome Kohl to their city: 'Every thinking person knows that after fifty-six years of barbarism and oppression *we're unable to pull ourselves out of the swamp*, all the successes of recent weeks notwithstanding.'[26] Increasingly, this shaded into rather wretched, begging

23 Krone, *Briefe*, p. 290 and *passim*.
24 Beck, 'Opposition', p. 24. Similarly, Hartung observes ('Radwechsel', p. 173) that 'for the masses' it represented 'the clearest formula for drawing a radical line under forty years of GDR and SED'.
25 Prokop, *Unternehmen*, p. 209.
26 Weber, *Alltag*, p. 58, emphasis added.

addresses to FRG politicians to come to the rescue of us poor East Germans. Demonstration banners turned from the ebullient to the imploring: 'Herr Kohl, help us!', and 'Only German unity can save us!'

Here, too, Hartung provides an astute analysis:

> The change from 'We are the people' to 'We are one people' is shocking, but not so much for its nationalism as for the dramatic decline in self-confidence. 'We are the people' is a clear expression of the consciousness of power; 'We are one people' is at best an appeal to the Federal Republic.

East Germans he goes on, 'emerged from shortage into poverty. Whereas in the GDR they could find no goods for their money, in the West they had no money for the goods.'[27] Their trips to West Germany involved curiosity and enthusiasm but were suffused with a painful – and disempowering – awareness of their lack of means, as the black-market value of the East-Marks in their pockets declined precipitously. A journey across the border would bring pleasures – the sheer thrill of travelling to places hitherto barred, visiting family and friends, and so forth – but could equally engender feelings of impotence and frustration – that a month's wage packet, changed to Deutschmarks, would buy only a cheap pair of shoes.

As the winter wore on, feelings of powerlessness strengthened and new anxieties took root. From December, many workers discovered that their bosses were preparing to fillet their firm – to sell bits to Western companies and ditch the rest. Hopes in well-paid jobs in a unified Germany balanced precariously against the fear of unemployment. It was as if a real-life game of musical chairs was about to begin, with jobs playing the role of chairs. Colleagues were increasingly seen as competitors and decreasingly as a source of support. The atmosphere in workplaces grew demonstrably 'colder'.[28] In this context, the demand for unification grew shriller. Like travellers crossing a rickety bridge, supporters of unification, increasingly alive to the fraying ropes and the roar of the water beneath, sought to reach the other (seemingly lush) side as expeditiously as possible. As they crossed, the nature of their collective constitution changed – from 'fused group' to 'series', as Sartre might say. The movement's focus shifted from the self-activity of ordinary people to appeals to the FRG state, increasingly seen as the only force capable of organising redress for East Germans' social and political demands.

As collective action involving colleagues and fellow citizens declined in centrality, faith was displaced onto the Father figure FRG; the movement

---

27 Hartung, 'Radwechsel', pp. 173, 176.
28 According to all employees in one typical Leipzig firm, interviewed by Francesca Weil ('Wirtschaftliche', p. 540).

became, as it were, more 'religious', if unification is seen as a secular salvation. Yet this did not necessarily imply an increasing irrationality, for the basic calculation by advocates of unification was eminently logical. Already in mid-autumn, as one journalist put it, 'people on the streets were analysing very realistically what formation is strong enough to topple the SED apparatus. The answer that they soon came to was: the West German parties.' By contrast – and here the final piece in the puzzle falls into place – the civic groups offered little. They considered austerity a virtue, viewed the Wall's fall with ambivalence and, displaying neither the will nor desire to assume power, were entering into an alliance with the SED even as revelations of the latter's mismanagement and corruption were stimulating an escalating clamour for an emphatic break with the GDR *nomenklatura*, Party, state and all. Revelations about the parlous state of the economy, meanwhile, put paid to hopes in a phoenix GDR. The alternatives the fledgling civic groups offered, as Garton Ash observes, 'were so vague, inchoate, uncertain. The alternative offered by West Germany was just so immediately, so obviously, so overwhelmingly plausible.'[29]

The civic groups and the German Question

Oppositionists tended to view unification with scepticism or hostility; some disapproved of the process *tout court* and many objected to its pace. They possessed a well-honed critique of western capitalism and possessed a relatively secure belief in East German independence, not least because their vision was of a continuing and successful movement for reform. Unlike much of the population, their trust in the SED was growing rather than collapsing. Already in mid-November, Wolfgang Ullmann (DJ) took a strong position, replying 'Yes, I'm not ashamed to say that' when asked 'On the question of sovereignty, is the opposition singing the same melody as the SED?' Like the Party, his organisation favoured confederation. Such an arrangement, it was hoped, would encourage both Germanies to reform; in the meantime, East Germany represented a welcome alternative to 'consumerist, Western' society. In the same period, New Forum and the SDP supported the status quo but emphasised that the issue was 'at present of no importance'.[30]

For their part, 'the demonstrators on the streets, who were ever more resolutely demanding unification, perceived the opposition's differentiated position to be more a delaying tactic than a constructive contribution to

29 Hartung, *Neunzehnhundertneunundachtzig*, p. 60; Ash, *People*, p. 72.
30 *die tageszeitung*, 18 November 1989; Müller-Mertens, *Politische*, p. 43.

shaping unification'.[31] At Leipzig rallies in late November, New Forum speakers who warned that unification would turn their country into the 'poor house of Greater Germany' received scant support – and not a few whistles.

As winter drew in, the positions of the civic groups fanned out along a spectrum. In the centre were those who favoured preserving the GDR's independence in the short to medium term. This was formally agreed as a joint goal by old and new forces at the round table. Indeed, one might say, with Ehrhart Neubert, that the former 'succeeded in exploiting' the oppositionists' advocacy of GDR sovereignty 'in order to exacerbate the alienation of the people from the opposition'.[32] Thereafter, as greater numbers swung behind unification, SDP, DJ, and most New Forum members followed; by late December they all supported unification, albeit at a gradual tempo.

At the pro-Western end of the spectrum, DA had come out for unification already in early December. In its origins a small band of dissidents, it had espoused an ethical socialism that appealed especially to left-leaning professionals who belonged to activist and/or Church milieux in the early autumn. But it had expanded quickly, drawing in other layers who, less rooted than their leaders in that oppositional culture for which morality was the yardstick of policy, were drifting with the pro-unification tide. Some DA spokespeople – those who placed power above principle or who had been sceptical of the principles from the outset – threw in their lot with the majority of the membership and declared for market capitalism and German unity. Before long, the long-standing socialist, Stasi agent and DA leader Wolfgang Schnur could be seen distributing propaganda with the (not especially socialist) message: 'For Nazis, Stasies and Sozis [Socialists]: one-way ticket to the Sahara desert!'[33]

Occupying the other end of the spectrum were the Green League, the VL and an important minority of New Forum, who marched against 'capitalist unification' in February. Of these, the VL was the most adamant. Originally at the radical edge of the opposition, with an orientation (at least in rhetoric) to working-class self-activity,[34] when that class began to march towards unification it jumped the opposite way: to the defence of

---

31 Neubert, *Opposition*, p. 889.
32 Preuss, 'Roundtable', p. 107; Neubert, *Opposition*, p. 893. See also von Plato, *Vereinigung*, pp. 164–70.
33 Schneider, *Revolution*, p. 119.
34 As one of its leaders lamented, the VL's overriding focus was on propaganda, even when, from late autumn onwards, opportunities for agitation in workplaces were abundant. Klein *et al.*, *Visionen*, p. 237.

the SED-state. In mid-November, with popular anger focusing upon the
Stasi and corrupt functionaries, the VL tilted instead at 'Mickey Mouse
and Coca-Cola'.[35] Its most impressive action is said to have been a
demonstration against 'selling-off the GDR and unification' on December
19, but one suspects that the bulk of the 60,000 who attended was
mobilised by the SED.

There are, I would suggest, two main reasons behind the oppositionists' sceptical approach to unification. In spite of their reluctance to
assume power, over long years of courageous political engagement they
had woven visions of an alternative GDR, one that *they* could help to
shape. With unification, these plans and dreams would be thrown uncer-
emoniously aside. As one VL member explained to me, 'Why are we
against unification? Because we have to use this unique opportunity to
really start something new, ourselves!'[36] More importantly, oppositionists had developed a critique not only of Soviet-style communism but
equally of market capitalism. Unification, they assumed, would be
offered on Helmut Kohl's terms. A joint press statement issued by the VL,
New Forum and Green Party warned that rapid unification would suf-
focate the revolutionary process, drive industries to the wall and sow illu-
sions that annexation to the FRG would bring West German living
standards. Unification conjured up spectres of NATO, mass unemployment, welfare erosion and an egotistic 'elbows society' – with East
Germans as second-class citizens. But, however accurate these prophe-
cies turned out to be, a sizeable segment of the public dismissed them,
and of those who did pay heed, many believed second-class citizenship
to be a price worth paying for an improved quality of life.

For Our Country

During the autumn uprising there were voices present that may be
described, loosely perhaps, as internationalist. I am thinking, for
instance, of a demonstration in Halle at which 'Cheers were raised for
[the revolution in] Czechoslovakia, accompanied by rhythmic clap-
ping'.[37] This spirit, one assumes, then migrated to the anti-unification
camp. Whereas supporters of unification were an aggressively nationalistic, flag-waving lot, this camp, including as it did a higher proportion
of oppositionists, inherited the 'non-violent' and internationalist ethos of
the early autumn. But this supposition, while not false in every detail, is

35 Neues Forum, *Jetzt*, p. 260.
36 Björn Kruger.
37 Editors of *Das Andere*, *Überraschung*, p. 113.

mistaken on the central count: at the core of the anti-unification argument was nationalism. Both camps concurred that the central question
was which state one should back. On the streets, the FRG flag-wavers
were met by counterdemonstrators. These carried not, say, rainbow
flags, but black–red–gold flags, too – albeit with the GDR emblem left
defiantly in the middle. East Germans were able to enjoy *a choice of
nationalisms.*

As with its pan-German rival, GDR nationalism was not of a virulent
'ethnic' strain but was bound up with economic and political goals. The
VL, to take an extreme example, championed GDR capital and saw the
'defence' of the *Kombinate* against western business as a prime goal.
Preventing the 'sell-off of the GDR' (by which was meant above all the
sale of 'people's own' firms to western capital) was the rallying cry. And
it was not without resonance among ordinary citizens. 'We're being
sold!', was how many workers experienced their company's purchase by
western capital. When – to give a typical example – the GDR light bulb
producer Narva began negotiations with its FRG counterpart, Osram,
Narva workers expressed their concern that management was organising a 'sell-off, at wretched terms, to the Osram capitalists'. But this
example exposes a mystifying aspect to the Left's campaign to 'defend
GDR *Kombinate*', for it was precisely the *Kombinat* directors who were
seeking western partners and buyers for their firms.

Objections to the 'sell-off of the GDR' were also somewhat eccentric,
for the SED regime – which the objectors were buttressing when not positively cheering – had, over the previous decade, been frenetically selling
anything it could lay its hands on to western buyers: cobblestones,
antiques, political prisoners, East German citizens' blood, sites for toxic
waste disposal and so on. Calls for the 'defence of people's property'
were scarcely less puzzling. Certainly, they 'fell on deaf ears among
workers, who didn't wish to defend what in any case didn't belong
to them'.[38]

The GDR patriots launched their manifesto two days before that of
the unification movement (Kohl's Ten-Point-Plan). Titled the 'Appeal for
an independent GDR' but more commonly known as 'For Our Country'
(FUL), its authors were SED academic Dieter Klein, DJ founder Konrad
Weiß, Protestant Church Generalsuperintendent Günther Krusche and
author Christa Wolf. Its original signatories also included prominent
figures in the SED (Berghofer) and opposition (Schorlemmer, Pflugbeil,
Ulrike Poppe, Bernd Gehrke), authors (Stefan Heym, Volker Braun),

---

38 *Die Zeit* 13 April 1990, p. 30; *die tageszeitung*, 3 March 1990, p. 8; Mosler,
   'Klassenkämpfe', p. 12.

Kombinat directors and church leaders. Within two months it had gathered over a million signatures.

The text of FUL offered its readers a choice. '*Either* we can insist upon GDR sovereignty', and build a socialist society of peace, justice, solidarity, freedom and environmental protection. '*Or* . . . powerful economic forces and unacceptable conditions imposed by influential West German business and political leaders' will lead to 'a sell-out of our material and moral values'.[39] The latter, it hinted, were rooted in 'the anti-fascist and humanist ideals from which we had earlier set out'. Given that the SED's foundation myth was that it was born of precisely those ideals, this formula appealed not only to democratic socialists and left-liberals but also to SED members, those of Stalinist disposition and otherwise. It was little wonder that early signatories included Egon Krenz and Hans Modrow. As a nationalist manifesto, it was no surprise either that the head of 'National Security' (formerly the Stasi), General Schwanitz, joined them – he even declared, with scant sensitivity to the new democratic norms, that every one of his officers supported the petition.

Coming as it did on the eve of the strike calls from Saxony, some of which were associated with pro-unification sentiment, FUL was a gift to the SED. 'Who could possibly sign For Our Country and yet advocate strike action?', *Neues Deutschland* editorialised on 2 December. For some early signatories, this was a scurrilous exploitation of FUL – it 'was misused as a campaign of the old style', in Heym's phrase.[40] In truth, however, its authors all but invited such mistreatment by lashing their call for progressive change to an insistence on the GDR's existence as a sovereign state.

FUL polarised East Germany. Two-thirds of Leipzig demonstrators rejected it, according to one survey. Counterpetitions were initiated. 'Whoever insists upon GDR sovereignty', one began,

> misunderstands the drastic extent of the crisis that the SED regime has presided over and must ask themselves if they are not being used as a tool of those still influential forces which continue, under the guise of socialism, to hanker for the old Stalinist structures.

The civic groups divided on the issue, too. Plauen New Forum, to give one example, issued an impassioned rebuttal:

> Since 28.11.1989 the drums in the media – which as always is controlled by the SED – have been beating to the sound of 'For Our Country'. All the registers of power are being deployed, in the old style. With no objective

39 Wolf was responsible for the 'either or' formulation. Wuttke, 'Entweder?'.
40 Heym, *Einmischung*, p. 272.

basis, government spokespeople are talking of majority support among the population for 'For Our Country'. With what right?!! In this conjuncture, in which conservative forces are beginning to feel the wind blowing their way and strive to stealthily bring back the old order, . . . the people are to be lulled to sleep with a dream . . . If there are anti-fascist and humanist ideals here, let us bring them into a federation for the benefit of both German states.

A referendum on the national question, the Plaueners concluded, should be called forthwith.[41]

In taking up cudgels on behalf of the East German state, a section of the opposition committed the fateful error of 'binding liberation from dictatorship, the struggle for direct democracy and the democratisation of society to the GDR's sovereign status'. For those goals had been advanced primarily through collective action – on the streets, in workplaces, universities and prisons. By contrast, the rise of the German Question up the political agenda, accelerated by FUL, tended to displace agency from ordinary people to political leaders, East and West, who were, at best, uninterested in 'direct democracy and the democratisation of society'. As they formed into choruses on behalf of rival national elites, East Germany's protestors and campaigners found themselves weakened, both through this division itself and through their transformation from autonomous actors into cheerleaders for one or other state. Although at least one of FUL's authors intended the petition to further the cause of 'participatory democracy', its actual effect was the opposite.[42]

As December passed into January, most of East German society, including the civic groups and *nomenklatura*, came to accept the inevitability of unification. As elections approached, the tempo and character of the unification process became the dominant issue of political debate, with political parties as the key actors. Yet the cycle of protest did not end therewith. Indeed, a revival occurred in January, and it is to that which we now turn.

41 Lindner, *Revolution*, p. 118; Küttler and Röder, *Volk*, p. 63; Renken, 'Oppositionsgruppen'.
42 Hartung, *Neunzehnhundertneunundachtzig*, p. 123; Weiß, *Macht*; Rochtus, *Utopie*, p. 216.

10

Protest swan-song, economic collapse

Now people are disappointed, because even capitalism is failing to bring about communism. (Pastor Hans-Jochen Vogel)[1]

We are in danger of losing our liberation from the dictatorship of a political party to the dictatorship of finance. (Friedemann Ehrig, DA)[2]

Popular histories of East Germany's revolution concentrate on a series of media-spectacular events: the summer exodus, 9 October in Leipzig and the fall of the Wall. A number of scholarly studies mention, in addition, the surge of protest in December. But the subsequent, and final, protest peak has suffered neglect in both academic and popular accounts. Except in the cities of Berlin and Leipzig, it was not in October or November that the greatest number of people took part in protests, but in January. That month also saw the highest number of protest events (aside from Berlin and Dresden), as well as peaks in other forms of protest, notably strikes and mutinies.[3] This chapter charts this final protest up-tick, traces the changing strategy of the regime and analyses the opposition's response, before concluding with a brief examination of the revolution's outcome.

'Events are getting ever less predictable'

Modrow's regime had weathered the storm, or so it appeared in mid-December. The SED had successfully re-founded itself and, by binding opposition leaders into its 'Great anti-chaos coalition', any immediate threat to its rule had been banished. By calling for a halt to protests over the Christmas period the Churches helped, too, as did Helmut Kohl, with

1 Interview with the author.
2 Opie, 'Views', p. 51.
3 Eberwein *et al.*, *Aufstand*, p. 35; Johnson, 'Massenmobilisierung', pp. 92–3.

his appeals to supporters of unification for patience.[4] Foreign leaders, meanwhile, were competing with one another for audiences with Hans Modrow, buttressing his credibility.[5]

Having restored a modicum of stability, the regime sought to regain the initiative and brake the pace of change.[6] It systematically obstructed the work of the round table and, in late December, announced that the Stasi's dissolution would be postponed until May and that its employees, when dismissed, would receive full salary for three years. Shortly thereafter, lurking repressive instincts were revealed in the form of a letter from a district Stasi headquarters, dated early December, which exhorted 'the armed organs of our common homeland . . . to unmask and paralyse the hate-filled machinations against the organs of state power' – such as the occupations of Stasi premises.[7]

Simultaneously, a campaign in the media, briefed by the police, high-lighted a new threat: neo-Nazism. Anti-Semitic graffiti was discovered at Jewish graveyards and 'ultranationalist' slogans appeared at the Soviet war memorial in Berlin-Treptow. However, the ulterior motives behind the campaign were not hard to spot. 'The impression is being given', Konrad Weiß argued, that since the Stasi had been shrunk into the Nasi, 'neo-Nazis have arrived. But they were already around when the Stasi still existed.' There were, moreover, rumours that some graffiti had been applied by Stasi hands. Whether true or not, these suspicions were strengthened when a rally at the Treptow memorial was expeditiously organised by the SED–PDS, which thousands of Communists and func-tionaries attended (and which the civic groups and CDU boycotted). Never above exploiting anti-fascist sentiment to further its own interests, the Party was seeking to exploit fears of a resurgent Right to justify the reconstitution of the Stasi. Gregor Gysi used his Treptow speech to call for 'the most decisive action' of the security organs, implying that the strengths of the Stasi and neo-Nazism were inversely related, while Stasi

4 With his visit to Dresden on 19 December, Helmut Kohl 'appeared to be sta-bilising a government that possesses no legitimacy . . ., but is at present the only stable factor in East Germany . . . For the German politicans in Dresden, unification was not on the agenda.' Hans-Jürgen Fink, quoted in Renken, 'Oppositionsgruppen'.
5 Notable amongst the latter was US Secretary of State James Baker, keen to get his visit in before that of François Mitterrand. Von Plato, *Vereinigung*, p. 150.
6 Falkner, 'SED', p. 41.
7 The document is reproduced in Krone, *Briefe*, pp. 400–1.

plainclothesmen could be seen in the crowd yelling slogans that called for a strengthened secret service.[8]

The regime's attempts to retrench only served to goad protestors to further efforts. At a mammoth, and especially militant, demonstration in Leipzig, banner slogans warned: 'For just two weeks we've stayed off the street, and already the SED's back on its feet!'[9] Parts of the country witnessed their largest demonstrations to date, including 160,000 in Karl-Marx-Stadt. But it was in workplaces that the sharpest reactions were seen. Political strikes broke out in Berlin, Suhl, Gera and a dozen other towns, against the SED–PDS and in particular the decision to extend salary payments to former Stasi employees.

The army, meanwhile, was in mutinous mood. At the Warnemünde Maritime College, students and trainees demanding the demilitarisation of the college and the abolition of uniforms marched, with weapons in hand, into the principal's office and forced him to resign.[10] On New Year's Day, several hundred conscript soldiers at Beelitz, near Potsdam, took command of their barracks, elected a soldiers' council and drafted a 24-point list of demands.[11] There was talk of founding a soldiers' union, and of forging links with their West German counterparts. According to one mutineer, their grievances were rooted in 'the interpersonal relations of superordinates and subordinates: it's not on for officers to vent their frustrations on us'. Local residents supported the striking soldiers, bringing coffee and sausages. Elsewhere, mutinous behaviour erupted over spartan barrack conditions, disciplinary issues and the length of compulsory military service (which, at eighteen months, was widely resented).[12]

Riding this new wave of revolt, the civic groups began to assert themselves. On 8 January, the round table delivered ultimatums to Modrow: to dissolve the Stasi, and to attend its next session in person. On 11

---

8 Krahulec, 'Dilemmata', p. 101; *die tageszeitung*, 5 January 1990. Canepa, *Germany's*; on neo-Nazism in the GDR, see Weiß, 'Neue'; Siegler, *Auferstanden*.
9 'Zwei Wochen nicht auf die Straße, schon hebt die SED die Nase.'
10 Nick Howard, personal communication.
11 The demands included: improved barracks conditions, a forty-hour week, reduction in the length of military service, an end to officers' privileges, the freedom to travel, no more deployments to fill labour shortages in industry and the right to refuse orders that contravene health, labour or environmental regulations.
12 *die tageszeitung*, 5 January 1990; *International Herald Tribune*, 1 March 1990.

January, oppositionists in Erfurt warned that close to a million workers in the South were prepared to strike. On the following day, almost all workplaces in nearby Weimar and the surrounding area, as well as several thousand workers in Erfurt itself, took part in a two-hour polit- ical strike.[13] 'Where demos are of no avail, strike action must prevail', read the slogans. Some New Forum groups, as well as SDP leader Markus Meckel, proposed calling political strikes over SED–PDS and Stasi retrenchment, a threat which, when rehearsed by opposition dele- gates at the round table, did at last force the Stasi to open sections of its files for inspection.[14]

Unfazed by the mounting pressure, Modrow informed the Volkskammer on 11 January that he would not waver from his intention of building a new security service. But even as parliament met, Berlin construction workers downed tools and marched into town. In addition to criticisms of SED–PDS and FDGB their banners read: 'Complete dis- solution of Stasi and Nasi!', 'Opposition at the Round Table – We build- ing workers support you!' and 'For rapid unification of both German states!' Encircling the parliament building, they hauled down its flag and cut out the GDR emblem. On the next day, taxi drivers followed suit. Forming a convoy around the Volkskammer, they called for a retraction of the decision to pay salaries to former Stasi employees, the dissolution of the FDGB and the formation of free trade unions. Parliament refused to pass the bill, and Modrow climbed down, promising that no new secu- rity service would be established until after a general election.[15]

Despite – or because of – this victory, the protest crescendo continued. On 15 January, workers at a Leipzig factory downed tools, demanding 'The SED–PDS must go!', and organised a demonstration, attended by employees from neighbouring workplaces. In Gera, Plauen and else- where, strikes broke out, with demands including the dissolution of the Stasi, democratisation, unification and the indictment of corrupt func- tionaries. But the highpoint of this, final, protest wave occurred at the Stasi's national headquarters in Berlin, to which New Forum had called a march. The event was, explicitly, a response to the regime's prevarica- tion over Stasi dissolution, but it evolved into a reprise and climax at the national level of the previous month's occupation movement. 'The crowd

---

13 New Forum backed this action, but several other opposition groups were opposed. Dietrich and Jander, 'Revolution', p. 325; Gehrke, 'Die "Wende"- Streiks', p. 262.

14 Schulz, 'Neues', p. 47; Neubert, *Opposition*, p. 896. SDP leaders were divided on this issue, with Ibrahim Böhme strongly opposed.

15 Pond, *Beyond*, p. 150; Renken, 'Oppositionsgruppen'.

was exceptionally aggressive', according to one report, 'and thousands pressed against the gates'. When these opened, tumult ensued, as demonstrators ransacked parts of the building. Hearing of the riot, opposition leaders rushed across Berlin to appease the crowds. Bärbel Bohley was to the fore, but her calming words were drowned out – 'She is shouted down before she can even say a word. "Wendehals", cries one of the demonstrators.' The irony was not lost on those present. 'The former victims of the Stasi', one commented, 'were summoned up to protect the Stasi from the mob'.[16]

Some mystery inevitably still attaches to the question of why the gates were opened. Stasi employees were responsible and, it seems, plain-clothesmen sought to direct the crowds toward 'safe' parts of the building. According to one citizens' committee member, 'all the regional headquarters had already been stormed, so the Stasi knew that it was only a matter of time before Berlin was targeted, and preferred to "enable" a situation there in order that it could exercise at least some control over events'. [17] Did Stasi officers hope to encourage, or even stage, scenes of vandalism in order to justify the government's continued attempts to shore up the security forces? Did they seek to give the impression that their organisation had been struck a mortal blow, so as to encourage the belief that the threat was gone, even as they continued hiding, selling, burning and manipulating information?[18] If the latter were true, then the gambit was partially successful. For although a citizens' committee was now permitted to control movements into and out of the building, many Stasi employees continued to enter and exit almost at will. However, the primary impact of the event was to hasten the Stasi's disintegration, force the release of more documents and guarantee at least some role for citizens' committees in overseeing the dissolution process. It was only on this day, 15 January, that the spectre of a resurrected secret service was finally abolished. Stasi General Grossmann now gave the order 'to destroy everything', and senior officers defected in droves to the FRG and US secret services, and to western multinationals.[19]

Although New Forum distanced itself from the occupation, and denounced the 'violence' involved, it marked the most decisive blow to the regime's attempted retrenchment. For Soviet ambassador Kochemassov,

16 *Tribüne*, 16 January 1990; *die tageszeitung*, 17 January 1990; *die tageszeitung* Journal 2, p. 60; Thompson, *Reluctant*, p. 55.
17 Steff Konopatzky, interview.
18 For speculation along these lines, see Reuth and Bönte, *Komplott*, p. 203.
19 Mitter and Wolle, *Untergang*, p. 12; *Der Spiegel*, 38, 1990, p. 41; 4, 1995, pp. 109–11.

15 January 'represents the beginning of a new phase [of the crisis]: Strikes are beginning, slogans against the State Security and SED/PDS [are proliferating]. Developments are getting ever less predictable.' In line with this perspective, the ambassador set up a crisis cabinet and a round-the-clock duty roster.[20] For US historian Robert Darnton, the day 'shook the government to its core'. Gerda Haufe agrees: it was 'hit in the bullseye'.[21] The SED–PDS now commenced its final retreat from power, beginning with an offer of government positions to the civic groups.

Butchers, bakers, potash miners

In terms of the severity of blows raining upon the regime and the extent of popular mobilisation, the last half of January bears comparison with the first week of December. The SED–PDS' ongoing disintegration was highlighted when Wolfgang Berghofer – its most popular figure after Modrow and Gysi – resigned, along with the entire Dresden leadership and prominent *Kombinat* directors. From within the Party rank-and-file, advocates of complete dissolution raised their voices yet again. The provision of consumer goods was deteriorating, too. With the dismantling of currency restrictions, foreigners – West Germans to the fore – could exploit the favourable exchange rate, buying goods cheaply and further emptying the shops. (By insinuating repeatedly that Poles and Vietnamese were responsible for goods shortages, the state media and government spokespeople only signalled their impotence; given the strength of protests directed against the regime, playing the 'race card' was futile.) Economic crisis was also intensified by continued emigration: fully 60,000 people left the country in January, a rise from the previous month's figure of 43,000.

The SED–PDS' continued grip on power was a major theme on the weekly demonstrations, which continued throughout January. Banners called for the 'expropriation of the SED' and even for its proscription. The same period also saw a proliferation of placards exhorting industrial action. For the first time since 1953, East Germans began to take action, on a large scale, as workers. There were demonstrations: of teachers, for their jobs; health workers, to protest the crisis in the health service; and kindergarten nurses, for a pay rise and for the provision of fresh fruit for the children. Even police demonstrated, for greater democracy in the police force. On 16 January a strike wave began, with industrial action in Schwerin. Ten more towns followed on the next day, and more again

20 Maximytschew, 'Mauerfall', p. 37.
21 Darnton, *Berlin*; Haufe and Bruckmeier, *Bürgerbewegungen*, p. 86.

on the 19th. By the end of January, the daily strike toll was in the region of twenty–twenty-five, concentrated in Thuringia.[22]

Strikes took place across the country and in a wide range of industries. Doctors and nurses took action, as did factory and construction workers, shop assistants and refuse collectors, tram and ambulance drivers, butchers, bakers and dairy workers. Many broke out over terms and conditions, including working hours and safety, and other workplace-related demands, such as the sacking of incompetent managers or the release of the company from state control. Health workers struck nationwide for better pay and conditions as well as health sector reform. Strikes over pay were often fuelled explicitly by a desire to close the gap with FRG counterparts. Many such strikes, over wages and other workplace-related issues, were successful – notably that of the Bischofferode potash miners, whose demands included a hefty pay rise and independence for their *Kombinat*.

In many other cases, overtly political demands were central. Strikes and strike threats continued to be deployed to drive the SED–PDS from workplaces, and many raised the demand for it to quit government, too. The dissolution of the Stasi, faster democratisation, and the sacking of ministers were also common themes. The demands of strikers in Strasburg, for example, included proscription of the SED–PDS, the sacking of all functionaries in senior political positions and their replacement, pending free elections, by representatives of the civic groups. Those of strikers at the Büromaschinenwerk Sömmerda included: 'Complete disclosure of all the Stasi's machinations, complete transparency about the SED's funds, and the expropriation of the SED's companies and their conversion into people's property', as well as 'complete equality of opportunity for parties and opposition groups standing in elections'.[23]

The strikes were oriented not only to 'old' issues but also to the challenges of the new. From December, *Kombinat* managements had been gearing up for 'rationalisation', including joint ventures with, or the outright sale of the enterprise to, western companies. Rationalisation meant layoffs, which were invariably justified with the argument 'it's unavoidable – the market is coming'. Although common responses to the looming threat of job cuts included the hope that one's own would be safe, and a faith in the 'flourishing landscapes' promised by the apostles of unification, in some cases workers were spurred to action. At the Berliner Bremsenwerk, for example, 'tumult' broke out when employees

22 *Linksruck*, 5 November 1999; Gehrke, ' "Wende"-Streiks'.
23 Langer, *Norden*, p. 203; Klenke, *Rationalisierung*.

learned that the company's western partner was to take on only 700 of its 2,300-strong workforce.[24]

As the above examples show, the strike wave witnessed an intertwining of economic and political issues, as well as of 'old' and 'new' issues. Consider, for example, the hostility to continued salary payments for former Stasi officers, which prompted much industrial action. The bitterness involved, trade union activist Bernd Gehrke has argued, 'resulted largely from the fact that the approaching unemployment for ordinary workers would not be accompanied by such generous interim payments, while the renewed privileges for the formerly privileged were becoming blatantly obvious.'[25]

Alongside strikes, progress was made in union and workplace organisation. Workers sought to reform the FDGB, or to establish independent trade union groups, while new-formed works councils demanded a say in negotiations with western firms – indeed, the first quarter of 1990 saw an upturn in all these forms of organisation. Groups such as the VL and the Initiative for Independent Trade Unions (IUG) contributed to the formation and networking of rank-and-file workplace organisations, and in early 1990, a national congress of works' councillors took place. The IUG maintained contact with some 170 workplace groups, each with a membership of between 5 and 500. According to one IUG activist, workers from across the country were continually 'ask[ing] us to establish independent union organizations'. The emergence of rank-and-file organisations, in turn, intensified pressure upon the FDGB – no longer seated at the highest tables of the state – to take seriously its nominal role of representing workers. At its congress in late January, a motion supporting a radical trade union law was passed, and the idea of lending it weight by calling a general strike found popularity among delegates.[26]

'A popular upsurge they could not fully control'

At the peak of a protest cycle, as described in chapter 8, one tends to see a proliferation of forms of protest, as well as bargaining between social movement organisations and the authorities. In East Germany, both these phenomena were witnessed in early December and again in mid-January. In both periods, negotiations between civic groups and

---

24 Roesler, *Ostdeutsche*, pp. 57–8.
25 Gehrke, ' "Wende"-Streiks', pp. 263–4.
26 Gehrke and Hürtgen, *Betriebliche*, pp. 420, 433–5 and *passim*; Dale, *Popular*, ch. 9; Ansorg and Hürtgen, *Initiative*, p. 5; Fuller, *Working*, p. 119; Müller ' "Oktoberrevolution" ', p. 94.

government reached a higher level. Both saw protest waves that included significant new actors and/or sites of action. As in December, the upsurge in January could well have consigned the government to history. The key date was 15 January. That day's riot in Berlin could easily have 'spread out across the whole country', East Germany's chief of police warned at the time. 'What would have happened', historian Eckhard Müller-Mertens has asked, 'if the occupation of the Stasi headquarters . . . had not been reversed? Who could have prevented New Forum from taking the buildings into its own hands? What would have happened if New Forum had proceeded in this way on 15 January?' Frank Renken, too, argues that East Germany was on the threshold of 'a full-scale social uprising'; the only missing ingredient 'was coordination amongst its various centres around the country'. US scholar Steven Pfaff makes a not dissimilar case:

> Had the civic movement been prepared to more fully exploit the situation, it is likely that the Modrow government could have been compelled to take much more radical steps or have collapsed completely. Of course, this is precisely what the civic movements feared – a popular upsurge they could not fully control.[27]

Needless to say, the prospect of 'a full-scale social uprising' did not tempt opposition leaders in the slightest, and most of them looked upon the strike wave with dismay. 'There are strikes everywhere and everyone wants something', they – in this instance a Leipzig feminist – would lament, but 'when there's nothing in the pot, people must hold down their expected living standards for two or three years'. Their western allies, notably Walter Momper of West Berlin's SPD, appealed for 'the incessant discussion about a general strike' to be quashed. A more forth-coming attitude from Modrow meanwhile confirmed the oppositionists in their stance.[28]

As Modrow himself saw it, the threat of 'chaos' had returned, oblig-ing him to broaden his base yet again, this time by engaging more con-structively with the round table and the civic groups. From 15 January, he repeatedly invited oppositionists to assume posts in government. Other SED–PDS leaders, notably Gysi, appealed to them to act, 'together with the SED–PDS, to calm the population down', and they responded warmly. Friedrich Schorlemmer, previously of DA but recently converted

27 Bahrmann and Links, *Chronik der Wende 2*, p. 62; Renken, 'Oppositions-gruppen'; Pfaff, 'Revolution', p. 425.
28 Ute Leukert, in Findeis, *Entzauberung*, pp. 146–7; *Berliner Zeitung*, 20 January 1990.

to the SDP, put the argument against 'chaos' and for cooperation with a singular gusto: 'I get incandescently angry when I notice that people are doing their utmost to trip Herr Modrow up. I need to work through this feeling, by making my views clear: Because I am concerned for peace, I wish for stability for Modrow's government.'[29]

If mainstream oppositionists such as Schorlemmer were bound to support the government in its battle against 'chaos', this was not true for the more radical currents. There were three main groupings: the IUG, VL and New Forum's left-wing minority. The IUG's prime aim was to encourage workers' networks outside the FDGB; it rejected the strategy of 'dialogue' in favour of grassroots organisation. Rather than mobilising around opposition to unification – as did the VL – the IUG mapped a radical agenda for the transition to the market: develop links with West German trade unionists, combat redundancies and campaign for wages and conditions to be raised to West German levels. Similarly, leftists in New Forum oriented to social and workplace issues as prerequisites for a radical democracy: the right of workers' representatives to veto management, a reduction in the working week, the rights to a home and to a job.[30]

The growing prominence of workers within the movement in the winter months presented these three groupings with opportunities. They could have 'made a concerted effort to build links with East Germany's workers', one North American scholar has speculated, 'particularly since this was a period marked by numerous strikes and initiatives to form independent labour organisations'.[31] Yet, for such efforts to count, the radical groupings were too small and/or arrived too late. The IUG was not founded until mid-December, yet only a month later the established FRG trade unions were beginning to arrive and, for many, they seemed a surer alternative to the FDGB than did the small circles of IUG-linked militants.[32] New Forum's left wing came into being in the same period as the IUG; it possessed only shallow roots among workers, and made little effort to extend them. As for the VL, it attempted to relate to the working-class radicalisation but its small numbers, coupled with its conversion into a vehicle of GDR patriotism, restricted its potential audience.

29 Modrow, *Aufbruch*, p. 79; *Neues Deutschland* 18 January 1990; Lindner, *Maß*, p. 131.
30 Jander, 'Formierung', p. 290; Krone, 'Keine'.
31 Allen, *Germany*, pp. 203–4.
32 In addition, the IUG was ill-equipped to relate to the wave of working-class radicalisation, for it was strongly political in nature, whereas the IUG's remit was restricted to a comparatively narrow range of syndicalist issues.

'If the streets take control of the German Question . . .'

The revival of protest in January was driven by a perception that the regime was attempting to retrench, and this same perception added an urgency, even desperation, to the calls for unification. The clamour was amplified by a second dynamic, namely that economic crisis, the continuing exodus and the crumbling of the Modrow government's legitimacy further diminished the belief that reconstruction could be accomplished without unstinting western assistance. On the streets, divisions widened over the German Question. Supporters of unification turned their fire on the GDR patriots, taunting them with chants of 'Communist pigs', 'Stalinists' and 'Reds out of the demo', to which the 'reds' replied with banners and chants attacking 'Konsum Rausch' (consumerism) and the 'Fourth Reich' (unified Gernany).

Name-calling escalated into skirmishes, in which fascists and their fellow travellers were sometimes involved. Despite this, the widely held supposition that 'the *Republikaner* and conservative chauvinists took over the Monday demonstrations in Leipzig' is an exaggeration. It is true that many protestors, initially, would accept propaganda brought by the *Republikaner* from the FRG. But this was early on, when all political literature was greedily read. Later, people tended to discriminate, and to challenge the fascists, chasing them from the demonstrations and tearing up their placards. Of the Leipzig demonstrators surveyed by Kurt Mühler, Steffen Wilsdorf and their students, only 1 per cent supported the *Republikaner* in November and December, rising to 4 per cent in January and falling back to 3 per cent in February.[33] In a general election at the year's end, neo-fascist parties achieved only 1.6 per cent in eastern Germany, considerably less than in the western *Länder*.

In contrast to the autumn, supporters of unification now found themselves in the company of substantial sections of the ruling class, notably company managers, as well as the 'bloc parties'. The latter had not hitherto been prominent actors of the *Wende*. (As Müller-Mertens puts it: 'They slotted themselves into the course of events, not making the slightest appearance as revolutionary or revolutionising forces that might fill the power vacuum.')[34] In December, the 'Democratic Bloc' had begun to collapse, with CDU, LDPD and the other bloc parties abandoning their alliance with the SED and commencing, in the words of one CDU leader,

33 Smith, 'Revolution', p. 242; Schomers, *Deutschland*, p. 216; Mühler and Wilsdorf, 'Montagsdemonstration', p. 43.
34 Müller-Mertens, *Politische*, p. 51

a process of 'self-cleansing'.[35] On the German Question, their positions diverged slightly from the SED–PDS. The CDU came out for the 'unity of the German nation' and for a 'growing together of the two German states', while the NDPD declared in favour of confederation, and added for good measure that East Germans should accept West Germany's president as their own.

The bloc parties were responding to public opinion but also to the growing influence of West Germany's political class. From January, Bonn began to force the pace on unification, and sought to destabilise Modrow's regime. Kohl's chief of staff, Horst Teltschik, warned that the GDR faced imminent collapse (a comment that a Free Democratic Party (FDP) government minister Otto von Lambsdorff likened to 'arson').[36] West Germany's CDU and FDP actively sought allies in the East; the former gathered up East Germany's CDU as well as a newly formed right-wing party, the DSU, and DA, while the NDPD and LDPD allied with the FDP. These alliances were potent, bringing together the funds and membership of the bloc parties with the funds and credibility of their western partners. Given that they betokened a marriage between previously hostile elites, the process was steeped in irony. For example, DA was led into alliance with Kohl's (strongly pro-market) CDU by a leader, Rainer Eppelmann, who had only a month before been arguing that 'state property must dominate' in East Germany's economy. Kohl's Eastern counterpart, CDU leader de Maizière, had been the GDR's deputy president since November. As late as December, his party had insisted that the GDR's constitution include a commitment to socialism, which he himself praised as 'one of the human imagination's most beautiful visions'. But the most priceless of ironies was the Stasi connections of de Maizière and his colleagues. 'All the three major players with whom Kohl formed the Alliance for Germany', Dirk Philipsen has pointed out, 'namely the General Secretary of the CDU, Martin Kirchner, the chairman of the CDU and later Prime Minister, Lothar de Maizière, and the chairman of Democratic Awakening, Wolfgang Schnur, had for many years served as Stasi informants' – a fact for which the FRG government, and Kohl himself, 'possessed conclusive evidence at the time'.[37]

---

35 Martin Kirchner, in *Zurück zu Deutschland*, p. 451. Kirchner himself didn't 'cleanse' thoroughly enough: some documents remained which proved he had acted as a Stasi informal agent.

36 The policy, argues Jürgen Habermas (*Revolution*, p. 212), was also aimed at weakening the opposition.

37 Pechmann and Vogel, *Abgesang*, p. 361; Teltschik, *329*, p. 38; Philipsen, *People*, p. 337.

It was not long before the bloc parties were joined in their support for unification by the SED–PDS. To many a Party member this seemed an extraordinary reversal. As late as 25 January, Gysi had been espousing the case for continued independence, but on that very same day Modrow conceded to Helmut Kohl's chief of staff that his regime was in an exceptionally tight corner: 'the state's authority is tumbling, the strike wave is growing, aggression is increasing, the Round Table no longer has any influence upon events.' Against a background characterised by the partial disintegration of local government, accelerating emigration, an ongoing strike wave and a swelling chorus demanding higher wages and pensions and, of course, unification, Modrow feared that the masses would 'become a law unto themselves', with 'the streets taking control of the German Question'.[38]

The possibility of unification being pushed 'from below' was a very real one. Demonstration banners warned: 'If the D-Mark comes, we'll stay. If it doesn't, we'll cross over to it.' In the middle of January, a remarkable case of 'exit-as-voice' occurred when around 70,000 inhabitants of the border region of Eichsfeld effected a mass exit to the FRG . . . and then returned, the message being: 'we came back this time, but if the SED stays in office we might just change our minds.'[39] After currency union had been agreed in the spring, East Germans kept up the pressure, with around a million trade unionists demonstrating in favour of conversion of East-Marks into D-Marks at parity, rather than at the 2:1 ratio favoured by the FRG establishment. In this context, and with Moscow acquiescing to a geopolitical redesign of Europe, Modrow faced a choice between provoking further radicalisation by defending GDR sovereignty to the last, or bowing to the growing pressure from below. He plumped for the latter and, at the end of January, announced his support for unification.

Elections and demobilisation

If the beginning of East Germany's 1989–90 protest cycle cannot be precisely dated, that is not true of its end. It came in the final four days of January, when Modrow announced his vision of 'Germany, United Fatherland' and also advanced the election date, originally due in May, by two months. The change of date was supported by the well-funded parties – CDU, SPD, SED–PDS, LDPD – but would clearly count against

38 Gysi, 'Sozialismus', p. 68; Teltschik, *329*, p. 115; *Tribüne*, 30 January 1990; Arnold, *Modrow*, p. 97.
39 Dietrich and Jander, 'Revolution', p. 327.

poorer and newer groups. ('The Opposition', gloated one SED–PDS supporter upon hearing the decision, 'lack structures and personalities; that will curb them'.)[40]

Preparations for the forthcoming election went into overdrive. The restructuring of political space continued apace, with the regime/opposition divide giving way to a competitive party system. Western parties muscled in on East German political territory; their allies rapidly became dependants. The civic groups – with the exceptions of DA and the SPD – gathered into two alliances, around New Forum and the Green Party, respectively.[41] As legal channels for political and industrial participation widened, protest declined. Reaching its zenith at the end of January, the strike wave then ebbed, while street protests steadily declined (in Leipzig the fall was from around 140,000 on 15 January to 11,000 six weeks later).[42] By February, the demonstrations were morphing into election rallies, with party activists distributing flyers, and banners displaying party slogans.[43]

A third decision, also at the end of January, saw the civic groups finally end their oppositional status and join a caretaker National Government. Prominent opposition figures such as Ullmann, Eppelmann and Gerd Poppe, as well as young unknowns such as the Green Party's Mathias Platzek, gained a taste of office. Some analysts interpret their invitation into government as the result of a shift in the balance of power 'in favour of the opposition forces' in consequence of the 15 January Stasi occupation. In fact, however, the civic groups were a dwindling force, with the popularity of those lacking western allies in rapid decline. It was not they that pressed Modrow to invite them into government but vice versa. With oppositionists occupying government posts, he hoped, its standing would be enhanced, enabling it to maintain control in the pre-election period. Citing the growth of fascism and the danger of 'chaos', the premier urged them to abandon their vestiges of hostility and give him their full confidence.[44]

---

40 Maximytschew, 'Mauerfall', p. 39.
41 An election alliance of all civic groups was mooted but was thwarted by the SPD. One of its leaders, Martin Gutzeit, told me gleefully: 'I blocked that plan! We had to have formal rules of membership. Formal principles! A programme! Structures! And New Forum couldn't possibly agree to any of that!'
42 Johnson, 'Massenmobilisierung'; Lohmann, 'Dynamics'.
43 Some of these retained the punning style of earlier demonstrations – such as 'Where there's a Willy there's a way!' (Willy refers, of course, to Brandt, the SPD's revered former Chancellor.) Schneider, *Kleine*, p. 405.
44 Bruckmeier und Haufe, *Bürgerbewegungen*, p. 98; Modrow, *Aufbruch*, p. 79; Gerlach, *Mitverantwortlich*, p. 412.

If the civic groups gained from participation in government the benefits are hard to spot. Of twenty-eight ministries, the opposition took
eight, all of which were in the low-status position of minister without
portfolio. Yet again, they had to confront the blocking tactics of the state
bureaucracies – for example, information on the state of the economy
and on the existence of GDR institutions' bank accounts abroad was
denied them. The former oppositionists, as Renken puts it, 'belonged to
a government which was nothing but a liquidator'. With the benefit of
hindsight, they themselves are hardly less scathing. Their ministers,
writes Mehlhorn, 'were nothing but guarantors that the period until the
elections would take place with as little chaos as possible'; the exercise
simply led 'to the stabilisation of the old forces within a new framework'.
In Neubert's assessment, 'the opposition groups had become a stabilising factor in the transition, without decisively influencing politics at the
state level'.[45]

A chief motivation of the decision to enter government was indeed, in
the words of a VL spokesperson, to contribute to 'a stabilisation of the
situation'.[46] The government to be stabilised represented the reformist
wing of the old regime. Its commitments included slowing the dismantling of the Stasi and ensuring that its officer caste not be redeployed 'into
production', as the demonstrators demanded, but into the interior ministry, customs authority and border police. Its priority was the security
of the existing elite, even as other groups faced mounting insecurity. The
latter included workers facing redundancy, particularly women, as well
as Vietnamese *Gastarbeiter* – a community that had received disgraceful
treatment under Honecker's government[47] and now faced worse under
Modrow's, which ordered the immediate deportation of the unemployed
and homeless and prepared the deportation of the remainder. Entering a
coalition government of this sort alienated the civic groups from a variety
of constituencies, including anti-communists and radical democrats. As
political scientist Ulrich Preuss has pointed out, they had 'derived their
influence mainly from their position as being the antipodes of the government. Consequently, this capital faded away when they radically

45 Renken, 'Oppositionsgruppen'; Findeis, *Entzauberung*, p. 167; Neubert,
    Revolution, p. 93.
46 *Neues Deutschland*, 31 January 1990. The VL itself quickly reversed its deci-
    sion to join the government as a result of Modrow's pro-unification decla-
    ration.
47 On arrival in the GDR their passports were withdrawn; they were housed in
    barracks, isolated from the rest of the community; they were paid less than
    their German counterparts and sent home if they bore children.

changed their position and complied with the prime minister's bid to join
his cabinet.'[48]

The new ministers were hopeful that their presence in government
would at least encourage one positive measure: that Bonn would loosen
its purse strings. Ever-optimistic, Modrow took the new ministers with
him on an expedition to Bonn. However, the FRG government signalled
clearly that it would not honour the moral credit that he had gained from
the opposition. 'We are sitting here with the rich brothers but we're to
keep quiet', commented cabinet minister Poppe on their humiliating trip
to Bonn.[49] No financial aid was forthcoming.

A vote 'for Coca-Cola and porn'?

As spring approached, East Germany was a curious cocktail of hopes and
fears. Free elections were imminent; the SED's rule was soon to be history.
Almost two-thirds of the population anticipated an 'economic miracle', a
utopian prospect that was assiduously propagated by scholars, journalists and politicians. Although 'many people will inevitably be put out of
work, they will be re-employed as new jobs are created', neoliberal economics professors predicted. But even if job losses were to be only for the
short term this was a still a concern, particularly for older workers. And
what would become of rents and incomes? And kindergartens? Worries
such as these fed into episodes of panic buying and into the belligerent
nationalism that could still be seen at demonstrations. What was remarkable about the period, observes Charles Maier, 'was the sense of unease
that accompanied the electoral process. How different from the euphoria
of the previous November . . . [T]he dominant mood of the country
seemed to be anxiety that the upcoming negotiations would undermine
their modest but secure standard of living.'[50]

Most observers expected to see a strong electoral performance from the
various parties – including the SDP, PDS and New Forum's 'Alliance '90' –
that preferred unification to be implemented according to article 146 of
the FRG constitution, which would entail founding a new state with a
new constitution. To different degrees, these all espoused reformist socialism which, opinion polls suggested, attracted 56 per cent support, as
against only 31 per cent for capitalism. The frontrunner was a party that
had been centrally involved in the uprising, possessed a powerful western

---

48 Preuss, 'Roundtable', p. 126.
49 Humann, *Geld*, p. 61.
50 Dennis, 'Perceptions', p. 89; *Financial Times*, 2 July 1990; Maier, *Dissolution*,
    p. 209.

ally and had historical roots in East Germany: the SPD. The alliances centred on New Forum and the Green Party were new and inexperienced and did not hope for victory, but could expect to perform creditably. They were untainted by association with the old establishment, and were the recognised leaders of the transition process. Like most of the electorate, they welcomed western capital but opposed NATO membership.[51]

In the event, less than one in twenty of the electorate cast their vote for the civic groups and less than a quarter voted SPD, with almost half preferring the CDU-led 'German Alliance'. The CDU's former ally in the National Front, the SED–PDS, also performed well, prompting one journalist to declare: 'The clear victors of this election are the old bloc parties, CDU and SED–PDS. The GDR is dying, long live the National Front.'[52] If this irony was apparent at the time, another emerged only in subsequent months, when the leaders of the two parties that profited most from what had been an overwhelmingly anti-Stasi vote were exposed as Stasi collaborators.[53]

There was something topsy-turvy about the CDU's triumph. Its voters were backing a party that only months earlier had condemned the protests which had broken open the path to elections. Its enemies missed no opportunity to remind the electorate of its tainted past – perhaps their best-known slogan was: 'Whoever learned recorder [*Block*flöte] with the SED should not play first violin after the elections.' Yet the CDU not only shook off this image but even had the gall, in what was a no-holds-barred campaign, to accuse its main rival, the SPD, of being in cahoots with Communism.

The CDU achieved a distance from its own past not through any rigorous *Aufarbeitung* but by more miraculous means – the blessed touch of the West German CDU and CSU. Thanks to Helmut Kohl's illegal party-funding activities, these pumped DM4.5 million to their allies in the East, three times the funds supplied by SPD and FDP, and this assistance could be put to efficient use thanks to the Eastern CDU's existing party machine. West Germany's media helped, too, by sowing fears that socialists and 'cosmopolitan intellectuals' were attempting to slow the unification process and by giving undue airtime and column inches to predictions that rapid unification would kick-start a growth miracle.[54]

51 Förster and Roski, *DDR*, p. 56; Denitch, *End*, pp. 40–2.
52 *die tageszeitung* Journal 2, p. 156.
53 In a further irony, the leader of the SED–PDS, appears *not* to have acted as an informal agent. See Miller, *Narratives*.
54 See *Die Zeit*, 1 June 1990, p. 52. The irony of the FRG media's intervention has been pointed out by Michael Schneider (*Revolution*, p. 103): 'The majority of

But to concentrate on party funding and media bias, as some post-election autopsies did, or to see it as 'a vote for Coca-Cola and porn movies', as one West Berlin newspaper sneered, would be to miss the main point. In essence, the election was a referendum on a union between two unequal states, of which the rich and stable one was governed by a CDU-led coalition. Kohl was the incumbent capitalist-in-chief; he held Bonn's purse strings. A US diplomat in the GDR has described a conversation with two young East Germans that alerted him to the coming CDU victory: ' "We are workers", one said. "We should vote SPD. Next time we probably will. But this country needs money. The West controls the money, and the CDU controls the West, so we will vote CDU." '[55] Similarly, for me, the CDU's advantage was summed up in the words of a student who, as an FDJ activist and proponent of unification via §146 (rather than the 'annexation paragraph' §23 favoured by the 'German Alliance'), was no natural conservative, yet nonetheless voted CDU. 'For the capital', she explained, matter-of-factly.

In its election campaign, the CDU played to these in-built strengths. It exaggerated the danger of economic and social collapse, indulged irrational fears of old-order retrenchment, and prophesied that monetary union and German unification would visit Edenic conditions upon the land. It tapped into a popular rejection of social 'experiments' and campaigned for unification 'with no ifs and buts'. In addition, it benefited from its existing party structures. In contrast, the SPD was a new organisation in the East; it presented a more sceptical face towards unification before later shifting tack to full-blooded support. Ultimately, it gained little either from the first path, which had been more popular in the West but was abandoned, or from the second, which appeared as a mere echo of the CDU's position.

Whereas most election post-mortems have focused on the nature and behaviour of the parties, the condition of the electorate should also be borne in mind. Ludwig Mehlhorn has drawn attention to

citizens' unease with themselves. Confidence in one's own strength was absent, and the [civic groups] were deemed too weak to take on the power structures of SED and Stasi. So the people said simply: 'We have to get through this as fast as possible, and the surest guarantee for that is the ruling CDU.'[56]

FRG media organs, especially the most influential ones, which never missed an opportunity to pillory the GDR media for its pro-SED partisanship . . . offered themselves as willing mouthpieces of the FRG government.'

55 Greenwald, *Berlin*, p. 302.
56 Findeis, *Entzauberung*, p. 167.

In this analysis, the CDU tapped that fervid desire for unification which, as suggested in chapter 9, expressed hostility to the SED–PDS combined with a consciousness of the country's abject situation. Conversely, the absence of 'confidence in one's own strength' militated against the civic groups, given that theirs was a politics dedicated to empowerment at the grassroots. Together with their lack of experience, shortage of time to develop brand recognition and divisions within and between their coalitions, this goes some way to explaining their calamitous performance.

Yet, must there not be something more? How could citizens' collective confidence have diminished so precipitously? Only nine weeks before the election, the storming of the Stasi headquarters in Berlin had threatened to spark a nationwide rising; it was eight weeks since a major wave of strikes and demonstrations, and seven weeks since Modrow had warned of 'the streets taking control of the German Question'. Had the mass movement simply evaporated, leaving a residue of disempowered individuals?

This question can be addressed in several ways, of which I would mention two. First, only a minority of the electorate, even if a large one, had participated in the protest movement. It was concentrated in the large towns and cities, whereas the German Alliance fared best in rural areas. Second, the movement had indeed demobilised, a process that the civic groups had, since November, sought to expedite. As protests took on a more plebeian and radical tone, the civic groups championed those issues that set them apart, such as personal austerity and economic nationalism. It was not only that the civic groups cultivated a 'lifestyle politics' and other issues with minority appeal, but also that they cooperated ever more closely with the despised regime. In consequence, a political vacuum arose, which the western parties and their 'self-cleansing' eastern partners were quick to exploit. By February, the civic groups were ensconced in government and engaged in drafting a future constitution; they paid little attention to the concerns of ordinary people. This latter point has been well made by Bernd Gehrke:

> The January strike wave, coupled with the mass demonstrations . . . convulsed the entire state which, without political leadership powers of its own, collapsed . . . While the opposition was winning, in a politically enervating manner, its months-long battle with the relics of the past, it ignored the social and economic conflicts around it and lost the battle for the future. On 18 March this outcome found its parliamentary expression.[57]

57 Gehrke, ' "Wende"-Streiks', p. 269.

For the most part, civic group activists were depressed by the election result, but some were indignant and felt betrayed by their fellow citizens. For Bohley, voters had behaved 'like sheep'. 'The masses', sniped Berlin anarchist Wolfgang Rüddenklau, had become 'blind aimless cogs, lacking initiative and obeying only their needs'. Another activist accused East Germans of 'lacking a talent for democracy', while a fourth (a 'highly prominent figure'), after berating them for having voted the wrong way, added: 'people are now worried about losing their jobs. I have to say it serves them right if they *do*, in fact, lose their jobs.'[58] In what was perhaps the revolution's final irony, some of the civic movement's leading lights, notably Bohley but also Vera Lengsfeld and Günter Nooke, recovered from their trouncing by the CDU and . . . joined it themselves.[59]

Of cream and spilt milk

The investiture of the CDU-led government marked the end of the revolution. The old structures were shattered; there could be no return. Intergovernmental negotiations over economic and monetary union and unification dominated the political agenda, and although protest activity revived around specific issues, notably the conversion of East-Marks into D-Marks, it was marginal. The actors involved in negotiating the terms of unification included the governments of both Germanies and of the four allied powers, as well as figures from the business community, including the heads of Germany's two largest private banks and of its Federation of Industry.

The modalities of the unification process were largely insulated from the citizenry. It was 'a bureaucratic process', writes Konrad Jarausch;

> To resolve difficult conflicts, an army of lawyers codified compromises in innumerable regulations. Instead of inspiring national town meetings, insistence on an orderly and swift transition produced a voluminous legal compendium. The complexity of re-unifying two estranged states took the process out of the public's hands and turned it over to distant bureaucrats.

Where the opinions of elites and citizenry divided, the former held sway. Thus, whereas a large majority of Germans on both sides of the Elbe desired withdrawal from NATO, keeping the new Germany in the

---

58 Pond, *Beyond*, p. 200; Rüddenklau *Störenfried*, p. 366; Fehr, *Unabhängige*, p. 263; Philipsen, *People*, p. 347, emphasis in original.
59 Neubert and Eppelmann also joined the CDU but, as DA members, had already been in alliance with it since January.

Alliance (and indeed extending it further eastward) was a prime objective for Washington and Bonn, and their position prevailed. While eastern Germans overwhelmingly favoured a mixed economy, the business community preferred fire-sale privatisation. Not only did the latter prevail, but the authority established to manage the process, the 'Treuhand', was deliberately and effectively sequestered from parliamentary scrutiny. This was not due to some innate Bismarckian strain in the German character, but in order to insulate the deindustrialisation *cum* asset stripping of the New *Länder* from democratic pressure. As the head of the Treuhand herself admitted: 'No cabinet would be able to make the kind of decisions that we [do], because it would be immediately voted out.'[60]

The withdrawal of citizens from the public sphere had complemented the goals and leadership style of the old regime, and likewise suited the new. If mobilisation for democratisation tends to foreground demands for political participation, the institutionalisation of parliamentary democracy serves to push them back. The 'demobilization of the eastern German electorate', according to US political scientist Jennifer Yoder, has been 'fostered by the new system itself. The institutions of representative party democracy do not necessarily encourage active support.' From the testimony of eastern Germans from elite and non-elite layers, Yoder portrays contemporary political participation as involving little more than occasional voting in parliamentary elections.

That a phase of mobilisation yields to the containment of social movements and consolidation of elite power is the normal progression in transitions to liberal democracy. In East Germany's case, however, it was overlayered by a second dynamic: the westernisation of the entire gamut of eastern institutions, in a process directed by 'an ersatz elite of managers and experts from West German political parties, bureaucracies, and other organizations'.[61] As a form of institutional transfer this doubtless appeared straightforward from a logistical point of view, but it came with a political price. Unification began to appear less a majority demand of the GDR citizenry than West German conquest. 'It's like after a war: the victor makes the rules', easterners say.[62] Some westerners agree. 'We are doing with the easterners what [the USA] did with us after World War II', said one official working in the east, 'we are reeducating them. Of

60 Jarausch, *Rush*, pp. 176, 168; Judt, 'Germany'; Förster and Roski, *DDR*, p. 70; Flug, *Treuhand-Poker*, p. 13; Kehrer, *Industriestandort*, p. 227.
61 Yoder, *From*, p. 12.
62 In this instance, guitarist Klaus Feldmann. 'Borderlands', BBC2, 26 November 2005.

course, we're not allowed to call it that, because we are supposed to be equals. But that's what it is.'[63]

It is little wonder that most easterners see themselves as second-class citizens in the new Germany (the figure fluctuates between seven and nine out of every ten), while almost as many hold that, despite sizeable transfer payments from the west, the GDR was 'conquered' in a 'colonial' manner.[64] Despite the March 1990 election victory of parties that favoured unification via 'Route 23' (incorporation into the FRG), an outright majority came to believe that the wholesale abolition of GDR institutions had been rash, and to the detriment of ordinary people. According to one survey, easterners rate the performance of the old regime as superior to the new on seven counts out of nine (healthcare, education, industrial training, law and order, gender equality, social security and housing).[65]

Had the post-1990 eastern economy experienced similar growth rates to post-1949 West Germany, unification might today be regarded as a miraculous event. But that was not to be. In 1989 West Germany itself was no longer a *Wunder*-economy (the dreams of easterners notwithstanding). Growth rates had lagged those of its rivals since the early 1970s and, in the decade from 1991, declined further to a sluggish 1–2 per cent. The eastern *Länder* entered a deep and lasting depression, centred on catastrophic deindustrialisation. 'Really existing' market capitalism revealed a more polarising and destructive character than even the most sceptical had feared.[66] Already six months after unification, nearly three-fifths of the workforce had experienced major dislocation (such as unemployment, premature retirement or reduced working hours), with women particularly hard hit, while for those fortunate enough to retain a job, work became far more demanding. Even today, the region suffers over 20 per cent unemployment and depends upon transfers totalling 4 per cent of Germany's GDP. In a withering

63 Yoder, *From*, p. 108.
64 Dennis, *Perceptions*, p. 94. Technically, and given that a large chunk of the transfers flow back to FRG-based companies, 'annexationist Keynesianism' may be a more appropriate term than 'colonisation'. See Jacoby, *Imitation*, p. 135.
65 *Financial Times*, 4 November 1999; Dennis, 'Perceptions'.
66 One commentator, an opponent of Communism, notes the irony that the sufferings of the eastern *Länder* have borne out 'some of the most vulgar accusations in Marxist–Leninist text-books – that capitalists are greedy and that capitalism as a system is immoral because it allows people to be thrown out into the street without either job or roof'. Kupferberg, *Communism*, p. 138.

assessment, *The Economist* observes that it houses the headquarters of 'hardly any companies' and has 'few prospects of attracting significant investment'.[67]

Eastern Germany's economic collapse, some say, was inevitable. The German historian Karl-Dietrich Bracher, for example, claims that all post-1989 problems are the result of the 'dreadful communist legacy', while many economists regard it as unfortunate but unavoidable. More common, though, are voices that criticise certain policy decisions but present these as 'already history' – a case of spilt milk, as it were. Perhaps the best-known figure to adopt this approach is former SPD chancellor Helmut Schmidt.[68] In 1990–91, Schmidt maintains, a litany of 'serious psychological and economic mistakes' was made. His list includes: the false promises made to East Germans, the 1:1 East-Mark conversion rate, the refusal to cancel *Kombinate* debts, the granting of property to western descendants of its one-time owners, and discriminatory punishment of crimes committed under the old regime, with Communists singled out and 'bloc party' members absolved. These were human errors, the former premier insists, upon which it would be dangerous to dwell. Instead of crying, whether from sorrow or rage, Germans should pull together and make the best of a botched job.

Although a widely held and influential position, it is an argument that skates over the considerable evidence that suggests that the 'mistakes' were not simply matters of human error. Like those of shopkeepers, the errors committed by those in charge of the unification process, including the Treuhand, seemed to favour one side of the balance sheet alone.[69] Almost all tilted the New *Länder* in one direction: towards rapid deindustrialisation and devaluation, complemented by a sacrifice of economic regeneration at the altar of private property norms. Although the CDU–FDP government had triumphed in the East on the back of a 'no experiments' mood, it utilised the New *Länder* as an *Experimentierplatz* – a testing ground for neoliberal reform; the initiatives and policies assayed there, such as the break-up of collective bargaining, were then transferred to the Old *Länder*. In this process, much of the 'spilt milk' was creamed off by (mainly western) property owners and entrepreneurs – a group that closely overlapped and intertwined with the businesspeople, bankers and politicians who controlled the unification process. For these classes, the 'development' of the New *Länder* has been highly profitable. Thanks to the timing and terms of currency union, together with the Treuhand's strategy

67 Jarausch, *Rush*, p. 195; *The Economist*, 20 August 2005, p. 64.
68 Bracher, *Wendezeiten*, pp. 329–50; *Die Zeit*, 41/2001.
69 For detailed discussion, see Dale, *Between*.

of 'shock' privatisation, the *Kombinate* were undervalued, enabling western businesses to acquire actual and potential rivals for a song. The pain of economic collapse was visited upon eastern workers and unemployed and upon western taxpayers, while the profits flowed to (largely western) property owners. Could it be just coincidence that the number of German millionaires soared by 40 per cent even as the *Kombinate* collapsed, in those merciless two years that followed unification?[70]

Generally speaking, easterners have felt let down by unification, and have reserved particular antipathy for its economic policies and institutions. According to the head of the Allensbach institute of public opinion research, the Treuhand, 'even today, attracts very strong resentment, with a widespread belief that numerous factories were ruined as West German enterprises' method of dealing with competition'. Its policies, Yoder concurs, 'have defined – both symbolically and practically – relations between the east and west. While many western businesses have profited from the restructuring of the east's economy, easterners have been the objects, rather than subjects, of Treuhand decisions.'[71]

Albeit with greater ambivalence, similar resentments were felt towards other aspects of the unification process. Even the institutionalisation of liberal democracy was not exempt. Here, disenchantment has been exacerbated by the region's economic travails. (The point has recently been made by Friedrich Schorlemmer, with his warning that: 'Many people no longer value the wonderful gift of freedom because they say what use is freedom if they are shut out from their jobs.') Yet the heart of the issue is the non-participatory nature of parliamentary democracy. Data from as early as November 1990 indicate that a paltry 10 per cent of easterners saw themselves as involved in 'shaping' German unity, as against an overwhelming majority who perceived their role as mere onlookers or even casualties of the process. Since then, numerous polls and studies have attested to endemic disaffection along these same lines. Easterners, Yoder has shown, 'complained of too few possibilities to participate in socio-political activities . . . Rather than feeling they are participants in the new system, many people feel they are once again passive observers.' Symptomatic of this disillusionment, participation in elections slumped, as did membership of the four main parties. Former oppositionists who had placed their hopes in the round tables and in participatory democracy experienced intense disappointment, too. One feminist, when elected to Berlin's municipal parliament, exclaimed that it resembled 'a dictatorship' rather than democracy. Sebastian Pflugbeil, when asked

70 *Junge Welt*, 4 March 2000.
71 *Wirtschaftswoche*, 27 September 2000; Yoder, *From*, p. 157.

whether 'citizens are again effectively divorced from political decision-making processes', replied: 'Yes. Absolutely. The degree of powerlessness toward what is being done "up there" is now very comparable to what it was before.' If the measure of the success of a transition to democracy is the extent of disaffection, as Samuel Huntington has proposed, East Germany's democratisation has been a triumph.[72]

If eastern Germans remain, on the whole, highly conscious of their region's particular history and culture and resentful at the consequences of unification, and perceive themselves to be second-class citizens, one might expect this to be reflected in a distinct regional political and cultural identity. And indeed, both an *Ostidentität* and, in the PDS, an *ostdeutsche Partei* have established themselves as enduring features of the new Germany. Yet there is no reason to assume that easterners' grievances will automatically find expression in a politics of regionalism. After all, most major contemporary issues are mediated by the national state, affecting citizens on both sides of the Elbe. Throughout the 1990s, all Germans have been affected by the progressive diminution of what Pierre Bourdieu calls 'the left hand of the state' (notably the spending ministries) and the strengthening of its 'right hand' (notably the Ministry of Finance). For each successive government, the lodestar has been neoliberal reform, centred upon privatisation, the deregulation of capital and labour markets and the placing of what former Chancellor Gerhard Schröder liked to call 'implacable budgetary obstacles' in the way of any expansion of public services.[73] (An exception that proved the rule was when Schröder's Minister of Finance, Oskar Lafontaine, suggested different priorities in the form of higher corporation tax. Following howls from the business community, he was forced out of office.)

It is workers and the poor, east and west, who have borne the brunt of 'reform', and the fall-out – whether in terms of alienation from politics ('*politikverdrossenheit*') or engagement in industrial action and social movements – has affected *Ossis* and *Wessis* alike.[74] In the country as a whole, criticism of the class nature of the democratic system runs high. An opinion poll taken shortly after the putsch against Lafontaine, in both parts of the country, showed 72 per cent of respondents agreeing with the statement that 'big business, not politics, has the say in our country', while 78 per cent thought that decisions made by big business came at

72 *Guardian*, ' "Gloom prevails" in Germany', 10 November 2005; Adler, 'Soziale', p. 204; Yoder, *From*, pp. 5, 165; Gabi Zekina, in Wainwright, *After*, p. 50; Philipsen, *People*, p. 319; Huntington, *Third*, p. 168.
73 Bourdieu, *Resistance*, p. 1; Schröder, 'German', p. 15.
74 For detailed discussion see Dale, *Between*.

the expense of democratic participation and 85 per cent held that veto rights should be put in place to rein in the big corporations.[75] Social movements, too, have tended to assume pan-German dimensions. In the early 1990s this was not the case. 1991 witnessed a revival of the Leipzig Monday demonstrations coupled with a tremendous wave of occupations and trade union-led campaigns in the New *Länder*, followed two years later by a major strike wave.[76] Subsequent movements, however – the massive labour protests of 1996–97 and the student movement of 1997, and the protest wave against the 'Hartz IV' austerity measures in 2004 – were more evenly spread.

The protests of the mid-1990s contributed to a left shift amongst voters that brought the SPD and Green Party into office, while those of 2004 contributed to a revival and realignment on the Left, with Lafontaine brokering an election alliance between western trade unionists and the PDS. At time of writing, this latter appears to have revived the fortunes of socialism in Germany. Far from marking the 'end of history', German unification produced a crisis-ridden and polarised country, and one in which renewed social movements have placed debates over the viability and desirability of capitalism back onto the political agenda

75 Bornost, 'Germany'.
76 Relative to the workforce, strike days in the New *Länder* in 1993 exceeded the western figure by over thirty times. Pritchard, 'National'; Turner, *Fighting*.

Conclusion

The causes of the East European revolutions of 1989 can be analysed in several different registers.[1] The first is that of inter-imperial competition. The key process here was the Soviet bloc's decreasing ability to match its western rivals in economic and military terms. This provided the context for developments in a second register, that of the internal economic and political decay of the various national economies and of the Soviet empire itself. The third register concerns the manner in which these structural changes catalysed political struggles. The politics of reform and crisis management were fought out within the ruling classes of Eastern Europe and, especially at times of crisis or intra-regime conflict, other social forces mobilised, too. In the 1980s, against a backdrop of blocwide economic crisis and turmoil in the heart of the imperium – Poland – and in the marches of Afghanistan, the policy consensus amongst Soviet elites began to fragment. Perceiving their own and the hegemon's decline, Eastern European ruling classes lost faith in the Soviet model and began to look to alternative methods for organising their power and securing the conditions for capital accumulation. Gradually, inexorably, the Soviet model hollowed out from within; ideas of a 'socialist market economy' and political pluralism gained ground.

In the East German case, contradictions arose between its 'national–economic' form and globalisation, and between its dependence upon Moscow and the economic attractive power of the West. East Germany's rulers found themselves seduced by the superior technologies, commodities and economic structures of the West, not to mention loans and transfers from Bonn. They were torn between ingrained loyalties to orthodox Communism and Moscow and their tacit awareness of the West's competitive edge. Locked into Soviet structures, which entailed the centralised fusion of political, economic and ideological institutions, major reform would necessarily be a fraught process. Creating a further

---

1 This paragraph draws upon Rees, 'Socialist'.

complication, the GDR, being the twin of the more prosperous and democratic FRG, was uniquely dependent upon its Soviet structures and alliance with Moscow. Honecker's regime was therefore loath to attempt major reforms, as Poland and Hungary did in the 1980s, and felt especially threatened by Gorbachev's 'new thinking'.

In East Germany, the 'hollowing out' of the old lagged behind the process in Poland and Hungary, but it caught up in late 1989. Almost all the country's new leaders had occupied prominent positions in the old regime, but they were willing to dismantle the structures to which they had hitherto been pledged. Far from abdicating, they restructured the political-party landscape, began to construct new frameworks for capital accumulation and attempted to carve positions for themselves within new or reformed institutions.

That Communism could so readily be exchanged for ideologies of the 'class enemy', such as social democracy and liberalism, has puzzled those who perceive the SED either as a totalitarian behemoth or as a vehicle of working-class emancipation. In fact, Communist parties in power had been committed, since the late 1920s, to a politics of authoritarian paternalism, at times more benevolent, at others more tyrannical. Their core goals were capital accumulation and military competition, in comparison with which their Soviet-type structures were of secondary importance – as became clear in 1989–90. If a distinction is made between the Soviet states *qua* class societies, in which the *nomenklatura* controlled the means of production, and the political system through which its control was secured, the apparent contradiction between the collapse of the old and the determination of powerholders to maintain their positions in the new order resolves itself. As elsewhere in Eastern Europe, transition in East Germany centred on '*nomenklatura* privatisation' and not '*nomenklatura* surrender' – the chief difference being that, here, Bonn's support for unification rendered the task more difficult.

In parts of the former Soviet bloc, one can be forgiven for wondering if much has changed since 1989. Is Russia freer under Putin than under Gorbachev? One Russian liberal politician has recently argued that his country 'has no independent judicial system . . . no elements of [an] independent parliament . . . no public or parliamentary control on secret services and law-enforcement structures', while an independent media exists only at the margins, and elections are subject to 'very substantial pressure from the authorities'. The economic system, he adds, 'is in fact a 100% merger between business and authorities . . . Every single important bureaucrat in Russian government or Russian administration is at the same time deeply involved in businesses or represents their interests.' *The Economist*, in which this interview appeared, glossed it with the suggestion that 'Russia today is arguably where it might have been if it had avoided *perestroika*, choosing instead a Chinese path of strictly limited freedom'.[2] The end of Communism in Russia appeared cataclysmic at the time, yet now, after the dust has settled, appears to have heralded only such changes that could have been launched under Communist auspices. The revolutionary image was a mirage.

Elsewhere, of course, 1989 signalled rather more dramatic departures. East Germany's *Wende* culminated in the transition to parliamentary democracy and market economy, exit from the Warsaw Pact and Comecon, and fusion with West Germany. Similar transformations occurred in other parts of Eastern Europe, and yet in many cases they were accompanied by scarcely a whisper on the streets. Here, one may ask in what sense, if any, were these developments revolutionary? And did collective action have any impact at all, or were the crowds on the streets merely historical froth?

Responses to these questions have diverged wildly. Jürgen Habermas managed to write an entire book on 1989 without even mentioning the protest movement, while Claus Offe accords it only a marginal, reactive role. It was not the movement, he writes, that brought about victory but just the opposite: 'the obvious weakness of the state apparatus encouraged and triggered the growth of a democratic movement.' The year 1989, he concludes, was an ' "exit revolution", not a "voice revolution". The GDR was not brought down by a victorious *collective* struggle for a new *political* order; instead, massive and suddenly unstoppable *individual* emigration destroyed its *economic* foundations.' For Robert Kurz, the GDR's collapse was catalysed by an exodus that expressed 'not conscious action directed against Prusso-Saxon war socialism' but merely 'blind and helpless flight', and was then overlayered by a protest movement fuelled by 'nothing but unconscious and untamed resentment'. ('That is what things are like during a power cut in New York', he sniffs, 'or when fire breaks out in a prison'.) Like Kurz, other western intellectuals cannot hide their contempt for the East German masses. Klaus Bittermann refers to their 'immaturity'; they acted like 'little children who hurl their toys into a corner and trample on them, under the thrall of an *idée fixe*', while for Thomas Schmid, student activist turned conservative publicist, the Leipzig masses were 'infantilised', 'immature' and 'bawling'.[3]

In a refreshing counterblast to these deterministic and patronising lines of argument, Harvard historian Charles Maier inveighs against his 'West

2 'A Survey of the EU's Eastern Borders', 25 June 2005, p. 12.
3 Offe, 'Wohlstand', pp. 293–4, *Varieties*, p. 21; Kurz, *Honecker's*, p. 48; Bittermann, *Rasende*, p. 108; Schmid, *Staatsbegräbnis*, p. 35.

German colleagues [who] have talked of an "implosion" of East
Germany as if some worn-out machine finally just broke down'. They

> argued that no revolution had occurred. Instead, they claimed that the GDR
> had collapsed as a result of its inner difficulties; it had suffered 'systems
> failure' or 'imploded'. These judgments were occasionally condescending.
> To a degree, the East German popular movement seemed actually embar-
> rassing to some West German social scientists [who] were used to thinking
> in terms of abstract processes, and the powerful intrusion of crowds and
> demonstrations seemed vaguely threatening . . . The East German protes-
> tors were like obstreperous children at an adults' dinner party.[4]

As regards specific flaws in the 'implosion' thesis, I would begin by mentioning its tendency to reify the distinction between state breakdown and
social movements – it is as if structural shifts occurred, which *then* contributed to an expanded space for collective action in 1989. In reality,
collective action had shaped East Germany history from the outset. In
the late 1940s the characters of the SED and mass organisations were
moulded as they sought to subjugate resistance; likewise the Stasi in the
mid-1950s. Although protest was systematically suppressed, and even
'innocent' forms of collective self-organisation were corralled by state
institutions, public opinion and industrial action still influenced the
regime's choices, whether in respect of toleration of western rock music,
the role of the Church, or work quotas. In the 1980s, emigration and
small-scale social movements became serious irritants to the regime, and
served as seedbeds from which organised resistance was to spring.

   In 1989, state crisis and the burgeoning of social movements were
mutually enhancing processes. Far from being a walk-on part, writes
Maier, 'at each critical juncture, the East Germans' collective action – no
matter how hesitant at first, and how filled with doubts later – impelled
decisive accommodations or allowed new initiatives'.[5] These moments
commenced with the summertime border breakthroughs and embassy
occupations, included the battle of Dresden Station and the rise of public
protests in Leipzig, and achieved its initial climax on 9 October, when
the scale of the demonstration overawed the local SED leadership and
security forces, weakening the will to open fire. It was only now – *after*
a showdown with the mass movement in which the state's omnipotent
image was decisively punctured – that the old regime truly began to
'implode'. It was collective action in Leipzig, and again on 9 November
in Berlin, that pushed the process of state erosion beyond the point of no

4 Maier, *Dissolution*, pp. xiv, 119.
5 *Ibid.*, p. xiv.

return. Crowd action deepened the crisis and collapse of the Soviet order, knocking any remaining diplomatic aces out of Gorbachev's meagre hand and accelerating the pace of German unification.

The movement, moreover, was more popular and enduring than generally thought. It arose in the southern towns of Leipzig, Plauen, Dresden and Arnstadt, but then diffused nationwide. For fifteen weeks, demonstrations of over 100,000 occurred each Monday – and that was just in Leipzig. Altogether, the city saw twenty-three mass demonstrations, as did Plauen. In terms of numbers, the movement crested in the first week of November; in addition to demonstrations of around 2 million, that week alone saw some 230 reported political meetings, attended by over 300,000 people.[6] Further peaks occurred in early December and again in January.

Raw data on the volume and duration of protest activities capture important aspects of the movement, but for a more detailed picture, anecdotal and journalistic evidence is required. This bears witness to the courage of participants – for this revolution was not so velveteen as sometimes thought – and their perseverance. (Thus, one elderly couple 'reported with pride that they had taken part in every demonstration in their town, he with walking stick and she weakened after a heart attack'.)[7] They displayed memorable wit and creativity, emblazoned on innumerable placards, and admirable tactical intelligence in their confrontations with the forces of 'law and order'. They sparked a conflagration of democratic debate and initiative; they proposed, defended and rejected aims and strategies, and initiated, developed or abandoned innumerable projects and organisations – and all in the space of a few short months. In the process, people discovered hitherto unsuspected capacities.

As discussed in chapter 3, participation in mass protests, with their elements of surprise and solidarity, could contain an emotional kick. 'That was quite some feeling, being in that mass of people', said one participant; 'it was so liberating. Even now, tears come to my eyes when I see footage of it on television. I'm actually a hard bloke, but that was such an experience, it was fantastic!' This was not routine protest, the stuff of petitions and pressure groups. Rather, as Maier observes, it possessed a revolutionary quality: at least in the first phase the crowds 'were bonded by a vision of an alternative public sphere; they shared a fraternal identity . . .; they demonstrated the exaltation of will that social theorists such as Durkheim and Victor Turner have emphasized; they helped bring down a regime'.[8]

6 Zwahr, 'Revolution', pp. 222–3; Mitter and Wolle, *Befehle*, p. 248.
7 Niethammer, *Erfahrung*, p. 381.
8 Lindner and Grüneberger, *Demonteure*, p. 34; Maier, *Dissolution*, p. 166.

If 1989 was, in the senses given above, a revolution involving mass collective action, what were its driving forces? Was the unrest a product of 'rising expectations', as Konrad Jarausch has argued, in a rebuttal of what he calls 'the Leninist model of revolution'?[9] This notion, whereby rising expectations clash with stable or diminishing needs satisfaction, derives from the theories of collective behaviour developed by James Davies and Ted Gurr. But these are largely discredited nowadays, having encountered effective criticism since their advent in the 1960s. The model centres on changes in expectations and achievements, which are notoriously difficult to measure. Even where yardsticks can be agreed, numerous cases can be found in which rising expectations do not lead to revolutionary situations. In addition, as aggregate social–psychological models, they ignore structural change. Few social movement theorists adhere to the approach any longer.

But what of 'the Leninist model'? A writer primarily of performative rather than systematic–theoretical texts, Lenin nowhere developed a comprehensive theory of revolution, yet he did sketch his views on the subject, including, most famously, three conditions necessary for the development of a revolutionary situation.[10] These are, first, that a country's ruling class be passing through a political crisis which substantially weakens the government and 'draws even the most backward masses into politics'; second, that the mass of the population experience an 'unusual degree of oppression', encouraging widespread demands for change; and third, that social movement activity enjoy a marked up-tick.

These three points may not a systematic theory make, but do they not accurately describe the run-up to East Germany's revolutionary crisis? The late 1980s witnessed a 'silent breaking' with the regime[11] (which helps to explain both the low morale of state-supporting sectors of the population and the force of protests when they arrived). In 1989, the old order became subject to internal scrutiny and serious fracture; through the resulting 'fissures', to quote Lenin, 'the indignation of the oppressed classes burst forth'. The crisis at the top of society sharpened the discontent below, giving encouragement to activists who interpreted grievances as political issues. Oppositionists and would-be emigrants scented and responded to the new opportunities, and organised a 'noisy breaking' in the form of public protest.

In its early stages, the movement gathered together individuals who shared a general sense that 'something must change'; its character was

9 Jarausch, *Rush*, p. 50.
10 Lenin, *Werke*, vol. 21, p. 206; *Communism*, p. 86.
11 For details, see Dale, *Between*; *Popular*.

shaped by the sense of 'we-ness' as individuals recognised one another as allies – 'We are the people!' being the defining slogan. Motivations to participate commonly drew upon 'particular and deeply personal concerns such as the desire to be free of a feeling of entrapment' rather than 'abstract ideals such as democracy'.[12] These traits are typical of the first stages of mass revolts, that tend to feature, as Hal Draper observed in 1965, a united campaign 'against the visible enemy', which involves 'greater certainty on what one is against than on what one is for (what we can call "anti-politics")'. However, once prospects of major political change appear, simple denunciations of the existing order or general appeals for dialogue or democracy no longer suffice to give direction to protest movements. At this point, 'the problems of perspective and program multiply, as more basic issues and powers are brought to the surface . . . Even to know what those basic issues are requires a broader and more general conception of what the fight is about – in effect, an ideology.'[13]

It is ironic that the section of the movement that possessed the most worked-through 'general conception' tended to perceive itself as non-ideological and 'anti-political'. The civic groups, whose cadre came largely from the church-linked 'grassroots groups' of the 1980s, were well placed to relate to the rising movement, in that they emphasised maximising citizens' involvement in the political process. As shown in chapter 6, they helped spark the uprising. However, as it progressed, the wider movement discussed and assessed their strategies and ideology; within a process of general politicisation, some became active supporters while others veered in a different direction. To a degree, the polarisation that ensued followed class lines, the civic groups tending to attract the middling layers, particularly professionals. Workers were not preponderant amongst the 'early risers' in September. Possessing lower levels of individual movement building resources, they tended to be less 'mobilised' during protest downturns. However, as in most recent uprisings – Chile, Portugal and Iran in the 1970s, Poland and South Africa in the 1980s, Bolivia in 2005 – breakthroughs depended upon their mass involvement.

As I have discussed in detail elsewhere, East German workers, their substantial shop floor strength notwithstanding, entered 1989 with little experience of public collective action and did not make their presence felt as an independent force in the revolt's early stages.[14] In the winter of

12 Dyke, *Dresden*, p. 237
13 Draper, quoted in Johnson, *Track*, pp. 8–9.
14 Dale, *Popular*, ch. 9.

1989–90 this began to change, as the movement's working-class component grew ever more central. Workers' involvement peaked in December
and January, two months in which the intensity and force of demonstrations and 'non-conventional' forms of protest was considerably greater
(and in potential far greater) than is usually acknowledged. Yet in the
same period, the civic groups moved towards GDR patriotism and into
coalition with the regime; and although a minority within the civic
groups had always advocated enhanced engagement with the movement's plebeian sections, it remained small. To the cold shoulder they
received from the civic groups, the plebs responded in kind, lending their
votes to other political forces and leaving the civic groups with little electoral support. 'Had we related to workers' demands', one of the few
workers in New Forum's leadership would later lament, 'we could have
become a lively, trade union-linked left-wing movement. Instead we
became a sect.'[15]

The divergence between civic groups and mass movement became overt
following the fall of the Wall, but its outlines had been visible earlier. In
the cloisters of the 1980s opposition, attitudes flourished that denigrated
'material' demands as consumerism and dismissed workers as 'a conservative class'. As with previous generations of dissidents, working-class
revolt was welcomed in so far as it widened space for oppositional agitation but feared for its potential to provoke the state to repressive measures. In autumn 1989, the civic groups were preoccupied with 'purely
political' questions, such as civil liberties and democracy, at the expense
of issues of economic injustice, conditions of work and living standards.
Their inclination to negotiate with the regime bore the stamp of pre-1989
dissident circles, which had tended to accept the existence of the SED and
its state as inevitable, even legitimate, power structures. (As Wolfgang
Rüddenklau lamented, 'we showed a misplaced loyalty towards the SED
over which, at best, a few Stasi officers will have sniggered'.)[16] Their
ambivalence towards the demonstrations, their willingness to engage in
'dialogue' with a despised regime, and their astonishment that 'apathetic'
workers would rise up, were all legacies of the pre-1989 opposition, for
which strictly policed limits to oppositional activity, together with the
influence of the Church, had produced an ingrained pessimism towards
strategies other than gradualist pragmatism and lifestyle politics.

The schism within the protest movement is commonly viewed through
a Cartesian lens, so to speak. In one camp, a movement of intellectuals,
concerned with matters of democracy, civil liberties and communication,

15 Uwe Rottluf, interview.
16 Rüddenklau, *Störenfried*, p. 13.

and described with epithets such as 'mature', 'responsible', 'autonomous' and 'living in truth'. In the other, a lemming-like materialist movement of workers, driven by greed and the 'seduction' of western commodities. Workers, according to one, typical, account, 'wanted to get better consumer goods' while intellectuals were motivated by 'human rights'.[17]

The grain of truth in this Cartesian framework is that material questions did figure strongly in the schism. However, workers were not only looking to their pay packets; democratic demands were important, too, as were 'non-materialist' issues such as the environment. Advocates of unification were interested not merely in changing their Trabant for an Audi, but perceived the Western system to be more democratic and offering greater scope for individual self-fulfilment. That workers tended to support unification says as much about their class situation as about material desires: they possessed the smallest stake in the existing system and could cut their ties with comparative ease.

The movement for unification, as shown in chapters 8 and 9, tapped into and then absorbed a working-class revolt against economic injustice and *nomenklatura* corruption. In early December, Klaus Wolfram recalls, with a leaderless SED, the apparatuses of power in disarray and the crowds clamouring for the root-and-branch destruction of the regime, 'the question of power' stood before us.[18] Opposition leaders, wary of the radical, social demands and pro-unification sentiment of the crowds, and embroiled in negotiations with the SED, declined the historic opportunity. Ironically perhaps, the former oppositionists who had braved repression in the long years preceding 1989 ultimately placed greater trust in the SED; they had internalised the limits of the status quo more than had the crowds. There is also irony in the fact that the civic groups increasingly sought to 'substitute' for the mass activity that they advocated in theory. In the process, the idea of 'grassroots democracy', which had at one stage seemed their defining feature, was jettisoned. Before 1989 was out, New Forum activists could be heard declaiming that traditional politician's phrase, 'the people wishes to be led', while some opposition intellectuals lost patience with the masses, dismissing them as a 'politically immature and politically stupid mob, under the grip of baneful unconscious drives'.[19]

As a result of the civic groups' aloofness from the bulk of the movement, the political vacuum that emerged in late autumn and which was filled, ideologically, by the demand for unification and, organisationally,

17 Jarausch, *Rush*, p. 47.
18 *Die Andere*, 40, 1991, p. 3.
19 Timmer, *Aufbruch*, p. 344.

by political parties with FRG connections, was greater than would otherwise have been the case. That FRG parties would gain influence in East Germany was inevitable, but that they gained hegemony so quickly and easily was thanks to the oppositionists' dismissal of plebeian social demands, their refusal to organise mass action as a lever of political change and their cooperation with the SED. It is ironic that when unification had been a radical demand – and would have provoked confrontation with the regime – the civic groups opposed it, but when it became inevitable, with the SED itself declaring for 'Deutschland einig Vaterland', they swung behind it, too.

This book has charted the radicalising dynamic at work within the East German revolution, drawing attention to critical conjunctures at which it could have been taken further. Had these opportunities been grasped, the outcome – in the broad sense of German unification – would have been unaltered, but Helmut Kohl would have faced greater pressure from eastern labour and a more spirited Left. As it was, the radicalising thrust was successfully contained, social movements rapidly demobilised, and eastern Germans were offered up as guinea pigs for neoliberal reform. Some of the practices that had fuelled protest were revived by the new overlords: corruption and the abuse of power, preaching water while drinking wine, selling arms to Third World dictatorships (despite an 'ethical' foreign policy) and joining imperial alliances. Dictatorship in the workplace was reinvented, this time with the whip of unemployment as disciplinary mechanism. 'Many people are once again scared to open their mouths for fear of being fired', one former protestor lamented; 'they've withdrawn back into their shells'. The social and economic blight that the New *Länder* have endured is reflected in demographic trends that are otherwise seen only during (or immediately after) war: a 60 per cent slump in the birth rate, and the emigration – over and above the 1989–90 exodus – of fully 2 million souls to the 'old *Länder*'.[20]

Unemployment, neoliberalism and second-class citizenship; these were not the goals of 1989, and it is small wonder that disillusionment set in so swiftly. Yet the revolution did bring several unqualified gains. The freedoms achieved – of speech, assembly, organisation and the vote – are invaluable victories in themselves. For many, participation in collective action was itself a rewarding venture. Interviews and surveys of former protestors bear witness to the degree of education and the leap in confidence that was experienced.[21] For me, this is symbolised by the story of a hotel worker who, before 1989, was so fearful of speaking in public

20 Lindner and Grüneberger, *Demonteure*, p. 105; Kolinsky, 'Meanings'.
21 *Opp et al.*, 'Data'.

that she was known to take tranquillisers even before attending a small workplace meeting but, some time afterwards, was amazed to find herself mounting a podium to address thousands of citizens at an anti-fascist rally – and with no chemical assistance.[22]

For Marxists, 1989 brought additional reasons for cheer.[23] It consigned Stalinism to history. That was significant far beyond Eastern Europe and the USSR. For over half a century, Stalinism dominated the world's Left ideologically and organisationally, perfecting the art of signalling left while turning right. Its demise assists the task of reclaiming Marxism as a theory of working-class self-emancipation. In addition, being the two-hundredth anniversary of the revolution, 1989 saw a thousand pundits proclaim the impossibility and undesirability of revolution. History replied: European revolutions were celebrated. And in that year, above all, East Germany furnished a glimpse of the potential that arises when established order breaks down in the face of collective protest.

22 Ramona Hübner, interview.
23 This paragraph borrows from Barker and Mooers, 'Theories'.

Bibliography

Documents

Official documents cited are, for the most part, published in collections listed under 'Books and articles' below. Of materials from the 1980s *Basisgruppen* and from the *Bürgerbewegung*, a large part is from my own collection. In addition, documents were sourced from the following archives: Stiftung/Archiv der Parteien und Massenorganisationen der DDR im Bundesarchiv (SAPMO), Berlin; Robert Havemann Archiv, Berlin; 15 Januar Archiv, Berlin; and the Umweltbibliothek, Berlin. Documents from Saxony's security services were provided by Hans-Jochen Vogel.

Interviews

Markus Bahr, Student, Schneeberg.
Michael Brie, SED reformer; member of the SED–PDS leadership in early 1990, Berlin.
Gabi Engelhardt, VL activist, Chemnitz.
Barbara Fuchs, Puppet theatre employee, Berlin.
Christian Führer, Pastor, Leipzig.
Steffen 'Gullimoy' Geißler, Opposition activist, Chemnitz.
Martin Gutzeit, Founder member of the SDP, Berlin.
Hilke, socialist; Christian and opposition activist, Berlin.
Ramona Hübner, Hotel worker and VL member, Chemnitz.
Mario Kessler, SED dissident and academic, Leipzig.
Jens König, Apprentice sailor, Rostock.
Bert Konopatsky, Student, church cleaner and supporter of Umweltbibliothek, Berlin.
Steff Konopatsky, Member, then employee, of the Citizens' Committee for the dissolution of the Stasi, Berlin.
Tina Krone, New Forum activist, Berlin.
Lily M., Junior official in government ministry, Berlin.
Helmut Meier, Director of the Academy of the Social Sciences, Berlin.
Petra N., Secondary school teacher, Berlin.
Antje Neubauer, Apprentice and college student, Berlin.
Ollie, Apprentice, Dresden.
Marianne Pienitz, Psychotherapist, Leipzig.
Rolf Richter, Deputy director of the Academy of the Social Sciences, Berlin.

Uwe Rottluf, Printer and leading member of New Forum, Berlin.
Hans-Jochen Vogel, Pastor and opposition activist, Chemnitz.
Andrea Vogt, Secretary, Berlin.
Klaus Wolfram, New Forum's national steering committee, Berlin.

Interviews were conducted in August–December 1989 and October 1994, except in the cases of Führer (October 2004) and Bahr (October 2005).

Newspapers and magazines

Die Andere, Berliner Zeitung, Friedrichsfelder Feuermelder, Junge Welt, Linksruck, Märkische Volksstimme, Neues Deutschland, Sozialismus von unten, Sozialistische Zeitung, Der Spiegel, die tageszeitung, Telegraph, Tribüne, Die Welt, Wirtschaftswoche, Die Zeit.
The Economist, Financial Times, Guardian, International Herald Tribune, Socialist Worker.

Books and articles

Adler, Frank (1991) 'Soziale Umbrüche', in Rolf Reißig and Gert-Joachim Glaessner, eds, *Das Ende eines Experiments*, Berlin: Dietz.
Adomeit, Hannes (1998) *Imperial Overstretch: Germany in Soviet Policy from Stalin to Gorbachev*, Baden-Baden: Nomos Verlagsgesellschaft.
Akerlof, George *et al.* (1991) 'East Germany In From the Cold', *Brookings Papers in Economic Activity*, 1.
Albrecht, Ulrich (1996) 'The Role of Social Movements in the Collapse of the German Democratic Republic', *Global Society*, 10 (2), 145–65.
Allen, Bruce (1991) *Germany East*, Montreal: Black Rose Books.
Aminzade, Ronald and Doug McAdam (2001) 'Emotions and Contentious Politics', in Ronald Aminzade *et al.*, *Silence and Voice in the Study of Contentious Politics*, Cambridge: Cambridge University Press.
Anderson, Perry (1994) 'Power, Politics and the Enlightenment', in David Miliband, ed., *Reinventing the Left*, Cambridge: Polity.
Andrews, Molly (1999) 'Criticism/Self-Criticism in East Germany: Contradictions Between Theory and Practice', *Critical Sociology*, 24 (1–2).
Ansorg, Leonore and Renate Hürtgen (1992) *Aber jetzt gibt es Initiative Leute und die müßte man eigentlich alle an einen Tisch bringen: Die 'Initiative für unabhängige Gewerkschaften' (IUG) 1989 bis 1990*, Freie Universität Berlin.
Arnold, Karl-Heinz (1990) *Die ersten hundert Tage des Hans Modrow*, Berlin: Dietz.
Ash, Timothy G. (1981) '*Und willst Du nicht mein Bruder sein . . .*', Reinbek: Rowohlt.
——(1990) *We The People: The Revolution of '89*, Cambridge: Granta.
Auer, Stefan (2004) 'The Paradoxes of the Revolutions of 1989 in Central Europe', *Critical Horizons*, 4 (1–2), Leiden: Brill.
Bahr, Eckhard (1990) *Sieben Tage im Oktober*, Leipzig: Forum.
Bahrmann, Hannes and Christoph Links (1994) *Chronik der Wende*, Berlin: Links.
——(1995) *Chronik der Wende 2: Stationen der Einheit*, Berlin: Links.

Barker, Colin (1987) 'Perspectives', in Colin Barker, ed., *Revolutionary Rehearsals*, London: Bookmarks.

——(1995) ' "The Muck of Ages": Reflections on Proletarian Self-Emancipation', *Studies in Marxism*, 2.

——(1996) ' "The Mass Strike" and "The Cycle of Protest" ', Paper given to 'Alternative Futures and Popular Protest' conference, Manchester Metropolitan University.

——(1997) 'Empowerment and Resistance', Paper given to British Sociological Association conference, York.

——(2001) 'Introduction', in Colin Barker *et al.*, eds, *Leadership and Social Movements*, Manchester: Manchester University Press.

——and Gareth Dale (1998) 'Protest Waves in Western Europe: A Critique of "New Social Movement" Theory', *Critical Sociology*, 24 (1–2).

——and Michael Lavalette (2002) 'Strategizing and the Sense of Context: Reflections on the First Two Weeks of the Liverpool Docks Lockout September–October 1995', in David Meyer *et al.* eds, *Social Movements: Identity, Culture and the State*, Oxford: Oxford University Press.

——and Colin Mooers (1994) 'Theories of Revolution in the Light of 1989 in Eastern Europe', Paper given to Political Studies Association conference, Swansea.

Barker, Peter (1998) 'From the SED to the PDS: Continuity or Renewal?', in Peter Barker, ed., *The Party of Democratic Socialism in Germany: Modern Post-Communism or Nostalgic Populism?*, German Monitor, 42, Amsterdam and Atlanta: Rodopi.

Bartee, Wayne (2000) *A Time to Speak Out: The Leipzig Citizen Protests and the Fall of East Germany*, Westport: Praeger.

Baule, Bernward (1991) 'Politische Bedingungsfelder der Freiheitsrevolution in der DDR', in Konrad Löw, *Ursachen und Verlauf der deutschen Revolution 1989*, Berlin: Duncker & Humblot.

Bauman, Zygmunt (1992) *Intimations of Postmodernity*, London: Routledge.

Beck, Ulrich (1991) 'Opposition in Deutschland', in Bernd Giesen and Claus Leggewie, eds, *Experiment Vereinigung, Ein sozialer Grossversuch*, Berlin: Rotbuch.

Behrend, Manfred and Monika Prenzel (1990) *Die Republikaner*, Leipzig: Urania.

Beyme, Klaus von (1996) *Transition to Democracy in Eastern Europe*, Basingstoke: Macmillan.

Bittermann, Klaus (1993) *Der rasende Mob*, Berlin: Edition TIAMAT.

Bleiker, Roland (1993) *Nonviolent Struggle and the Revolution in East Germany*, Cambridge: Albert Einstein Institution.

Bornost, Stefan (2005) 'Germany: The Rise off the Left', *International Socialism*, 2nd series.

Bourdieu, Pierre (1998) *Acts of Resistance*, Cambridge: Polity.

Bracher, Karl Dietrich (1992) *Wendezeiten der Geschichte*, Stuttgart: dva .

Braun, Volker (1990) 'Kommt Zeit, kommen Räte', in Michael Naumann, ed., *'Die Geschichte ist offen'; DDR 1990: Hoffnung auf eine neue Republik*, Reinbek: Rowohlt.

Bruckmeier, Karl (1993) 'Die Bürgerbewegungen in der DDR im Herbst 1989', in Gerda Haufe and Karl Bruckmeier, eds, *Die Bürgerbewegungen in der DDR und in den ostdeutschen Bundesländern*, Opladen: Westdeutscher Verlag.

Brzezinski, Zbigniew (1990) *The Grand Failure*, London: Macdonald.

Büscher, Wolfgang and Peter Wensierski (1984) *Null Bock auf DDR*, Reinbek: Rowohlt.

Callinicos, Alex (1991) *The Revenge of History*, Cambridge: Polity.

Canepa, Eric (1994) 'Germany's Party of Democratic Socialism', *Socialist Register*.

Clemens, Elizabeth (1996) 'Organizational Form as Frame', in Doug McAdam *et al.*, eds, *Comparative Perspectives on Social Movements*, Cambridge: Cambridge University Press.

Connelly, John (1990) 'Moment of Revolution: Plauen (Vogtland), October 7, 1989', *German Politics and Society*, 20.

Dale, Gareth (2004) *Between State Capitalism and Globalisation: The Collapse of the East German Economy*, Oxford: Peter Lang.

——(2005) *Popular Protest in East Germany, 1945–1989*, London: Routledge.

——(2006) ' "A Very Orderly Retreat": Democratic Transition in East Germany, 1989–90', *Debatte: Journal of Contemporary Central and Eastern Europe*, 14 (1).

Darnton, Robert (1991) *Berlin Journal*, New York: W. W. Norton.

Debray, Régis (1973) *Prison Writings*, New York: Random House.

Degen, Christel (1992) 'Das Neue Forum: Eine Plattform für alle?', Diplom Arbeit, Freie Universität Berlin.

——(2000) *Politikvorstellung und Biografie*, Opladen: Westdeutscher Verlag.

Denis, Mathieu (2006) 'Industrielle Interessengegensätze und der Zusammenbruch der DDR', in Sandrine Kott and Emmanuel Droit, eds, *Die ostdeutsche Gesellschaft aus europäisher Perspective*, Berlin: Ch. Links.

Denitch, Bogdan (1990) *The End of the Cold War: European Unity, Socialism, and the Shift In Global Power*, Minneapolis: University of Minnesota Press.

Dennis, Mike (2000) 'Perceptions of GDR Society and its Transformation: East German Identity Ten Years after Unity', in Chris Flockton *et al.*, eds, *The New Germany in the East: Policy Agendas and Social Developments since Unification*, London: Frank Cass.

Dietrich, Christian and Martin Jander (1999) 'Die Revolution in Thüringen: Die Sonderrolle des "Südens" im Jahr 1989', in Günther Heydemann *et al*, eds, *Revolution und Transformation in der DDR*, Berlin: Duncker & Humblot.

Dönert, Albrecht and Paulus Rummelt (1990) 'Die Leipziger Montagsdemonstration', in Jürgen Grabner *et al.*, eds, *Leipzig im Oktober*, Berlin: Wichern.

Dornheim, Andreas (1995) *Politischer Umbruch in Erfurt, 1989/90*, Weimar: Böhlau Verlag.

Draper, Hal (1977) *Karl Marx's Theory of Revolution, Volume 1: State and Bureaucracy*, New York: Monthly Review Press.

Dyke, Elizabeth Ten (2001) *Dresden; Paradoxes of Memory in History*, London: Routledge.

Eberwein, Wolf-Dieter *et al.* (1991) *Vom Aufstand der Massen zum Ende der DDR*, FIB Papers P91–308, Wissenschaftszentrum Berlin für Sozialforschung.

Eckelmann, Wolfgang *et al.* (1990) *FDGB intern: Innenansichten einer Massenorganisation der SED*, Berlin: Treptower Verlagshaus.

Edgar, David (1990) *The Shape of the Table*, London: Nick Hern Books.

Editors of *Das Andere Blatt* (1990) *Keine Überraschung Zulassen! Berichte und Praktiken der Staatssicherheit in Halle bis Ende November 1989*, Halle.

Eigenfeld, Frank (2001) 'Bürgerrechtsbewegungen 1988–1990 in der DDR', in Andrea Pabst *et al.*, eds, *Wir sind das Volk? Ostdeutsche Bürgerrechtsbewegungen und die Wende*, Tübingen: Attempto Verlag.

Eigenfeld, Katrin (2000) ' "Neues Forum" – eine Erinnerung', in Hermann-Josef Rupieper, ed., *Friedliche Revolution 1989/1990 in Sachsen-Anhalt*, Halle: Mitteldeutscher Verlag.

Elster, Jon (1996) 'Introduction', in Jon Elster, ed., *The Roundtable Talks and the Breakdown of Communism*, Chicago: University of Chicago Press.

Eyerman, Ron and Andrew Jamison (1991) *Social Movements*, Cambridge: Polity.

Falkner, Thomas (1991) 'Von der SED zur PDS: Weitere Gedanken eines Beteiligten', *Deutschland Archiv*, 1.

Fantasia, Rick (1988) *Cultures of Solidarity*, Berkeley: University of California Press.

Fehr, Helmut (1996) *Unabhängige Öffentlichkeit und soziale Bewegungen: Fallstudien über Bürgerbewegungen in Polen und der DDR*, Opladen: Westdeutscher Verlag.

Findeis, Hagen *et al.* (1994) *Die Entzauberung des Politischen*, Leipzig: Evangelische Verlagsanstalt.

Fine, Bob (1984) *Democracy and the Rule of Law*, London: Pluto.

Fischbeck, Hans-Jürgen (1989) 'Marktwirtschaft im Sozialismus', in Hubertus Knabe, ed., *Aufbruch in eine andere DDR*, Reinbek: Rowohlt.

Flam, Helena (1998) *Mosaic of Fear*, Boulder: Westview.

Flug, Martin (1992) *Treuhand-Poker*, Berlin: Links.

Förster, Peter and Günter Roski (1990) *DDR zwischen Wende und Wahl*, Berlin: Links.

Fricke, Karl-Wilhelm (1991) 'Honecker's Sturz mit Mielkes Hilfe', *Deutschland Archiv*, 24.

Fuchs, Jürgen (1977) *Gedächtnisprotokolle*, Reinbek: Rowohlt.

Fukuyama, Francis (1992) *The End of History and the Last Man*, Harmondsworth: Penguin.

Fulbrook, Mary (1995) *Anatomy of a Dictatorship*, Oxford: Oxford University Press.

Fuller, Linda (1999) *Where Was the Working Class? Revolution in Eastern Germany*, Urbana: University of Illinois Press.

Funder, Anna (2003) *Stasiland: Stories From Behind the Berlin Wall*, London: Granta.

Gedmin, Jeffrey (1992) *The Hidden Hand*, Washington, DC: AEI.

Gehrke, Bernd (2001) 'Demokratiebewegung und Betriebe in der "Wende" 1989: Plädoyer für einen längst fälligen Perspektivwechsel?' in Bernd Gehrke and Renate Hürtgen, eds, *Der betriebliche Aufbruch im Herbst 1989: Die unbekannte Seite der DDR Revolution*, Berlin: Bildungswerk.

——(2001) 'Die "Wende"-Streiks: Eine erste Skizze', in Bernd Gehrke and Renate Hürtgen, eds, *Der betriebliche Aufbruch im Herbst 1989: Die unbekannte Seite der DDR Revolution*, Berlin: Bildungswerk.

Gehrke, Bernd and Renate Hürtgen, eds (2001) *Der betriebliche Aufbruch im Herbst 1989: Die unbekannte Seite der DDR Revolution*, Berlin: Bildungswerk.

Gerlach, Manfred (1991) *Mitverantwortlich*, Berlin: Morgenbuch.

Gill, David and Ulrich Schröter (1991) *Das Ministerium für Staatssicherheit: Anatomie des Mielke-Imperiums*, Berlin: Rowohlt.

Glaessner, Gert-Joachim (1991) *Der schwierige Weg zur Demokratie*, Opladen: Westdeutscher Verlag.

——(1992) *The Unification Process in Germany*, London: Pinter.

Görtemaker, Manfred (2001) 'Zusammenbruch des SED-Regimes', in *Der Weg zur Einheit. Deutschland seit Mitte der achtziger Jahre*, Bundeszentrale für politische Bildung.

Greenwald, Jonathan (1993) *Berlin Witness: An American Diplomat's Chronicle of East Germany's Revolution*, Pennsylvania: Pennsylvania State University Press.

Grix, Jonathan (2000) *The Role of the Masses in the Collapse of the GDR*, Basingstoke: Macmillan.

——(2000) 'Recasting Civil Society in East Germany', in Chris Flockton *et al.*, eds, *The New Germany in the East: Policy Agendas and Social Developments since Unification*, London: Frank Cass.

Gutzeit, Martin (1993) 'Der Weg in die Opposition', in Walter Euchner, ed., *Politische Opposition in Deutschland und im internationalen Vergleich*, Göttingen: Vandenhoeck.

Gysi, Gregor (1990) 'Wird es einen demokratischen Sozialismus in der DDR geben?' in Frank Blohm and Wolfgang Herzberg, eds, *'Nichts wird mehr so sein, wie es war': Der Zukunft der beiden deutschen Republiken*, Frankfurt/Main: Luchterhand.

Habermas, Jürgen (1973) *Legitimationsprobleme im Spätkapitalismus*, Frankfurt/Main: Suhrkamp.

——(1987) *The Theory of Communicative Action, Volume Two*, Cambridge: Cambridge University Press

——(1990) *Die nachholende Revolution*, Frankfurt/Main: Suhrkamp.

Hager, Kurt (1996) *Erinnerungen*, Leipzig: Faber & Faber.

Hall, Peter, ed., (1990) *Fernseh-Kritik*, Mainz: Hase & Koehler.

Hartung, Klaus (1990) *Neunzehnhundertneunundachtzig*, Frankfurt/Main: Luchterhand.

——(1990) 'Der große Radwechsel oder Die Revolution ohne Utopie', in Frank Blohm and Wolfgang Herzberg, eds, *'Nichts wird mehr so sein, wie es war': Der Zukunft der beiden deutschen Republiken*, Frankfurt/Main: Luchterhand.

Haufe, Gerda and Karl Bruckmeier (1993) *Die Bürgerbewegungen in der DDR und in den ostdeutschen Ländern*, Opladen: Westdeutscher Verlag.

Haug, Wolfgang (1990) *Das Perestrojka-Journal*, Hamburg: Argument.

Hawkes, Nigel *et al.*, eds (1990) *Tearing Down the Curtain*, London: Hodder & Stoughton.

Hay, Colin (1996) *Re-Stating Social and Political Change*, Buckingham: Open University Press.

Henrich, Rolf (1989) *Der vormundschaftliche Staat*, Reinbek: Rowohlt.

Herles, Helmut and Ewald Rose (1990) *Vom Runden Tisch zum Parlament*, Munich: Bouvier.

Hertle, Hans-Hermann (1996) *Der Fall der Mauer*, Opladen: Westdeutscher Verlag.

——(1996) *Chronik des Mauerfalls*, Berlin: Links.

——and Gerd-Rüdiger Stephan, eds (1997) *Das Ende der SED: Die letzten Tage des Zentralkomitees*, Berlin: Links.

Herzberg, Guntolf (1994) 'Der Zusammenbruch der Staatssicherheit 89', *die tageszeitung*, 9 December.

Herzberg, Wolfgang and Patrick von zur Mühlen (1993) *Auf den Anfang kommt es an*, Bonn: Dietz

Heym, Stefan (1990) 'Aschermittwoch in der DDR', in Michael Naumann, ed., *'Die Geschichte ist offen': DDR 1990: Hoffnung auf eine neue Republik*, Reinbek: Rowohlt.

——(1990) *Einmischung*, Bertelsmann.

Hilsberg, Stefan (1993) 'Interview', in Wolfgang Herzberg and Patrick von zur Mühlen, eds, *Auf den Anfang kommt es an*, Bonn: Dietz.

Hoffman, Michael and Dieter Rink (1990) 'Der Leipziger Aufbruch: Zur Genesis einer Heldenstadt', in Jürgen Grabner *et al.*, *Leipzig im Oktober*, Berlin: Wichern.

Hollitzer, Tobias (1999) 'Der friedliche Verlauf des 9. Oktober 1989 in Leipzig – Kapitulation oder reformbereitschaft? Vorgeschichte, Verlauf und Nachwirkung', in Günther Heydemann *et al.*, eds, *Revolution und Transformation in der DDR*, Berlin: Duncker & Humblot.

——and Reinhard Bohse, eds (1999) *Heute vor 10 Jahren. Leipzig auf dem Weg zur Friedlichen Revolution*, Bonn: InnoVatio Verlag.

Hough, Jerry (1990) 'The Logic of Collective Action and the Pattern of Revolutionary Behavior', *Journal of Soviet Nationalities*, 1 (2).

Humann, Klaus, ed. (1990) *Wir sind das Geld*, Berlin: Rowohlt.

Huntington, Samuel (1993) *The Third Wave: Democratization in the Late Twentieth Century*, Norman: University of Oklahoma Press.

Hürtgen, Achim (1989) 'Rolf Henrichs Umwälzung der Wissenschaften', *Friedrichsfelder Feuermelder*, summer.

Israel, Jürgen, ed. (1991) *Zur Freiheit berufen*, Berlin: Aufbau.

Jackson, Paul, ed. (1994) *DDR – Ende eines Staates*, Manchester: Manchester University Press.

Jacoby, Wade (2000) *Imitation and Politics*, Ithaca: Cornell University Press.

Jäger, Wolfgang and Ingeborg Villinger (1997) *Die Intellektuellen und die deutsche Einheit*, Freiburg: Rombach.

Jander, Martin (1995) 'Formierung und Krise politischer Opposition in der DDR: Die "Initiative für unabhängige Gewerkschaften"', in Ulrike Poppe *et al.*, eds, *Zwischen Selbstbehauptung und Anpassung: Formen des Widerstandes und der Opposition in der DDR*, Berlin: Links.

Jänicke, Martin (1964) *Der dritte Weg*, Cologne: Neuer Deutscher Verlag.

Jarausch, Konrad (1994) *Rush to German Unity*, Oxford: Oxford University Press.

Johnson, Alan (1997) 'New Track May Have to be Laid', paper presented to *Alternative Futures and Popular Protest III*, Manchester Metropolitan University.

Johnson, Carsten (1992) 'Massenmobilisierung in der DDR im Jahre 1989', MA thesis, Freie Universität Berlin.

——(n.d.) Collated data on protest activities GDR 1989–90, in possession of the author.

Joppke, Christian (1995) *East German Dissidents and the Revolution of 1989*, Basingstoke: Macmillan.

Judt, Tony (1997) 'New Germany, Old NATO', *New York Review of Books*, 44 (9).

Kehrer, Gerhard (2000) *Industriestandort Deutschland*, Berlin: FIDES.

Keithly, David (1992) *The Collapse of East German Communism*, Westport: Praeger.

Kirsch, Sarah (1990) 'Kleine Betrachtung am Morgen des 17. Novembers', in Michael Naumann, ed., *'Die Geschichte ist offen': DDR 1990: Hoffnung auf eine neue Republik*, Reinbek: Rowohlt.

Klandermans, Bert (1984) 'Mobilization and Participation: Social–Psychological Expansions of Resource Mobilization Theory', *American Sociological Review*, 49.

——(1992) 'The Social Construction of Protest and Multiorganizational Fields', in Aldon Morris and Carol Mueller, eds, *Frontiers in Social Movement Theory*, New Haven: Yale University Press.

Klein, Thomas (1999) 'Außer Reden nichts gewesen?', in Bernd Gehrke and Wolfgang Rüddenklau, eds, . . . *das war doch nicht unsere Alternative: DDR-Oppositionelle zehn Jahre nach der Wende*, Münster: Westfälisches Dampfboot.

——(2004) 'Modrow-Regierung in der Zwickmühle', in Stefan Bollinger, ed., *Das letzte Jahr der DDR*, Berlin: Dietz.

——*et al.* (1996) *Visionen: Repression und Opposition in der SED*, Frankfurt/Oder: Editionen.

Klemm, Volker (1991) *Korruption und Amtsmißbrauch in der DDR*, Stuttgart: dva.

Klenke, Olaf (2007) *Zwischen Rationalisierung und sozialem Konflikt: Das Mikroelektronik-Programm in der DDR (1977–1989)*, Berlin: Links

Knabe, Hubertus, ed. (1989) *Aufbruch in eine andere DDR*, Reinbek: Rowohlt.

——(1990) 'Politische Opposition in der DDR: Ursprünge, Programmatik, Perspektiven', *Aus Politik und Zeitgeschichte*, 5 January.

Knauer, Gerd (1992) 'Innere Opposition im Ministerium für Staatssicherheit', *Deutschland Archiv*, 25.

Koch, Peter-Ferdinand (1992) *Das Schalck-Imperium lebt*, München: Piper.

Kocka, Jürgen (2003) 'Bilanz und Perspektiven der DDR-Forschung: Hermann Weber zum 75. Geburtstag', *Deutschland Archiv*, 5.

Kolinsky, Eva (2004) 'Meanings of Migration in East Germany and the West German Model', in Eva Kolinsky and Mike Dennis, eds, *United and Divided: Germany since 1990*, Oxford: Berghahn.

Königsdorf, Helga (1990) *Adieu DDR*, Reinbek: Rowohlt.

Koopmans, Ruud (2004) 'Protest in Time and Space', in David Snow *et al.*, eds, *The Blackwell Companion to Social Movements*, Oxford: Blackwell.

Kopstein, Jeffrey (1997) *The Politics of Economic Decline in East Germany, 1945–1989*, Chapel Hill and London: University of North Carolina Press.

Kowalczuk, Ilko-Sascha (1994) 'Artikulationsformen und Zielsetzungen von widerständigem Verhalten in verschiedenen Bereichen der Gesellschaft', in the German Parliament's 'Enquête-Kommission' for the 'Aufarbeitung von Geschichte und Folgen der SED-Diktatur'.

Krahulec, Peter (1990) 'Dilemmata des "verordneten Antifaschismus" ', in Christoph Butterwegge and Horst Isola, eds, *Rechtsextremismus im vereinten Deutschland: Randerscheinung oder Gefahr für die Demokratie?*, Berlin: Links-Druck-Verlag.

Krejci, Jaroslav (1976) *Social Structure in Divided Germany*, London: Croom Helm.

Krenz , Egon (1990) *Wenn Mauern fallen*, Wien: Paul Neff Verlag.

——(1999) *Herbst '89*, Berlin: Neues Leben.

Krone, Martina (1990) 'Keine Chance mehr für uns?', in Frank Blohm and Wolfgang Herzberg, eds, *'Nichts wird mehr so sein, wie es war': Der Zukunft der beiden deutschen Republiken*, Frankfurt/Main: Luchterhand.

Krone, Martina ed. (1999) *'Sie haben so lange das Sagen, wie wir es dulden':* *Briefe an das Neue Forum September 1989-März 1990*, Berlin: Robert-Havemann-Gesellschaft.

Küchenmeister, Daniel (1993) *Honecker-Gorbatschow*, Berlin: Dietz.

Kuczynski, Jürgen (1991) *Probleme der Selbstkritik: Sowie von flacher Landschaft und vom Zickzack der Geschichte*, Cologne: PapyRossa.

Kuhn, Ekkehard (1992) *Der Tag der Entscheidung*, Berlin: Ullstein.

Kumar, Krishan (1993) 'Civil Society', *British Journal of Sociology*, 44.

Kupferberg, Feiwel (1999) *The Break-up of Communism in East Germany and Eastern Europe*, Basingstoke: Macmillan.

Küttler, Thomas (1995) 'Die Wende in Plauen', in Alexander Fischer and Günther Heydemann, eds, *Die politische 'Wende' 1989/90 in Sachsen*, Weimar: Böhlau.

——and Jean Curt Röder, eds (1993) *Es war das Volk; Die Wende in Plauen*, Plauen: Vogtländischer Heimatverlag Neupert.

Kurz, Robert (1991) *Honecker's Rache*, Berlin: Edition TIAMAT.

Lang, Ewald, ed. (1990) *Wendehals und Stasi-Laus*, München: Wilhelm Heyne.

Langer, Kai (1999) *'Ihr sollt wissen, daß der Norden nicht schläft . . .': Zur Geschichte der 'Wende' in den drei Nordbezirken der DDR*, Bremen: Edition Temmen.

Lasky, Melvin (1991) *Wortmeldung zu einer Revolution*, Frankfurt/Main: Ullstein.

Lenin, V. I. (1975) *'Left-Wing' Communism: An Infantile Disorder*, Peking: Foreign Languages Press.

——(1980) *Werke*, vol. 21, Berlin: Dietz.

Leonhard, Wolfgang (1990) *Das kurze Leben der DDR*, Stuttgart: dva.

Liebold, Cornelia (1999) 'Machtwechsel vor Ort: Die SED und ihr Apparat in Leipzig vom Oktober 1989 bis Mai 1990', in Günther Heydemann *et al.*, eds, *Revolution und Transformation in der DDR*, Berlin: Duncker & Humblot.

Liebsch, Heike (1991) *Dresdner Stundenbuch*, Wuppertal: Peter Hammer.

Light, Margot (1997) 'The USSR/CIS and democratisation in Eastern Europe', in Geoffrey Pridham *et al.*, eds, *Building Democracy? The International Dimension of Democratisation in Eastern Europe*, revised edition, London and Washington, DC: Leicester University Press.

Lindner, Bernd (2001) *Die demokratische Revolution in der DDR 1989/90*, Bundeszentrale für politische Bildung, Bonn.

——and Ralph Grüneberger, eds (1992) *Demonteure*, Bielefeld: Aisthesis Verlag.

Lindner, Gabriele (1994) 'Das Maß der Macht: Runder Tisch und Modrow-Regierung', in Siegfried Prokop, ed., *Die kurze Zeit der Utopie*, Berlin: Elefanten Press.

Links, Christoph and Hannes Bahrmann (1990) *Wir sind das Volk*, Berlin: Aufbau.

Lohmann, Susanne (1994) 'The Dynamics of Informational Cascades', *World Politics*, 47.

Lohmar, Henry (1995) 'Die Entwicklung des Runden Tisches der DDR – eine vertane Chance', in Wolfgang Dümcke and Fritz Vilmar, eds, *Kolonialisierung der DDR*, Münster: Agenda-Verlag.

Luft, Christa (1991) *Zwischen Wende und Ende*, Berlin: ATV.

Maier, Charles (1997) *Dissolution*, Princeton: Princeton University Press.

Marcuse, Peter (1990) *A German Way of Revolution*, Berlin: Dietz.

Maron, Monika (1991) 'Writers and the People', *New German Critique*, 52.

Maximytschew, Igor (2001) 'Vom Mauerfall bis Archys', *Deutschland Archiv*, 34.

——and Hans-Hermann Hertle (1994) 'Die Maueröffnung', *Deutschland Archiv*, 27.

McAdam, Doug (1982) *Political Process and the Development of Black Insurgency*, Chicago: University of Chicago Press.

——*et al.* (2001) *Dynamics of Contention*, Cambridge: Cambridge University Press.

MccGwire, Michael (1991) *Perestroika and Soviet National Security*, Washington, DC: Brookings.

McFalls, Laurence (1995) *Communism's Collapse, Democracy's Demise?*, Basingstoke: Macmillan.

Meinel, Reinhard and Thomas Wernicke, eds (1990) *Mit tschekistischem Gruß*, Potsdam: Edition Babelturm.

Menge, Marlies (1990) *Ohne uns läuft nichts mehr*, Stuttgart: dva.

Merkel, Wilma and Stefanie Wahl (1991) *Das geplünderte Deutschland*, Bonn: IWG.

Miller, Barbara (1999) *Narratives of Guilt and Compliance in Unified Germany: Stasi Informers and their Impact on Society*, London: Routledge.

Minnerup, Günter (1984) 'The GDR and the German Question in the 1980s', in Ian Wallace, ed., *The GDR in the 1980s*, Dundee: GDR Monitor.

——(1989) 'Politische Opposition in der DDR', in Ilse Spittmann and Gisela Helwig, eds, *Die DDR im vierzigsten Jahr*, Cologne: Deutschland Archiv.

Mitter, Armin and Stefan Wolle (1990) *'Ich liebe euch doch alle . . .'*, Berlin: BasisDruck.

——(1993) *Untergang auf Raten*, Munich: Bertelsmann.

Modrow, Hans (1991) *Aufbruch und Ende*, Hamburg: Konkret.

——(1998) *Ich wollte ein neues Deutschland*, Berlin: Dietz.

Mögenburg, Harm (1990) *Die Revolution in der DDR*, Frankfurt/Main: Diesterweg.

Mosler, Volkhard (1994) 'Klassenkämpfe in der Revolution 1989', *Sozialismus von unten*, 2, Frankfurt/Main.

Mühlen, Patrik von zur (2000) *Aufbruch und Umbruch in der DDR: Bürgerbewegungen: kritische Öffentlichkeit und Niedergang der SED-Herrschaft*, Berlin: Dietz.

Mühler, Kurt and Steffen Wilsdorf (1991) 'Die Leipziger Montagsdemonstration – Aufstieg und Wandel einer basisdemokratischen Institution des friedlichen Umbruchs im Spiegel empirischer Meinungsforschung', *Berliner Journal der Soziologie*, 1.

Müller, Hans-Peter (1991) 'Die "Oktoberrevolution" und das Ende der FDGB', in Konrad Löw, *Ursachen und Verlauf der deutschen Revolution 1989*, Berlin: Duncker & Humblot.

Müller-Mertens, Eckhard (1997) *Politische Wende und deutsche Einheit*, Berlin: FIDES.

Musch, Reinfried (1990) 'Die Linke und die Revolution in der DDR', in Axel Lochner, ed., *Linke Politik in Deutschland*, Hamburg: Galgenberg.

Mushaben, Joyce (2001) 'Die Lehrjahre sind vorbei! Re-Forming Democratic Interest Groups in the East German Länder', *Democratization*, 8 (4).

Nakath, Detlef *et al.*, eds (1998) *'Im Kreml brennt noch Licht'*, Berlin: Dietz.

——and Gert-Rüdiger Stephan, eds (1996) *Countdown zur deutschen Einheit*, Berlin: Dietz.

Neubert, Ehrhart (1989) *Gesellschaftliche Kommunikation im sozialen Wandel*, Berlin: editionKontext.

——(1990) *Eine protestantische Revolution*, Berlin: Kontext.

——(1998) *Geschichte der Opposition in der DDR, 1949–1989*, Berlin: Links.

Neues Forum (1990) *Wirtschaftsreform der DDR*, Berlin: Nicolai.

Neues Forum Leipzig (1989) *Jetzt oder nie – Demokratie*, Leipzig: Bertelsmann.

Niemann, Heinz (1995) *Hinterm Zaun*, Berlin: edition ost.

Niethammer, Lutz *et al.* (1991) *Die volkseigene Erfahrung*, Berlin: Rowohlt.

Oberschall, Anthony (1973) *Social Conflict and Social Movements*, Englewood Cliffs, NJ: Prentice Hall.

Offe, Claus (1993) 'Wohlstand, Nation, Republik: Aspekte des deutschen Sonderweges vom Sozialismus zum Kapitalismus', in Hans Joas and Martin Kohli, eds, *Der Zusammenbruch der DDR*, Frankfurt/Main: Suhrkamp.

——(1996) *Varieties of Transition: The East European and East German Experience*, Cambridge: Polity.

Oktober 1989 (1989) Berlin: Neues Leben.

Olson, Mancur (1990) 'The Logic of Collective Action in Soviet-Type Societies', *Journal of Soviet Nationalities*, 1 (2).

Opie, Gerald (1995) 'Views of the *Wende*', in Derek Lewis and John McKenzie, eds, *The New Germany: Social, Political and Cultural Challenges of Unification*, Exeter: Exeter University Press.

Opp, Karl-Dieter *et al.* (1993) *Die volkseigene Revolution*, Stuttgart: Klett-Cotta.

——(1995) *Origins of a Spontaneous Revolution: East Germany, 1989*, Ann Arbor.

——(n.d.) *Eine Umfrage über die Entstehung und den Verlauf der Proteste in der DDR 1989–1990*, Unpublished data, in possession of the author.

Ost, David (1989) 'The Transformation of Solidarity and the Future of Central Europe', *Telos*, 79.

Owen, Ruth (2005) ' "Wenn ein staat ins gras beißt, singen die dichter": The *Wende* in poetry', in Silke Arnold-de Simine, ed., *Memory Traces: 1989 and the Question of German Cultural Identity*, Berne: Peter Lang.

Pechmann, Roland and Jürgen Vogel, eds (1991) *Abgesang der Stasi*, Braunschweig: Steinweg-Verlag.

Peterson, Edward (2002) *The Secret Police and the Revolution: The Fall of the German Democratic Republic*, Westport: Praeger.

Pfaff, Steven (1996) 'Collective Identity and Informal Groups in Revolutionary Mobilization: East Germany in 1989', *Social Forces*, 75 (1).

——(1999) 'From Revolution to Reunification: Popular Protests, Social Movements and the Transformation of East Germany', PhD thesis, New York University.

——(2001) 'The Politics of Peace in the GDR: The Independent Peace Movement, the Church, and the Origins of the East German Opposition', *Peace and Change*, 26 (3).

——and Hyojoung Kim (2003) 'Exit-Voice Dynamics in Collective Action: An Analysis of Emigration and Protest in the East German Revolution', *American Journal of Sociology*, 109 (2).

Philipsen, Dirk (1993) *'We Were The People'*, Durham: Duke University Press.

Piven, Frances Fox and Richard Cloward (1977) *Poor People's Movements*, New York: Pantheon.

Pizzorno, Alessandro (1986) 'Some Other Kinds of Otherness: A Critique of "Rational Choice" Theories', in Alejandro Foxley *et al.*, eds, *Development, Democracy, and the Art of Trespassing*, Notre Dame: University of Notre Dame Press.

Plato, Alexander von (2003) *Die Vereinigung Deutschlands – ein weltpolitisches Machtspiel*, Berlin: Links.

Pollack, Detlef (1994) 'Von der Volkskirche zur Minderheitskirche: Zur Entwicklung von Religiosität und Kirchlichkeit in der DDR', in Hartmut Kaelble *et al.*, eds, *Sozialgeschichte der DDR*, Stuttgart: Klett-Cotta.

——(1997) 'Bedingungen der Möglichkeit politischen Protestes in der DDR', in Detlef Pollack and Dieter Rink, eds, *Zwischen Verweigerung und Opposition*, Frankfurt/Main: Campus.

——*et al.* (1992) *Was ist aus den politisch alternativen Gruppen in der DDR geworden?*, Study commissioned by the Kommission für die Erforschung des sozialen und politischen Wandels in den neuen Bundesländern.

Pond, Elizabeth (1993) *Beyond the Wall*, Washington, DC: Brookings.

Poppe, Ulrike (1989) 'Bürgerbewegung "Demokratie Jetzt" ', in Hubertus Knabe, ed., *Aufbruch in eine andere DDR*, Reinbek: Rowohlt.

——(1995) ' "Der Weg is das Ziel": Zum Selbstverständnis und der politischen Rolle oppositioneller Gruppen der achtziger Jahre', in Ulrike Poppe *et al.*, eds, *Zwischen Selbstbehauptung und Anpassung: Formen des Widerstandes und der Opposition in der DDR*, Berlin: Links.

Porta, Donnatella della and Mario Diani (1999) *Social Movements: An Introduction*, Oxford: Blackwell.

Preuss, Ulrich (1996) 'The Roundtable Talks in the German Democratic Republic', in Jon Elster, ed., *The Roundtable Talks and the Breakdown of Communism*, Chicago: University of Chicago Press.

Pritchard, Gareth (1996) 'National Identity in a United and Divided Germany', in Robert Bideleux and Richard Taylor, eds, *European Integration and Disintegration*, London: Routledge.

Probst, Lothar (1991) *Bürgerbewegungen und politische Kultur*, Bremen: Institut für kulturwissenschaftlichen Deutschlandstudien.

——(1992) 'Bürgerbewegungen im Prozeß der Vereinigung', *Forschungsjournal Neue Soziale Bewegungen*, 1.

——(1993) *Ostdeutsche Bürgerbewegungen und Perspektiven der Demokratie*, Cologne: Bund-Verlag.

Prokop, Siegfried (1993) *Unternehmen 'Chinese Wall': Die DDR im Zwielicht der Mauer*, Frankfurt/Main: R. G. Fischer.

Prunier, Gérard (1995) *The Rwanda Crisis 1959–1994: History of a Genocide*, London: Hurst.

Pryce-Jones, David (1995) *The War That Never Was*, London: Weidenfeld & Nicolson.

Przybylski, Peter (1991) *Tatort Politbüro, Band 1: Die Akte Honecker*, Berlin: Rowohlt.

——(1992) *Tatort Politbüro, Band 2: Honecker, Mittag und Schalk-Golodkowski*, Berlin: Rowohlt.

Rees, John (1999) 'The Socialist Revolution and the Democratic Revolution', *International Socialism*, second series, 83.

Reich, Jens (1990) 'Reflections on Becoming an East German Dissident, on Losing the Wall and a Country', in Gwyn Prins, ed., *Spring in Winter*, Manchester: Manchester University Press.

——(1991) *Rückkehr nach Europa*, Munich: Carl Hanser.

——(1992) *Abschied von den Lebenslügen*, Berlin: Rowohlt.

——(1998) 'Freiheit, Einheit: Die friedliche Revolution von 1989', in Hans Sarkowicz, ed., *Aufstände, Unruhen, Revolutionen: Zur Geschichte der Demokratie in Deutschland*, Frankfurt/Main: Insel.

——(2001) 'Ich habe mich in der DDR nie zu Hause gefühlt', in Eckhard Jesse, ed., *Eine Revolution und ihre Folgen: 14 Bürgerrechtler ziehen Bilanz*, Berlin: Links.

——(2001) 'Revolution in der DDR – und zehn Jahre danach', in Andrea Pabst *et al*, eds, *Wir sind das Volk? Ostdeutsche Bürgerrechtsbewegungen und die Wende*, Tübingen: Attempto Verlag.

Reicher, Steve (1996) 'Collective Psychology and the Psychology of the Self', *The BPS Social Psychology Section Newsletter*, 36.

Rein, Gerhard, ed. (1989) *Die Opposition in der DDR*, Berlin: Wichern.

Remnick, David (1994) *Lenin's Tomb*, Harmondsworth: Penguin.

Remy, Dietmar (1999) 'Wir waren die letzten', *Deutschland Archiv*, 32.

Renken, Frank (1999) 'Die Rolle der Oppositionsgruppen in der ostdeutschen Revolution 1989/1990', Masters dissertation, Freie Universität Berlin.

Reum, Monika and Steffen Geißler, eds (1991) *Auferstanden aus Ruinen — und wie weiter? Chronik der Wende in Karl-Marx-Stadt/Chemnitz*, Chemnitz: Verlag Heimatland Sachsen.

Reuth, Ralf Georg and Andreas Bönte (1993) *Das Komplott*, Munich: Piper.

Richter, Michael (1996) *Die Staatssicherheit im letzten Jahr der DDR*, Cologne: Böhlau.

——(2001) 'Friedliche Revolution und Transformation', *Deutschland Archiv*.

——and Erich Sobeslavsky (1999) *Die Gruppe der 20: Gesellschaftlicher Aufbruch und politische Oppostion in Dresden 1989/90*, Cologne: Böhlau.

Richter, Michaela (1994) 'Exiting the GDR: political movements and parties between democratization and westernization', in Donald Hancock and Helga Welsh, eds, *German Unification: Process and Outcomes*, Boulder: Westview Press.

Riecker, Ariane *et al*. (1990) *Stasi intim*, Leipzig: Forum.

Rochtus, Dirk (1999) *Zwischen Realität und Utopie: Das Konzept des 'dritten Weges' in der DDR 1989/90*, Leipziger Universitätsverlag.

Roesler, Jörg (2003) *Ostdeutsche Wirtschaft im Umbruch, 1970–2000*, Bonn: Bundeszentrale für politische Bildung.

Rosenau, James (1992) 'The Relocation of Authority in a Shrinking World', *Comparative Politics*, April.

Rucht, Dieter (1996) 'German Unification, Democratization, and Social Movements', *Mobilization* 1 (1).

Rüddenklau, Wolfgang (1992) *Störenfried*, Berlin: BasisDruck.

Rule, James (1988) *Theories of Civil Violence*, Berkeley: University of California Press.

Sarotte, M. E. (2001) *Dealing With the Devil: East Germany, Détente, and Ostpolitik, 1969–1973*, Chapel Hill: University of North Carolina Press.

Sartre, Jean-Paul (1976) *Critique of Dialectical Reason*, London: Verso.

Schabowski, Günter (1990) *Das Politbüro*, Reinbek: Rowohlt.
——(1991) *Der Absturz*, Berlin: Rowohlt.
Schäfer, Eva (1990) 'Die fröhliche Revolution der Frauen', in Gislinde Schwarz and Christine Zenner, eds, *Wir wollen mehr als ein 'Vaterland': DDR-Frauen im Aufbruch*, Reinbek: Rowohlt.
Schlegelmilch, Cordia (1995) 'Die politische Wende in der DDR am Beispiel der sächsischen Stadt Wurzen', in Alexander Fischer and Günther Heydemann, eds, *Die politische 'Wende' 1989/90 in Sachsen*, Weimar: Böhlau.
Schmid, Thomas (1990) *Staatsbegräbnis*, Berlin: Rotbuch.
Schneider, Michael (1990) *Die abgetriebene Revolution*, Berlin: Elefanten Press.
——(2000), *Kleine Geschichte der Gewerkschaften: Ihre Entwicklung in Deutschland von den Anfängen bis heute*, Bundeszentrale für politische Bildung.
Schneider, Wolfgang, ed. (1990) *Leipziger Demontagebuch*, Leipzig: Kiepenheuer.
Schomers, Michael (1990) *Deutschland ganz Rechts*, Cologne: Kiepenheuer & Witsch.
Schorlemmer, Friedrich (1990) *Träume und Alpträume*, Berlin: Verlag der Nation.
Schröder, Gerhard (1998) 'German Economic Policy from a European and Global Perspective' in Dieter Dettke, ed., *The Challenge of Globalization for Germany's Social Democracy*, Oxford: Berghahn.
Schüddekopf, Charles, ed. (1990) *'Wir sind das Volk'*, Reinbek: Rowohlt.
Schulz, Marianne (1991) 'Neues Forum', in Helmut Müller-Enbergs *et al.*, eds, *Von der Illegalität ins Parlament*, Berlin: Links.
Schwabe, Uwe (1999) 'Die Entwicklung der Leipziger Opposition in den achtziger Jahren', in Günther Heydemann *et al*, *Revolution und Transformation in der DDR*, Berlin: Duncker & Humblot.
Scott, James (1990) *Domination and the Arts of Resistance*, New Haven: Yale University Press.
Siegler, Bernd (1991) *Auferstanden aus Ruinen*, Berlin: Edition TIAMAT.
Sievers, Hans-Jürgen (1990) *Stundenbuch einer deutschen Revolution*, Zollikon: G2W.
Simon, Günter (1990) *Tischzeiten*, Berlin: Tribüne.
Sinn, Gerlinde and Hans-Werner Sinn (1992) *Jumpstart: The Economic Unification of Germany*, London: MIT Press.
Smith, Helmut (1991) 'Socialism and Nationalism in the East German Revolution, 1989–1990', *East European Politics and Societies*, 5 (2).
Smyser, William (1999) *From Yalta to Berlin: The Cold War Struggle over Germany*, New York: St Martin's Press.
Snow, David and Robert Benford (1992) 'Master Frames and Cycles of Protest', in Aldon Morris and Carol McClurg Mueller, eds, *Frontiers in Social Movement Theory*, New Haven: Yale University Press.
Snow, David *et al.* (1986) 'Frame Alignment Processes, Micromobilization, and Movement Participation', *American Sociological Review*, 51.
Sorel, George (1950) *Reflections on Violence*, New York: Collier Books.
Stark, Isolde (1995) 'Wirtschaftspolitische Vorstellungen der DDR-Opposition, *Deutschland Archiv*, 28.
Steinberg, Mark (1998) 'Tilting the Frame: Considerations on Collective Action Framing from a Discursive Turn', *Theory and Society*, 27.

Steinberg, Mark (1999) 'The Talk and Back Talk of Collective Action: A Dialogic Analysis of Repertoires of Discourse among Nineteenth-Century English Cotton Spinners', *American Journal of Sociology*, 105 (3).

Steiner, André (2004) *Von Plan zu Plan: Eine Wirtschaftsgeschichte der DDR*, Munich: dva.

Stent, Angela (1998) *Russia and Germany Reborn*, Princeton: Princeton University Press.

Stephan, Gerd-Rüdiger, ed. (1994) *'Vorwärts immer, rückwärts nimmer!'*, Berlin: Dietz.

Stokes, Raymond (2000) *Constructing Socialism: Technology and Change in East Germany 1945–1990*, Baltimore: Johns Hopkins University Press.

Stolle, Uta (2001) *Der Aufstand der Bürger: Wie 1989 die Nachkriegszeit in Deutschland zu Ende ging*, Baden-Baden: Nomos Verlagsgesellschaft.

Süß, Walter (1991) 'Bilanz einer Gratwanderung', *Deutschland Archiv*, 24.

——(1991) 'Mit Unwillen zur Macht', *Deutschland Archiv*, 24.

die tageszeitung (1990) *DDR Journal Nr. 1: Vom Ausreisen bis zum Einreissen der Mauer*, Berlin.

——(1990) *DDR Journal Nr. 2: Die Wende der Wende: Januar bis März 1990*, Berlin.

Tarrow, Sidney (1994) *Power in Movement: Social Movements, Collective Action and Politics*, Cambridge: Cambridge University Press.

Teltschik, Horst (1991) *329 Tage*, Berlin: Siedler Verlag.

Tetzner, Reiner (1990) *Leipziger Ring*, Frankfurt/Main: Luchterhand.

Thaysen, Uwe (1990) *Der Runde Tisch der DDR*, Opladen: Westdeutscher Verlag.

Therborn, Göran (1980) *The Ideology of Power and the Power of Ideology*, London: Verso.

Thompson, Mark (1996) 'Why and How East Germans Rebelled', *Theory and Society*, 25.

——(1999) 'Reluctant Revolutionaries: Anti-Fascism and the East German Opposition', *German Politics*, 8 (1).

——(2004) *Democratic Revolutions: Asia and Eastern Europe*, London: Routledge.

Timmer, Karsten (2000) *Vom Aufbruch zum Umbruch: Die Bürgerbewegung in der DDR 1989*, Göttingen: Vandenhoeck & Ruprecht.

Tiryakian, Edward (1995) 'Collective Effervescence, Social Change and Charisma', *International Sociology*, 10 (3).

Torpey, John (1995) *Intellectuals, Socialism and Dissent: The East German Opposition and its Legacy*, Minneapolis: University of Minnesota Press.

Tschiche, Hans-Joachim (1991) 'Herbst 1989 in Magdeburg', in *Anstiftung zur Gewaltlosigkeit*, Magdeburg: Impuls Verlag.

Turner, Lowell (1998) *Fighting for Partnership*, Ithaca: Cornell University Press.

Ullmann, Wolfgang (1990) *'Demokratie – jetzt oder nie!'*, Munich: Kyrill-und-Method-Verlag.

Villain, Jean (1990) *Die Revolution verstösst ihre Väter*, Bern: Zytglogge.

Wagner, Harald, ed. (1994) *Freunde und Feinde*, Leipzig: Evangelische Verlagsanstalt.

Wainwright, Hilary et al. (1991) *After the Wall: Democracy and Movement Politics in the New Europe*, Amsterdam: Transnational Institute.

Weber, Christian (1990) *Alltag einer friedlichen Revolution*, Stuttgart: Quell.

Weil, Francesca (1999) 'Wirtschaftliche, politische und soziale Veränderungen in einem Leipziger Betrieb 1989/90', in Günther Heydemann *et al*, eds, *Revolution und Transformation in der DDR*, Berlin, Duncker & Humblot.

Weinert, Rainer (1993) 'Massenorganisationen in mono-organisationalen Gesellschaften', in Hans Joas and Martin Kohli, eds, *Der Zusammenbruch der DDR*, Frankfurt/Main: Suhrkamp.

Weiß, Konrad (1989) 'Die neue alte Gefahr', *Kontext*, 8 March.

——(1989) 'Vierzig Jahre in Vierteldeutschland', in Hubertus Knabe, ed., *Aufbruch in eine andere DDR*, Reinbek: Rowohlt.

——(2001) 'Was macht ihr, wenn ihr die Macht habt?', in Eckhard Jesse, ed., *Eine Revolution und ihre Folgen: 14 Bürgerrechtler ziehen Bilanz*, Berlin: Links.

Werdin, Justus, ed. (1990) *Unter uns: Die Stasi. Berichte der Bürgerkomitees zur Auflösung der Staatssicherheit im Bezirk Frankfurt (Oder)*, Berlin: Basis Druck.

Wielepp, Christoph (1990) 'Montag Abends in Leipzig', in Thomas Blanke and Rainer Erd, eds, *Ein Staat vergeht*, Frankfurt/Main: Fischer.

Wielgohs, Jan and Carsten Johnson (1997) 'Entstehungsgründe, Handlungsbedingungen, Situationsbedeutungen', in Detlef Pollack and Dieter Rink, eds, *Zwischen Verweigerung und Opposition*, Frankfurt/Main: Campus.

Wielgohs, Jan and Helmut Müller-Enbergs (1991) 'Die Bürgerbewegung Demokratie Jetzt', in Helmut Müller-Enbergs *et al.*, eds, *Von der Illegalität ins Parlament*, Berlin: Links.

Wilkening, Christina, ed. (1990) *Staat im Staate*, Berlin: Aufbau.

Wilkens-Friedrich, Wilfried (1992) 'Die Beziehungen zwischen Neuem Forum und Gewerkschaften in Berlin', Diplom-Arbeit, Universität Hamburg.

Wolfram, Klaus (1991) 'Das NEUE FORUM und die Machtfrage', *Die Andere*, 40.

Wolle, Stefan (1998) *Die heile Welt der Diktatur*, Berlin: Links.

Worst, Anna (1991) *Das Ende eines Geheimdienstes*, Berlin: Links.

Wuttke, Carola (2005) '" Für unser Land": Entweder?– Oder!', in Stephan Bollinger, ed., *Das letzte Jahr der DDR*, Berlin: Dietz.

Yoder, Jennifer (1999) *From East Germans to Germans? The New Postcommunist Elites*, Durham: Duke University Press.

Zurück zu Deutschland (1990) Bonn: Bouvier.

Zwahr, Hartmut (1993) *Ende einer Selbstzerstörung*, Göttingen: Vandenhoek & Ruprecht.

—— (1994) 'Umbruch durch Ausbruch und Aufbruch: Die DDR auf dem Höhepunkt der Staatskrise 1989', in Hartmut Kaelble *et al.*, eds, *Sozialgeschichte der DDR*, Stuttgart: Klett-Cotta.

—— (1995) 'Die Revolution in der DDR 1989/90 – Eine Zwischenbilanz', in Alexander Fischer and Günther Heydemann, eds, *Die politische 'Wende' 1989/90 in Sachsen*, Böhlau: Weimar.

Index

Lightning Source UK Ltd.
Milton Keynes UK
UKOW03f1241091013

218730UK00001B/33/P